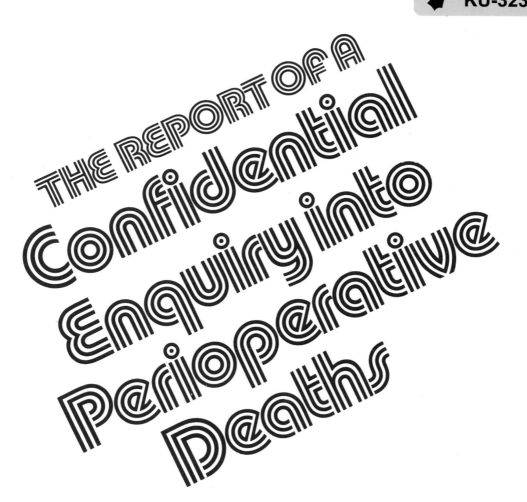

THE REPORT OF A Confidential Enquiry into Perioperative Deaths

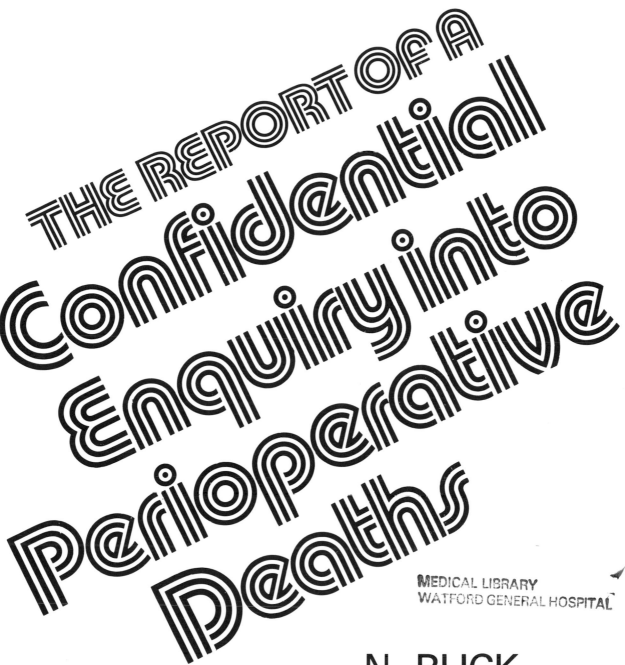

THE REPORT OF A Confidential Enquiry into Perioperative Deaths

THIS REPORT HAS BEEN PREPARED BY **N. BUCK**

H. B. DEVLIN and **J. N. LUNN**

The Nuffield Provincial Hospitals Trust

The King's Fund

Published by the
Nuffield Provincial Hospitals Trust
3 Prince Albert Road, London NW1 7SP

King's Fund Publishing Office,
14 Palace Court, London W2 4HT

ISBN 0 900574 67 4

© Nuffield Provincial Hospitals Trust

Acknowledgements

The acknowledgement of various groups' help is described at the end of Part 1 in this report. However it is appropriate here to record the authors' gratitude, firstly to the Nuffield Provincial Hospitals Trust who, together with the King Edward's Hospital Fund for London readily provided substantial financial support. In particular, we would like to thank Mr Gordon McLachlan, CBE, (retired Secretary of the Trust) for his continued personal support and both Dr Michael Ashley-Miller (current Secretary of the Trust) and Dr Robert Maxwell (Secretary to King's Fund) for their guidance and encouragement throughout the Enquiry. Secondly, our ability to deal with the large amounts of data about anaesthesia was facilitated by the enthusiasm, hard work, and dedication of Dr R D Jack who was an additional anaesthetist coordinator. Finally our particular thanks to Bernard Crossland for all his patience and skill in achieving this publication.

Designed by Bernard Crossland
PRINTED IN GREAT BRITAIN BY
BURGESS & SON (ABINGDON) LTD
ABINGDON OXFORDSHIRE

Contents

v

Foreword

In 1977 the Nuffield Provincial Hospitals Trust, in accord with its general policy relating to the quality of medical care, gave a grant to the Association of Anaesthetists of Great Britain and Ireland for a confidential enquiry into deaths associated with anaesthesia. The results of this enquiry were published under the Trust's imprint by Lunn and Mushin in 1982. This significant contribution to quality assurance suffered the defect that, at that time, it had not been possible to secure collaboration with members of the surgical specialties. The authors, well aware of the difficulty of assigning causative factors responsible for post-operative deaths due to the anaesthetic or surgical procedure, recommended that future epidemiological studies should involve **both** anaesthetists and surgeons. And so, it gave us great personal pleasure to learn that our colleagues in the Association of Surgeons of Great Britain and Ireland had agreed to collaborate with the Association of Anaesthetists in conducting a Confidential Enquiry into Perioperative Deaths. This decision found favour with the Nuffield Provincial Hospitals Trust and the King Edward's Hospital Fund for London; they also agreed to collaborate in funding the study. This book provides the results of the Enquiry.

The reader may tend to be deterred by large numbers of tables and figures but justifiable conclusions and sound recommendations must be based on the presentation of hard data; this the authors have done. They are to be congratulated on the organisation and completion of this major project, the results of which merit wide dissemination: if this does not occur through sales of this book, there would be merit in preparing a short pamphlet, giving the recommendations and conclusions, for distribution to all practitioners.

An overall death rate of 0.7% in over half a million operations is reassuring, particularly as death was attributable to avoidable surgical or anaesthetic factors in a very small proportion of patients. However, the report reveals several less than satisfactory practices including inadequate consultant supervision of trainees, lack of regular joint meetings between members of the two disciplines, and deficiencies in the Hospital Activity Analysis data; offence will only be taken at these and other valid conclusions by those who are not guiltless.

In recent years there has been a growing interest in quality assurance in medical care and in some hospitals audit committees provide peer review of clinical practice, but **some** is not acceptable; it should be **all** hospitals. The conduct and outcome of this Enquiry will provide a much needed stimulus, and may also encourage the establishment of further enquiries into other areas of clinical practice. The public has every right to expect such a sense of responsibility and we doctors should respond by giving a clear indication of our honest and determined endeavour to improve patient care.

Although perhaps tangential to the content of this book, we cannot resist the temptation to urge a major step towards assuring quality assurance. It is the traditional function of the Royal Colleges and their Faculties to maintain and raise the professional standards of their members; an inter-collegiate decision to insist on instruction in this area, and the inclusion of a compulsory question in the Fellowship and Membership examinations would be salutary.

SIR ANDREW WATT KAY.
SIR GORDON ROBSON, C.B.E.

Conclusions

1. The overall death rate after anaesthesia and surgery, analysed in this Enquiry was low. The mortality of over half a million operations was 0.7% and most of these were in the elderly (over 75 years old) and were unavoidable due to progression of the presenting condition, such as advanced cancer, or co-existing diseases such as heart and (or) respiratory failure. Death was solely attributable to avoidable surgical or anaesthetic factors in a very small proportion of operations.

2. The majority of clinicians in the relevant disciplines co-operated in this system of clinical audit.

3. There were important differences in clinical practice between the three Regions studied.

4. There were deficiencies in the Hospital Activity Analysis data. There were also problems with the storage, movement and retrieval of patients' notes, particularly those of deceased patients.

5. Many surgeons and anaesthetists did not hold regular audits of their operation results (mortality and morbidity meetings). The proportion varied with the sub-specialty but joint meetings between the two disciplines were very rare.

6. There were important differences in the consultants' supervision of trainees.

7. There were a number of deaths in which junior surgeons or anaesthetists did not seek the advice of their consultants or senior registrars at any time before, during or after the operations.

8. The pre-operative assessment and resuscitation of patients by doctors of both disciplines was sometimes compromised by undue haste to operate. This was a greater problem than delayed operations and it is possible that pressure to fit an operation into a very tight theatre schedule was one of the responsible factors.

9. There were instances of patients who were moribund or terminally ill having operations that would not have improved their condition.

10. There were examples of surgeons operating for conditions for which they were not trained or performing operations outside their field of primary expertise.

11. There were examples of difficulties in transferring patients for specialised treatment to other hospitals in the area.

Recommendations

Quality assurance

1. There is a need for an assessment of clinical practice on a national basis. Our experience suggests that our colleagues would welcome this.

2. Consultants in every District should ensure that their own coding and input to information systems (including the Körner systems) is accurate and up-to-date; without this, any audit is flawed. Every District should urgently review the storage, movement, and retrieval of patients' notes, particularly those of deceased patients. (See tables 4.1, 4.48 and Part 1).

3. Clinicians need to assess themselves regularly. Effective self assessment needs time; time to attend autopsies, mortality/morbidity meetings and clinical review with other disciplines. (See tables 1.11, 4.19, 4.20, 4.50, 4.51, 4.52, 4.108, 4.109, 4.145, 4.146, 4.152).

Accountability

4. All departments of anaesthetics and surgery should review their arrangements for consultants' supervision of trainees. Locally agreed guidelines are important to ensure appropriate care of all patients, but particularly when responsibility is transferred from one clinical team, or shift, to another. No senior house officer or registrar should undertake any anaesthetic or surgical operation as an emergency or urgent matter without consultation with their consultant (or senior registrar). (See tables 3.24, 4.12, 4.24–4.27, 4.59, 4.79–4.83, 4.123, 4.142, 4.143, 4.161, 4.176).

Clinical decision making

5. Resuscitation, assessment and management of medical disease take time and may determine the outcome; their importance needs to be re-stated. Arrangements which permit this in every case are important. (See tables 3.4, 3.5, 3.9, 3.13, 3.15, 4.30, 4.31, 4.42, 4.70, 4.71, 4.87, 4.88, 4.89, 4.126–4.129).

6. The decision to operate on the elderly and the very sick is important and should be taken at consultant (or senior registrar) level. For the most seriously ill patients, consultant anaesthetists and surgeons should consult together before the operation. (See Part 2).

7. The decision **not** to operate is difficult. Humanity suggests that patients who are terminally ill or moribund should not have operations (*ie.* non life saving), but should be allowed to die in peace with dignity. (See tables 3.6, 3.7, 3.8, 4.56, 4.57, 4.111, 4.112, 4.158, 4.159, 4.168, 4.170 and fig. 1.1).

Recommendations

Organisational issues

8. Districts should review their facilities for out-of-hours work and concentrate anaesthetic, surgical and nursing resources at a single location. A fully staffed and fully equipped anaesthetic room, rescuscitation room, operating room, recovery area and high dependency or intensive therapy unit should be available at all times. (See tables 4.8, 4.9, 4.13, 4.25, 4.76, 4.77, 4.78).

9. The implementation of the CEPOD classification of operations (emergency, urgent, scheduled and elective) would concentrate the attention of all staff on the fact that very few operations need to be performed at night. (See table 1.9).

10. Operations should only be performed by consultants or junior surgeons (accountable to consultants) who have had adequate training in the specialty relevant to the operation. Health Authorities should therefore balance surgical specialties so that appropriate urological and vascular trained surgeons are provided in each District. In the case of small Districts this may necessitate sub-Regional units to ensure adequate sub-specialty care. Neurological and neonatal surgery should be carried out at special Regional units. (See Part 2).

List of Figures

List of Tables

PART 4

In the following tables, any differences between the Regions of 5% or less has been classed as no Regional differences.

GENERAL INFORMATION

SURGICAL DATA

TABLE

SURGEON ASSESSORS' OPINIONS

ANAESTHETIC DATA

ANAESTHETIST ASSESSORS'
OPINIONS

TABLE

ANAESTHESIA-ASSOCIATED DEATHS

SURGICAL AND ANAESTHETIC DATA

COMPLETE DATA: SURGEON ASSESSORS' OPINIONS

COMPLETE DATA: ANAESTHETIST ASSESSORS' OPINIONS

COMPLETE DATA: SURGICAL & ANAESTHETIC DATA

part 1

general information

NIGEL BUCK

M.Sc.

Administrator, Confidential Enquiry into Perioperative Deaths,
9 Bedford Square, London WC1B 3RA

part 1

general information

CONTENTS

general information

INTRODUCTION

All data pertaining to this report, has now been destroyed. It is, therefore impossible retrospectively to identify clinicians, patients, hospitals or Districts.

The protocol stated that "The medical profession has a responsibility to the public and to itself to assess its own standards and to be in a position to meet criticism, from whatever source, in an authoritative fashion. Accurate audit can establish current standards of medical organisation and care; it allows for comparisons and helps to determine the value of procedures. It also directs future developments and influences teaching and training". This statement is the genesis of the Confidential Enquiry into Perioperative Deaths (CEPOD). This audit is a systematic review of medical work undertaken by doctors themselves.

Following closely the previous work by the Assocation of Anaesthetists and using a similar methodology, in this instance the enterprise was a joint venture between the Association of Surgeons of Great Britain and Ireland and the Association of Anaesthetists of Great Britain and Ireland. A Joint Working Party under the chairmanship of Professor M D Vickers was created to guide the work. The Enquiry investigated all deaths within 30 days of an operative procedure in order to clarify the current "state of the art" of surgery and anaesthesia throughout three Regional Health Authorities in England in 1986.

The Working Party appointed three clinical coordinators and one administrator to liaise with participating clinicians, direct the work in the CEPOD office and refer cases to the assessors. The coordinators were accountable to the Joint Working Party of the Confidential Enquiry into Perioperative Deaths.

The Joint Working Party produced a protocol for the Enquiry, this is reprinted here, together with the supplementary notes in the form seen by supporting bodies and consultants prior to the start of the Enquiry (appendix 3).

The original discussions[1] that led to the Confidential Enquiry into Perioperative Deaths began in 1982. The formation of the Working Party and the development of a workable protocol took many months of meetings and conferences. Simultaneously support was widely sought among professional bodies and those offering their support are listed in the protocol (appendix 3). In 1983, the Nuffield Provincial Hospitals Trust, together with the King Edward's Hospital Fund for London agreed to provide financial support for the venture and thereafter the preparatory work, including the pilot study, were started.

QUALITY OF CARE STUDIES

Previous attempts to assess the quality of medical care, both in the United Kingdom and overseas have tended to concentrate, in the main, on one particular aspect of the quality of medical care itself, and to be structure, process, or outcome orientated.[2,3]

Outside the United Kingdom

Quality assessment outside the United Kingdom has been used most notably in the United States of America. A detailed history of its evolution there has been reported by Lembcke.[4] The early work by Codman,[5] before World War I, who followed up all his surgical patients and initiated the "end result" study, was a powerful reform in the medical auditing world. Although the intervention of the war temporarily halted such developments. In 1918 the American College of Surgeons, under their director, Dr J G Bowman, took over the responsibility for the peer review programme and replaced the "end result" technique with one of standardisation of hospital programmes. The American College of Surgeons undertook a survey of the hospitals in the USA and Canada with the intention of implementing such a scheme.

This initiative by the American College of Surgeons grew into the Professional Standards Review Organisation (PSRO), which was replaced in 1951 by a unified quality assurance programme monitored by the Joint Commission on Accreditation of Hospitals (JCAH). The JCAH surveys American hospitals, measuring performance against standards. The surveys are voluntary and depend on the profession setting yardsticks of measurement, it is not nation-wide and has generally been aimed at cost containment.

Other examples of peer review include the American Medical Association self-assessment programme which enables surgeons to keep up with the surgical process, to identify areas of weakness and plan educative programmes. This involves the use of clinically orientated multiple choice questions completed by the clinicians themselves.[6] A number of other studies attempted to investigate the quality of clinical care by retrospective analysis of hospital records.[7] Some studies attempted to find "unwarranted" operations, for example one study examined all the hysterectomies carried out in thirty five Californian hospitals.[8] Further smaller studies have been done on the same basis to investigate the treatment of appendicitis, and of myocardial infarction.[9]

A comparison of different types of peer review methods has also been carried out in the United States where up to five peer review methods have been evaluated in a single study.[10] Not all studies were of a surgical nature, some looked at the "appropriate" use of hospital beds using a consensus review approach,[11] whilst others attempted to create a system of "unnecessary and untimely" disease, disability and death[12] occuring in hospitals with the intention of creating indicators of the quality of care.

Anaesthetic studies in the USA are highlighted by Beecher and Todd.[13] Coincidentally these researchers worked at the same hospital as Dr E A Codman who pioneered the early research on "end results". Beecher and Todd aimed to identify all anaesthetic deaths and to calculate all administrations for the population from which deaths occurred; they collected data in ten hospitals over five years. This was followed by further "anaesthetic deaths" studies, some based in particular American states[14,15] covering all anaesthesia. Other groups investigated particular types of anaesthetics, eg. spinal[16] or paediatric anaesthesia.[17] These localised studies were followed later by attempts to investigate anaesthesia on a long term basis.[18]

Other countries have involved themselves in the quality assessment of medical care. In Australia, the Australasian College of Physicians introduced auditing in 1978, and by 1983 it had become an absolute requirement for accreditation of hospital training of physicians in Australia. The anaesthetic specialty in Australia have also been involved in setting up a committee to investigate anaesthetic deaths in New South Wales,[19] and there have been other investigations of anaesthetic related mortality.[20,21] Canada also introduced audit as a requirement for accreditation of hospitals for training.[22] Several anaesthetic studies have investigated the link between anaesthesia and mortality.[23,24] Studies are also underway in Canada[25] and in France.[26] Other anaesthetic studies of note include a South African study,[27] and work in Finland.[28]

However, the wide-ranging methodologies used in these and other studies and the different organisation of medical work in each country makes their conclusions and results inapplicable to, and uncomparable with work of this type carried out in the United Kingdom.

United Kingdom

In the United Kingdom there are many examples of quality of care assessment, the Educational Accreditation of hospitals for Training Purposes carried out by the Royal Colleges and the Health Advisory Service and National Development Teams who study the long-stay sector of hospitals.

Other groups rely on participating (volunteer) groups to become involved; for example there is a UK national quality control scheme for clinical chemistry which relies on the standardisation of commonly performed tests and feedback on performance to the participating laboratories. Similar schemes operate for haematology and bacteriological services developed by the Royal College of Pathologists. The Royal College of General Practitioners set up a peer review system in 1980 as have the Royal College of Physicians who initiated a study on deaths in the under fifty year-olds. Formal audit has also been achieved by physicians in several hospitals according to a review by clinical tutors.[29] A scheme by physicians based in Swansea was able to gain support from the Area Medical Officer to set up formal auditing procedures.[30] The Confidential Enquiry into Maternal Deaths, set up in the 1930s by the Royal College of Obstetricians and Gynaecologists and on a formal footing with the DHSS since 1952 is an example of peer review similar to CEPOD.

The Department of Health and Social Security (DHSS) has promoted the idea of performance indicators as a method of assessing quality of care and performance of hospitals. Their use was intended for Regional and District Health Authorities as an attempt to give a nation-wide perspective on a particular hospital's performance by use of cluster analysis. For a description of performance indicators see Yates[31] whilst a definitive critique may be found in Pollitt.[32] Other groups also interested in the quality of health care include the College of Health, whose recent report on hospital waiting lists attempted to bring the assessment of performance into the public arena,[33] and the Office of Health Economics, who have presented outcome data in a clear manner.[34] On a wider basis, the establishment of the King Edward's Hospital Fund Quality Assessment Project is to be welcomed as an important initiative in this area.

Surgery. There have been a few medical peer review efforts on a smaller scale attempted either on a single Regional basis,[35] or on a more localised system in certain hospitals. There are also studies which compare two different hospitals in terms of their outcome characteristics supplied by the General Registry Office.[36] Teaching and non-teaching hospitals have been compared on the basis of their treatment and fatal outcome of hyperplasia of the prostrate.[37] Others have included the outcomes following appendicitis[38] or using appendicitis (or appendicectomy) as the criteria for entering the study and following up each case.[39] Some have attempted to measure the output of a hospital and develop a classification of morbid status,[40] whilst others have concentrated on investigating the surgical service provided by one hospital [41,42] or by two hospitals.[43] The influence of neurosurgical intervention on patients and the incidence of avoidable factors has also been scrutinised.[44,45] The UK Cardiac Surgical Register run by the British Thoracic Society has audited the work of such specialist cardiac units. The European Dialysis and Transplant Organisations audit the results of end stage renal disease. Perinatal deaths are studied with the intention of identifying failures in structure and process.[46,47] A comprehensive study of surgical activity in the UK is the St. Mary's Large Bowel Cancer study.[48]

Anaesthesia. John Snow started anaesthetists' interests within this field[49] and his skills as an anaesthetist and epidemiologist have led to him being claimed by both groups as their "godfather". However, even Dr Snow was unable or failed to collect denominator data, a criticism which reappeared in studies to be carried out over one hundred years later.

The Association of Anaesthetists of Great Britain and Ireland has commissioned, over the last thirty five years, three reports on mortality associated with anaesthesia.[50,51,52]

In 1956 the study by Edwards *et al.* relied upon the voluntary reporting of anaesthetic deaths and distribution of reply paid questionnaires to all hospitals. Information was collected on a thousand deaths over a five and half year period in the early 1950's but it was impossible to estimate the relative frequency (incidence) of the events reported due to the lack of denominator values (*ie.* the number of operations). However, it was successful in discovering "that in the great majority of the reports there were departures from ideal practice" and was able to pinpoint misadventures in the practice of anaesthesia.

In 1964 Dinnick followed up the 1956 study by examining a further six hundred deaths which had been reported. Although neither of these studies covered all deaths associated with anaesthesia, it was interesting to note that the conclusions in the latter report generally mirrored those of the former. It was also noted that the demise of many poor risk patients was related to surgical factors as well as anaesthesia. This final point was more strongly made by the next anaesthetic mortality study in 1980,[52] where the request for the inclusion of a surgical element in such a study was refused. This study was, however, able to present denominator data upon which to base its conclusions. Other types of investigations into anaesthesia related deaths have been carried out using claims to medical defence organisations.[53]

It has been recognised that the interdependence of anaesthesia and surgery together with the need to assess quality of care on a sufficiently large basis to allow for comparisons and to protect anonymity, has led to the requirement for audit of anaesthetic and surgical practice today.

Surgery with anaesthesia. The examples cited above, both at home and overseas, have tended to concentrate on the role of one or other discipline in the review of clinical practice. Very few studies have included surgery and anaesthesia together[13,54] and,[55,56] the former two studies and the latter study concentrating on anaesthesia, whilst the third example studied morbidity. These studies still leave a gap in the assessment of standards of practice, that is, a joint review by surgeons and anaesthetists. Hence the Confidential Enquiry into Perioperative Deaths was established.

This study is unique because both surgery and anaesthesia were jointly involved together. The two disciplines are not only different but also anaesthetists are already involved in the Confidential Enquiries into Maternal Deaths and the Association of Anaesthetists has recent experience in this field. This was not the case for the surgical discipline; with some notable exceptions,[48] no similar study has been made in the United Kingdom. The data which surgeons were able to collect was thus neither as clinical nor as detailed as that available to anaesthetists. The latter two parts of the report reflect this difference.

The Joint Working Party agreed to limit the Enquiry to National Health and Forces (MOD) Hospitals in three Regional Health Authorities, using only Regions which had not been subject to any previous mortality studies. Therefore Metropolitan and "south of England" Regions were included. The three Regions were the South Western, the Northern and North East Thames Regional Health Authorities.

Role of coordinators

Their function was to initiate the study and they visited each District to explain the Enquiry to the clinicians, they explained the procedures and the intended use of the data collected. The clinical coordinators were responsible for the scrutiny of each completed questionnaire for further information and to decide which assessor would be suitable for the particular case. Where necessary a clinical coordinator wrote to the participating consultant in order to obtain further information requested by the assessors. In cases where more than one assessor had been used and there was a difference of opinion, the clinical coordinator acted as arbitrator and decided one corporate assessment and the scores for feedback.

CASE SELECTION

The protocol proposed that all patients who died within thirty days of an operative procedure carried out by an anaesthetist and/or surgeon should be included in this study. There was an attempt to include patients who underwent the preparations for an operation, *eg.* induction of anaesthetic or booking of theatre in an emergency case, but who died before an operation could take place. However, the local reporters form, and both the surgical and anaesthetic forms began with the operation date or the operation performed. This resulted in the above "non-operated" patients being ignored and classed as "irrelevant" by some participants to the CEPOD study, although eleven cases were reported in which there was no operation:

Case A was to repair a fractured femur but the operation was abandoned because of ventricular failure.

Case B was to be a mastectomy but the patient died at induction from cardiac arrest.

Case C was to be an aortic aneurysm repair but the patient had cardiac arrest prior to induction of anaesthesia.

Case D according to the anaesthetist no operation was carried out; on the other hand, the surgeon claimed there was no anaesthetic with the sigmoidoscopy.

Case E was a road traffic accident victim who had cardiac arrest before any operation could begin.

Case F suffered cardiac arrest three minutes after induction of anaesthesia, the operation planned was a strangulated femoral hernia repair.

Case G also suffered cardiac arrest just before the planned total cystectomy.

Case H the anaesthetist left the operation blank, did not send on the anaesthetic record and no surgical questionnaire was returned.

Case I a laparotomy was booked but the patient died just before it started, from cardiac arrest.

Case J died just before reaching the theatre from a myocardial infarction, the planned operation was an exploratory laparotomy.

Case K was similar to case H.

Therefore CEPOD investigated the work of surgeons and anaesthetists. Other procedures carried out by non-surgeons even under anaesthesia were excluded from study. Similarly, where other audit mechanisms were in place, CEPOD excluded them from the enquiry, *eg.* maternal deaths, cardiac surgery (see supplementary notes appendix 3). In addition, the enquiry did not include deaths relating to diagnostic or therapeutic procedures carried out by physicians or other non-surgeons, radiological procedures performed solely by a radiologist without a surgeon present and endoscopies performed without the use of sedation or anaesthetic. Deaths following pain therapy were also excluded.

The logistical difficulties of enlisting the help of all the General Practitioners throughout the three Regions prevented us from establishing a mechanism to collect all the CEPOD cases which occurred at home. The Family Practitioners Committees within the three Regions were informed of the Enquiry and local reporters were encouraged to report such deaths to us. We were most grateful to the District Medical Officers in Gateshead and Darlington Health Authorities who undertook to identify these cases in their respective Districts and inform the relevant local reporters.

CONFIDENTIALITY

In spite of criticism that the medical profession in Britain is *collectively allergic to rational examination of the case for medical audit in any form*[57] CEPOD has succeeded in overcoming this national allergy. Any audit system has to maintain the highest levels of confidentiality such that the clinicians can be assured they would never be named, sued, or otherwise personally denigrated by information contained in this study. The benefits of an audit system[58,59] can only be reaped if confidentiality is assured. The CEPOD proposal could not proceed without anonymity.

There were four major areas in which confidentiality had to be secured. The first was non-identification of the patient, hospital or clinician involved to a third party. The second was the non-identification of individual assessors to the clinician who completed questionnaires (or *vice versa*). The third was the requirement to give feedback to the clinician involved in the case. The fourth was the necessity to avoid medicolegal action.

Third party access. The first item was achieved by the use of scissors and whitex to ensure that upon arrival at the office, all identifiable features were removed from the questionnaire and from any additional papers also retrieved, *eg.* operation notes. This ensured that no places or names could be identified except by a code number (the key to which was held by the two CEPOD staff only). So that if a questionnaire fell into the wrong hands, it was unidentifiable with regards to persons or places. This limited the number of people (to two) who had access to identifiable data and thereby the numerical concept of secrecy was upheld.

Blind assessment. The second requirement was again achieved by the use of codes such that an assessor knew that any case came from a hospital outside of his/her Region but he/she would be unable to identify places, or persons. In addition, the participants knew that the assessment was carried out by one or more of the assessor(s) on the list (see appendix 2).

Feedback. The third requirement concerning feedback led us to establish a mechanism by which only the clinician who completed the questionnaire could receive feedback.

The medicolegal aspects. These were tackled in two ways, primarily by the shredding of original data such that the information was destroyed before any medicolegal action was initiated. The second approach was to obtain "crown privilege" on the data held by CEPOD such that it became "in the public interest" that our data could **not** be subpoenaed by a court (see supplementary notes, appendix 3).

It was necessary to reject the use of precoded questionnaires so that the completed forms were not seen by the computer punching bureau. The Data Protection Act was not applicable to the Enquiry because all data related to deceased patients.

PILOT STUDY

It was agreed that three pilot studies would be set up to test the protocol and the procedures. The clinical coordinators visited the three chosen hospitals to explain the study and its methodology. The areas were the Exeter District Health Authority, Darlington District Health Authority and the Middlesex Hospital, London. The pilot study lasted for nine months in Exeter and Darlington (1/12/84 to 30/8/85) and for seven months at the Middlesex (1/5/85 to 30/11/85). Many versions of a questionnaire to be completed by the clinicians were tested and developed in the light of comments received. Pilot study forms were also sent to assessors who made comments on these and the assessors' forms. These comments were also taken into consideration prior to the production of the forms used in the main Enquiry. We would like to take this opportunity to thank all the staff who helped us in the pilot study areas.

MAIN STUDY

Arrangements were made for the coordinators to visit each District in the three Regions at least once and discuss the implemention of The Confidential Enquiry into Perioperative Deaths with the anaesthetists and surgeons during the running of the pilot studies and testing of the protocol. The corporate agreement of the District/hospital was requested at these meetings. The main Regional Enquiry began on 1/11/85 in the Northern and South Western Regions and ended on 31/10/86. The North East Thames Regional Enquiry ran from 1/12/85 to 30/11/86.

Hospitals. In addition to all the National Health Service acute hospitals within the three Regional Health Authorities, the following hospitals also agreed to join in the Enquiry: The Royal Navy Hospital in Plymouth and St Michael's Hospital in Cornwall. Some hospitals were not included, *eg.* hospitals with their own Special Health Authority; Moorfields Eye Hospital, The Hospital for Sick Children Great Ormond Street, National Hospital for Nervous Diseases, Cirencester Hospital (which is staffed by consultants from the Wessex Region).

Private Hospitals were not included in the study because of the lack of available denominator data, (the numbers of operations performed are not collected nationally or Regionally). When NHS pay beds were involved, deaths were included in the CEPOD study only if the patient's details were entered in the NHS Hospital Activity Analysis (HAA) data collection system. It is estimated that in the United Kingdom, private hospitals carry out half a million operations. Whilst we may estimate that one-fifth of these (100000) may have occurred in three Regions studied, we have no idea of the number which result in death within thirty days (the case mix of private patients is probably different and younger in age than CEPOD patients).

Visits. Initially, using the hospitals under Regional Health Authorities in England listed in the Medical Directory, an introductory letter, requesting a visit to explain the Enquiry, was sent to a consultant anaesthetist and surgeon in each hospital in three study Regions. Protocols were sent with each letter. This led to arrangements for visits, *via* the cogwheel or divisional chairmen, *via* the college/faculty tutor or in other cases on an *ad-hoc* basis. Some visits included staff from more than one hospital and some with representatives of more than one District. An attempt was made to include at least one consultant of each surgical specialty and an anaesthetist at these meetings to which all clinicians were invited. Staff were asked to agree corporately to enter the study and to appoint a local reporter.

Once the corporate agreement of a hospital had been obtained, each consultant surgeon and anaesthetist was individually invited to participate and give his/her consent in writing. Lists of consultant staff were initially obtained from the Regional Health Authorities and, where incomplete, from the District Health Authorities. These lists were checked for accuracy and completeness with those supplied by local reporters. Consultants were each sent an explanatory letter informing them of the appointment of a local reporter and enclosing the protocol, notes and a consent form to be returned in a pre-paid envelope. Participating consultants are listed in the appendix 2.

Local reporters. The task of the local reporter was to identify all deaths within thirty days of an operation with a few exceptions. They entered the following details on a local reporting form; names of consultant anaesthetist, consultant surgeon, anaesthetising anaesthetist, and operating surgeon, dates of death, birth and operation; then sent this form to the study centre in a pre-paid envelope. The report of a death to the CEPOD office required a number of questions to be answered:

1. Were the consultants both participating?
2. Was the death reported previously?
3. Was the death within the definitions of the protocol?

Questionnaires. (See appendix 3). If the above were answered correctly they were then sent to the participating consultants for completion; they were asked to return the completed questionnaires to the study centre within three weeks, in a pre-paid envelope provided. It was our recommendation that consultants asked their trainees to complete the questionnaire using the patients' notes, and when the form was completed the consultant and his junior should review it together. Consultants who refused to take part in the study were not sent questionnaires following the report of a death. If either of the pair of consultants (surgeon or anaesthetist) had refused to participate, neither of the two were sent a form and only the. details on the local reporting forms were recorded.

The next stage of the Enquiry was to follow up cases where the questionnaires were not returned, this was normally done at approximately five to eight week intervals for a first, and ten to sixteen weeks for a second follow up to encourage the return of the questionnaire. Questionnaires which were returned to the CEPOD office were processed in order for an assessment to take place:

1. Was the questionnaire complete?
2. Was it completed for the correct operation?
3. Was the operation note/autopsy report enclosed?
4. Removal of identifiable factors before assessment.

Assessors. Assessors were invited to join the CEPOD from all specialties of surgery and anaesthesia, together with a selection of assessors from other disciplines (see appendix 2). Five assessors' seminars were held prior to the start of the study and the assessors were asked to comment on the forms and other aspects of the study. Assessors were initially nominated by the supporting bodies and specialist associations listed on the protocol (see appendix 3).

Questionnaires (without identifying features) were sent to assessors, together with an assessors' form and notes (see appendix 3) *via* the clinical coordinator. They were asked to return the completed assessment in the pre-paid envelope within three weeks. Assessors who did not return forms received a letter at approximately three weeks, a telephone call at five weeks; and at eight weeks a further letter was sent by one of the clinical coordinators to encourage return.

The questionnaires contained a self-marking scheme of marks out of ten for the pre, per, and post-operative management. The assessors were also asked for three scores on the same basis. Where an assessor indicated that he did not feel competent to assess the case or where they suggested a further assessment, this was done *via* the clinical coordinators. Where assessors scored less than seven for any of the three phases, a further assessor was approached for a second opinion, again chosen by the clinical coordinators. In addition, a random ten percent of those cases where the first assessor had scored seven or more were also sent for a second opinion. Upon receipt of a second assessment, if the scores between this and the first assessor differed by four points or more, it was sent for a further third opinion and so on (assessors did not know the other assessors' opinion).

Classification of mortality. Based on the assessor's opinion and completion of an assessment form criteria for which were based on the definitions produced by an international symposium on Preventable Anaesthetic Mortality and Morbidity[60] the classification of mortality was as follows:

1. Surgery, and (or)
2. Anaesthesia, and (or)
3. Presenting surgical disease, and (or)
4. Intercurrent disease

Within section 1. *Surgery*, the surgeon assessors were required to specify which of the following aspects could be associated with a particular death:

a. Inappropriate operation
b. Inappropriate pre-operative management
c. Inappropriate grade operating surgeon
d. Failure of organisation (system)
e. Technical failure by surgical team due to:

i. Inadequate knowledge
ii. Failure to apply knowledge
iii. Lack of experience
iv. Inadequate supervision

v. Fatigue
vi. Physical impairment
vii. Mental impairment
viii. Other – specify

Within section 2. *Anaesthesia* the anaesthetist assessors were required to specify which of the following aspects were involved :

a. Failure of organisation
b. Failure of equipment
c. Drug effect
d. Human (anaesthetist) failure:

i. Lack of knowledge
ii. Failure to apply knowledge
iii. Lack of care
iv. Lack of experience

v. Fatigue
vi. Impairment
vii. Other – specify

There were also further sub-groups for unknown and not-assessable cases (see assessors' forms reprinted in appendix 3).

Criteria used by assessors. Explicit criteria have a number of positive features; they may be stated in advance, they may be used consistently and they may reduce inter-assessor variations,[61] but these types of criteria are known to be incomplete and misleading.[9] On the other hand, implicit criteria may tend to be the least severe in judgement.[10,62] The uniform education and high level of expertise in the assessors guarantees the reliability of results obtained, particularly when so many specialties are involved.

Clinical coordinators and assessors. The clinical coordinators were responsible for checking assessments; where there was a discrepancy between assessors, the clinical coordinators would act as arbitrators to produce a final assessment, or if this was not possible, (for example, where there were widely differing opinions or where scores differed by more than four) a further assessment was sought by the clinical coordinators. This ensured that each death was assessed by at least one surgeon and one anaesthetist. When the clinical coordinators or one of the assessors requested specialist advice on a particular case, the form was also sent to one of the other assessors. Any assessor requiring further information had to return his/her papers to the CEPOD centre where the details would be requested from the consultant involved in the case. Further details, if available, also had identifying data removed and were sent to the assessor in order to facilitate an assessment.

Once an assessor's form had been returned to the CEPOD office it was processed:

1. Was it complete ?
2. Had all the data been returned?
3. Was further information required?

4. How does it compare with other assessments on the same case?

5. Were any scores of six or less?

6. Ten percent of cases with scores of seven or more were sent for further assessment.

The assessments were then sent to the clinical coordinators for confirmation and production of a corporate assessment required for computer analysis. Storage of this information was required in a readily retrievable form to satisfy the individual feedback mechanism.

Feedback. There were three formal methods of feedback in the protocol. The first method of feedback was on a **personal** basis to the clinician who completed the questionnaire: Six weeks after a form had been returned to the CEPOD office, the clinician could, by telephone request only, obtain the assessors' scores on the pre, per and post-operative management of the patient. The consultant had to telephone the CEPOD office, identify him/herself, the patient, the CEPOD code number, the telephone number he/she had written on the questionnaire and the assessors' scores would be read to him/her. No further discussion with the clinician was held because time was limited and the staff were not clinical. No correspondence was conducted, on legal advice, so that anonymity would be preserved. Written material could be open to subpoena from the courts should any medicolegal action arise, as would any document held by the consultant. Even if non-attributable feedback were sent by letter, the fact that it could possibly be the only one attributable to a particular surgeon or anaesthetist meant that its unique nature would make feedback in writing immediately identifiable.

The second method of feedback was on a **Regional** basis; all cooperating clinicians were invited to attend a "closed" meeting midway through the study. The third method of feedback is **this report.**

The use of personal and Regional feedback systems was extremely low, (see Part 4, table 4.146) despite the claim to want information in 46% of cases by surgeons and anaesthetists. In the event few anaesthetists and surgeons actually telephoned for their scores with only five cases where both surgeon and anaesthetist had feedback. Invitations to over 1300 participating consultants to attend a Regional feedback meeting were accepted by 10%. On the day of these closed meetings (one held in each Region) only 5% actually attended.

Reasons for failure of methods of feedback. The interval between the operation and the end of the peer review was too long. In cases, for example, where the report of a death was delayed and completion of a form was also delayed, the resulting temporal interval between the event and the feedback may have made feedback appear to be irrelevant. It is possible that any feedback required by a clinician could be obtained by other means (*eg.* at local mortality/morbidity meetings). It is possible that the instructions given for feedback were misunderstood and too complicated. Indeed, the scores alone may have had little meaning to clinicians who wished to have further details of any assessors' review. It is also possible that the clinician present at the operation had moved from the hospital by the time feedback was available.

We found that three Districts in North East Thames, six Districts in the North and four Districts in the South West contained consultants of both disciplines who never asked for feedback throughout the entire study.

Indirect feedback. Most assessors (93%) were able to make an assessment on the information available in the questionnaire but in those cases for which more information was requested, it is possible that these questions acted as a type of feedback. Indeed, there was one case where the consultant surgeon withdrew from the study rather than answer the assessors' questions.

The total number of deaths reported to CEPOD during the twelve-month period were:

1359 in the Northern Region
1307 in the South Western Region
1368 in the North East Thames Region
(This does not include deaths outside the protocol).
The total number of operations during the same period from HAA sources were:
192421 in the Northern Region
143435 in the South Western Region
219402 in the North East Thames Region

We were able to obtain from one Regional Health Authority an indication of the number of operations and 30-day deaths which occurred during a 12-month period excluding all cases which were not relevant to the CEPOD study, *eg.* maternal deaths. This led us to revise downwards our original HAA totals of 555258 operations and 5807 deaths (see Part 4, table 4.1) by a factor of 0.875 to 485850 operations and 5081 deaths, thus the crude death rate using CEPOD deaths as a numerator rose from 0.7% to 0.8% of all relevant operations.

At the start of the study six out of four hundred and fifty nine consultant anaesthetists declined to take part. At the end of the study eleven consultant anaesthetists had declined to participate. At the start of the study thirty one out of nine hundred and thirty seven consultant surgeons declined to take part. At the end of the study sixty eight consultant surgeons had declined to participate. The withdrawal of the seventy nine consultants meant that approximately five hundred cases could not be investigated.

Return of forms

Of the 4110 deaths reported by local reporters, we found seventy six were not within the CEPOD protocol, *ie.* they already been reported, or had operations which occurred more than thirty days prior to the patients demise, or were excluded types of cases *eg.* maternal deaths, cardiac deaths etc. This resulted in 4034 deaths which could be legitimately called perioperative deaths. However, we were prevented from requesting further information in cases where one, or both consultants had refused to take part in the study. Of the remaining cases, we expected to receive information on all of them from the surgeons and slightly fewer of them from the anaesthetists (the difference was due to the use of local anaesthetics by surgeons). We did in fact receive 2784 surgical forms, and 2928 anaesthetic forms by the closing date of 16/2/87. There were 2391 cases where both the anaesthetic **and** relevant surgical forms were received.

Forms received. 4034 deaths reported

69.0% surgical forms returned
72.6% anaesthetic forms returned
59.3% (anaesthetic and surgical) forms returned
13.3% anaesthetic forms returned, but no surgical form
9.7% surgical forms returned, but no anaesthetic form
8.2% neither anaesthetic nor surgical forms returned
12.7% cases with consultant(s) not participating

Partial return. Only one of the pair of consultants returned a questionnaire in 930 cases. There were 537 cases with an anaesthetic but no surgical form and 393 cases with a surgical but no anaesthetic form. The former is high because of the late non-participation of a number of surgeons after the questionnaire had been issued. The latter is high partly because of a number of local anaesthetics given by surgeons.

We analysed the various sets of forms independently (both partial and complete data sets) and found that the data sets did not differ from each other in age distribution of patients, (*ie.* 80% over 65 years old), or in the period from operation to death (*ie.* 50% of cases occurred in the first 7 days). The assessors' opinions of the cases, (*ie.* the answers given by assessors) did not differ in their distribution between complete and partial data sets. (See Part 4, tables 4.155-4.176).

When we only had one form we were able to check if the consultant thought the other form was important for the assessors to look at; 7.4% of surgeons and 18.6% of anaesthetists claimed the other form was of importance. The assessors for each discipline did not incriminate the other discipline in any different manner from the whole data set.

Cooperation of individuals

The coordinators were very pleased with the response of the profession in general to the Enquiry. 95% cooperation is a very satisfactory figure but there was cooperation of different degrees. One centre managed to return a mere 8% of the deaths, which a study of HAA data indicated occurred. Another teaching hospital consultant regularly wrote disparaging comments on the questionnaires which, in addition, he filled out incompletely. His standards of anaesthesia, as reflected on the several forms which he returned, indicated little self-awareness to an extent that is frightening. His surgical colleague, who completed a form with exemplary thoroughness, was able by this means to demonstrate to us the anaesthetist's standards; should we list two cooperators, or only one? There were a few consultants who ceased to cooperate suddenly and we noticed that this was often a simultaneous event with receipt in the office of a form from the other discipline. That form often indicated suboptimal care and sometimes even avoidability. We assume that the withdrawal of cooperation was not coincidental.

Cases unavailable to the Enquiry

There were a number of cases reported to the CEPOD office which could not be followed up with an enquiry form to either the anaesthetist nor the surgeon.

Non-participants. This was the largest group, *ie.* where the consultant of either (or both) disciplines did not agree to participate.

Reasons for not participating:
   A *I have not enough time to fill in the questionnaire forms*
   B *I do not wish to participate*
   C *Mr . . . is too busy at Upper Wimpole Street*
   D *I find it quite impossible . . . to take on any further commitments*

Reasons for withdrawal after CEPOD began:
   A *We must withdraw from the project as medical manpower at this hospital is very much at a premium*
   B *I find it is impossible to participate due to the volume of work involved in addition to my clinical commitment*
   C *I believe each hospital should have a surgical assessor*
   D *Our records are not sufficiently detailed to give the answers to many of your questions*
   E *I feel it would serve no useful purpose and there are rather more important calls on my time*
   F *The proforma is too long and too complicated*
   G *We do not have half the information you require on the form*
   H *The conclusions being drawn without controlled data cannot be justified in terms of the data collected*

There were five hundred and twenty "non-participating" cases. Most (89%) of these were because the consultant surgeon would not take part, 7.9% were because the consultant anaesthetist would not take part, 2.4% were where neither surgeon nor anaesthetist would take part and the remaining 0.7% involved cases where the local reporter had not indicated any consultants names but had stated it was a death from a non-participating consultant.

Late forms. We also received, in addition to the above, a number of cases after the closure date (16/2/87): Two local reports of deaths, eighty nine surgical forms and fifty four anaesthetic forms.

An attempt was made to see if these above two groups differed from the main data set. Of the **non-participants** group, although we were unable to obtain any clinical details of these cases, the **patients' demographic** data were known from the local reports. The age distribution of non-participant deaths was the same as that for all CEPOD cases. The sex ratio was also similar. In addition, the interval from operation to death did not differ from that shown by the main CEPOD data. Of the late forms it was found that once again the age and sex distribution of these cases was no different from the whole CEPOD data set. We were also able to establish from these that the grades of surgeons and anaesthetists were similar in their distribution to the main study.

Questionnaire completion

In order to assess the amount of clinical time involved in the completion of questionnaires during the pilot study all consultants were asked how long each form took to complete.

The average time for a first form was one hour, the range being 30 minutes to three and a half hours. After this first form the average time for subsequent form completion was 40 minutes, ranging from 15 minutes to one and a half hours. It must be stressed that this is **actual** questionnaire completion. It was pointed out to us on more than one occasion that the retrieval of patients' notes could take six months or more before the clinician could attempt to complete the questionnaire. It was therefore unsurprising to find that after a period of six months, the motivation to spend 40 minutes completing a questionnaire was not at a high level. Indeed, our undertaking to provide feedback on individual cases within six weeks of the events relied heavily upon the availability of patients' notes to the consultants.

Once a consultant had agreed to participate and had received forms to complete, there was a large variation in the speed with which forms were returned. On one hand, a consultant returned a fully completed form to us on the Friday following the Monday it had been posted to him. On the other hand, another consultant who was sent a form at the very beginning of the study (December 1985) returned it to us 432 days later with neither explanation nor apology. We were sometimes told the reasons for failure to return forms; some were lost and we had seventy nine requests for further copies because the original had been lost. Other forms were filed in the notes of the patient and forgotten. The CEPOD staff, upon checking a set of patient's notes did come across a blank CEPOD form filed, uncompleted, in the patient's notes and, at that time, nine months overdue. Some consultants claimed that the patient's notes were "irretrievably lost"; on fifty five occasions. We were told in one hospital that "what happens here when a patient is known to be dead is that no attempt is made to file his/her notes which are then put into a room full of similar notes and their retrieval is not a practicable proposition".

Where it was impossible at times to retrieve patients' notes, the CEPOD office enlisted the help of the District Medical Officer in those hospitals with serious deficiencies but the problem remained largely unsolved.

Some consultants claimed a lack of junior staff to complete a form or indeed that such staff had "moved on" before completing the CEPOD form. There were nine cases in which the clinician claimed that a form had been completed and returned, but never reached the CEPOD office. The chances of questionnaires being lost in the post were reduced by the use of pre-paid, pre-addressed, envelopes. It is also possible that selective returning operated; some consultants did not wish to complete forms on certain cases.

We accept that clinicians are working hard and that no extra work is welcomed but over the year one consultant was sent fifty three forms and he completed and returned all of them. Others were sent only one or two, and failed to return a single one.

Age of patients

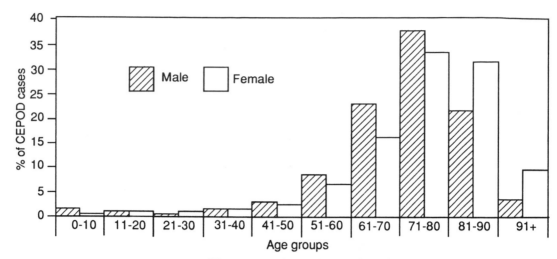

Figure 1.1 Ages of CEPOD patients

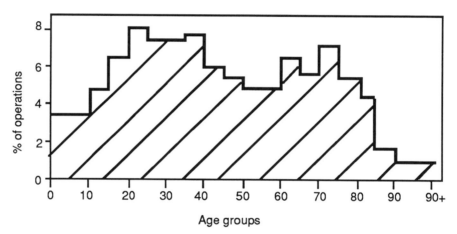

Figure 1.2 Age distribution of HIPE* operations
*Source : O.P.C.S.Hospital InPatient Enquiry.1986.
Trends 1979-84 England.

The overwhelming impression gained from the study of patients' ages was one of an elderly population. In fact, 79% of CEPOD patients were over 65 years old. This compares with only 22% of surgical patients included in Hospital Inpatient Enquiry (HIPE) statistics. There was a difference between the sexes with regard to the age structure such that CEPOD female patients tended to be older than the male patients and the righthand skew seen on the graph is more pronounced amongst the female CEPOD population. The under 15 year-olds account for 12% of all the operations in England (HIPE) but only 1% of the CEPOD cases (figs. 1.1,1.2). CEPOD patients account at all ages over 60 for proportionately more of the deaths than would be expected from HIPE data.

As a percentage of deaths from **all** causes (see table 1.1) within the three Regions CEPOD cases accounted for 3% of all deaths.

TABLE 1.1
CEPOD deaths as a percentage of all deaths
(all causes) within the three Regional Health
Authorities

Age range	All deaths in 3 regions all causes* (approximate number of deaths)	CEPOD deaths as a percentage of all deaths
0 - 4	1456	1.8
5 - 9	118	2.5
10 - 14	162	2.5
15 - 19	382	4.9
20 - 24	476	3.6
25 - 34	906	3.6
35 - 44	1916	4.4
45 - 54	4782	3.2
55 - 64	14680	3.3
65 - 74	29000	3.8
75 - 84	41100	3.5
85+	23180	2.9
All ages	118140	3.4

*Estimated from O.P.C.S. *Population Trends* ,
Winter 1986 ;**46.**

Weight and sex

We were able to establish that a greater proportion of men than women were weighed (table 1.2), the differences being consistent throughout each Region. In order to establish if this phenomenon was associated with fractured femurs, these cases were removed from the data and the same analysis carried out. In this instance the percentage of men and women weighed was approximately the same. This indicated that it is the female patients with fractured femurs who are not routinely weighed in hospital.

TABLE 1.2
Weighing of patients by sex

	% Patients					
		Male			Female	
Weight recorded	SW	N	NET	SW	N	NET
By region	40.2	37.7	38.7	35.7	29.8	34.0
All cases		39.0			33.0	

Period from operation to death

Many patients (50%) who died within 30 days of an operation died within one week of the procedure. Seventy five percent of the 30-day deaths occur within the first 15 days (see fig. 1.3).

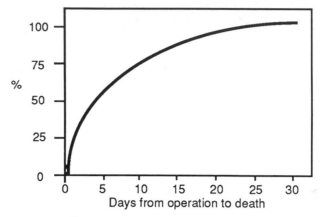

Figure 1.3 Period from operation to death
(Cumulative Percent)

Times of operations

There were three times of day at which CEPOD operations were most likely to start: 0900, 1100, and 1400 hours (see fig. 1.4). Most (80%) operations were carried out between 0800 and 1800 hours. However, during the night operations continued to take place, reaching a minimum in the small hours of the morning; most night-time CEPOD operations started before midnight.

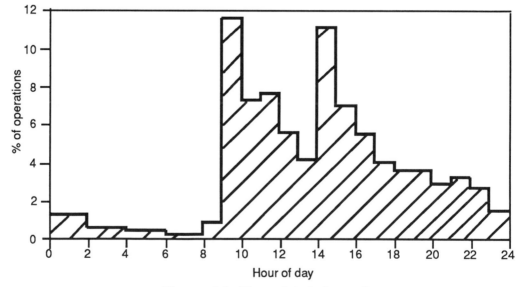

Figure 1.4 Times of start of operations

Day of week of operation

Most CEPOD operations took place Monday to Thursday. On Friday there was a slight decline in the numbers of operations, and Saturday and/or Sunday accounted for 11% of the operations.

The grades of clinicians involved in operations remained consistent for Monday to Thursday operations (see figs. 1.5,1.6) *ie.* consultant surgeons and trainee anaesthetists were involved in a majority of cases. On Fridays there was a slight decline in the numbers of operations taking place and a reversal of the Monday to Thursday theme with more trainee surgeons operating on a Friday than consultants. There were more trainee anaesthetists anaesthetising on a Friday than consultants, as during Monday to Thursday, however, the differential between the two was more pronounced.

At the weekends there were many fewer operations carried out, especially on a Sunday, however, on both days the trainee anaesthetists and trainee surgeons were involved in the great majority of CEPOD cases. The figure 1.5 for surgical work also indicates the type of operations carried out on each day by each group.

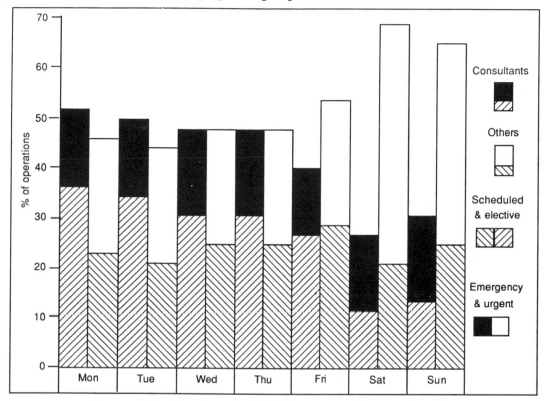

Figure 1.5 Day of week of CEPOD operations (Surgeons' grades)

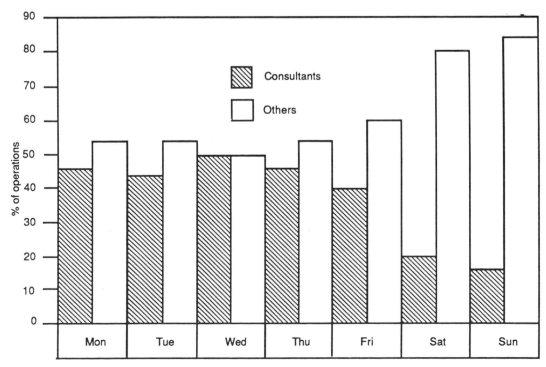

Figure 1.6 Days of week of CEPOD operations (anaesthetists grades)

19

THE QUESTIONNAIRES

Was the questionnaire relevant, *ie.* did it obtain the type of information it was designed to obtain?

The purpose of the questionnaire was to provide enough information for the assessors to complete an assessment form; and to provide a data base for computer analysis. Assessors meetings were therefore held where sample questionnaires were discussed and their content altered accordingly.

Did the questionnaire collect all the relevant information?

The requests for further information from assessors was perhaps the most telling indication of whether enough information was available to make an assessment. This was 6.4% of cases throughout the study, although some assessors always asked for more and others never asked for more. Those assessors who were also participants fell mainly into the latter category. It was considered desirable that each questionnaire completed and returned be accompanied by the relevant operating note or anaesthetic record, together with a copy of the autopsy report where one was carried out. We found that 67.8% of surgeons sent a copy of the operating note and 90.5% of anaesthetists, the anaesthetic record. In some cases the assessors would make a specific request for such information and a number of participants were specifically requested subsequently to send copies of records to us. Where an autopsy was known to have taken place we were supplied with 55.5% of the autopsy reports. Some clinicians thought the delay in obtaining copies of post-mortem reports were such that it was not feasible to wait for them and questionnaires would be returned anyway and the autopsy report sometimes arrived later.

Generally speaking, the questionnaires were completed well enough for assessors to make an assessment, especially when these were considered in conjunction with a copy of the operating note or anaesthetic record. Only 2.5% of the cases ended up as "unknown" or "not assessable" because of the lack of information. There were a number of cases where questions were left blank by the clinician completing the form, for example, "Where did the patient die?"; 1.9% did not answer and left this blank (see Part 3, table 3.2). Some forms were returned partially or wholly blank because of lost or incomplete notes. Two percent of local reporters missed one of the three dates they were asked to supply and in 10% of questionnaires the operation time was left blank.

Was the questionnaire accurate?

Even the "hard" data varied between the surgeon, anaesthetist and local reporter. For example, the date of death should be a simple characteristic upon which clinicians would agree. In approximately 15% of all cases disagreement on this date appeared. One case when received contained four different dates of death, depending on which of the local report, surgical, anaesthetic or autopsy report was analysed! Indeed, even the sex of the patient was sometimes in doubt with 1% of the cases showing disagreement between surgeon and anaesthetist. The time of death was even more widely disputed at the 20% level. Some of these discrepancies may be accounted for by the (mis)use of the 24-hour clock. The date of operation was also open to discrepancy in those cases where the patient had multiple operations in a short space of time. In addition 4% of surgeons and anaesthetists disagreed on whether an autopsy was carried out. In the realm of data which involved judgemental factors, there was even larger disagreement, *eg.* on ASA grade of patient or the operation type (see table 1.9).

There were other obvious cases of internal inaccuracy, *eg.* sending a patient to an intensive therapy unit (ITU) which the clinician had said in the previous question did not exist (eight cases); further complicating this matter some clinicians at the same hospital claimed there was in fact an ITU. This phenomena of clinicians within the same hospital and specialty disagreeing also appeared in response to the question "Do you have regular mortality review meetings", with some answering "yes", (see Part 4, table 4.155), and others (in the same hospital) claiming "no". These inconsistencies should be borne in mind by anyone considering the setting up of a data base supplied by clinicians.

Did the questionnaire have face validity?

Did it look as though it measured what it was supposed to measure? Some consultants returned their forms because they did not think the form had face validity, ie. it was "irrelevant" to the operation they had done or "irrelevant" to that type of patient or "irrelevant" because they "obviously" died of overwhelming disease. There was a view put forward by consultants that CEPOD was only interested in "disasters" and other cases were of no interest despite our original explanation that we were attempting to assess **overall** standards in the three Regions and wanted information on **all** cases.

Did the questionnaire have content validity?

Did the questionnaire probe the area it was supposed to measure? In some cases, eg. clinical experience, it was obvious that surgeons were reporting having done more than twenty five cases, ie. the maximum figure in the question, despite some being quite rare operations. For example, there was one case where an assessor claimed it was "remarkable" that a consultant surgeon had done more than twenty five "debridement of scrotum" operations. In another case the likelihood that a surgical senior house officer had done more than twenty five operations for strangulated hernias was considered "very slim" by another assessor.

Repeatability

Clinicians. When, and if, the questionnaires were sent out twice, (thirty four cases of double reporting), there were very few cases where this was not spotted by the clinician, and in one instance, where a questionnaire was completed by the same clinician on the same patient, we found that some different answers were received, for example on the use of drugs, the differences were mainly those of omission where questions were answered on one form and left blank on the other. Re-testing of assessors was found to be difficult because of their recognition of having seen the case before.

Assessors. Where more than one assessor was used it was possible in rare instances to find every question answered differently. The use of implicit criteria of "how would I have done" could account for some of these differences. With regard to the scores it was possible in very few cases to have a score of 3 from one assessor and 10 from another (see table 1.3).

During the pilot study we were able to use multiple assessors on one particular case in order to gauge the variation between assessors at an early stage (see table 1.4).

Each questionnaire and assessment form required a score out of 10 on the performance of each part of the operation, ie. the pre, per and post-operative phases. A score of 10 could be regarded as no fault, 7 as adequate, 3 avoidable errors and 0 as total failure. It was intended that the whole scale would be used. However, we found that the majority of clinicians and subsequently the assessors, scored 7 for each phase (see figs. 1.7,1.8). We were able to compare the assessors' scores with those of the clinicians completing the forms and found that whilst there was some agreement between the scores, the assessors generally gave lower scores than the clinicians who completed the questionnaires. The individual participants were much more likely than the assessors to score themselves 7 or more for each case, with 90% of the cases containing scores of 7 or more from the participants in both disciplines.

When the assessors scored there was no difference between disciplines to be seen, with 80% of anaesthetic cases and 77.8% of surgical cases being scored 7 or more by the relevant

TABLE 1.3
Random cases seen by more than one assessor

| | Scores by assessor | | | | | Scores by assessor | | | |
Case no	First	Second	Third	Fourth	Case no	First	Second	Third	Fourth
1	7	5	6		6	9	10		
	10	5	7			10	10		
	7	5	6			9	5		
2	9	5			7	8	3	10	10
	7	7				10	-	10	10
	9	7				10	-	10	10
3	8	10			8	7	3	10	
	8	10				7	7	10	
	8	7				-	7	10	
4	3	6	10		9	3	3	3	3
	6	6	10			3	0	3	3
	3	5	5			-	-	-	3
5	10	8			10	6	7	7	
	10	8				7	8	10	
	10	8				7	8	10	

NB The four assessors are not the same in each case.

TABLE 1.4
One pilot study case assessed by 14 assessors

| | | | | Assessors' opinions | |
Assessor	Scores			Avoidable elements	Departures from ideal practice
A	10	10	10	NO	NO
B	6	7	6	YES	YES
C	3	3	3	YES	YES
D	3	7	3	YES	YES
E	3	5	10	YES	YES
F	Not assessable			N/A	YES
G	3	7	3	YES	YES
H	5	5	5	YES	YES
I	6	5	8	YES	YES
J	Not assessable			N/A	N/A
K	6	10	10	N/A	NO
L	9	10	10	N/A	NO
M	8	5	N/A	N/A	YES
N	9	10	10	NO	NO

N/A = Not assessable.

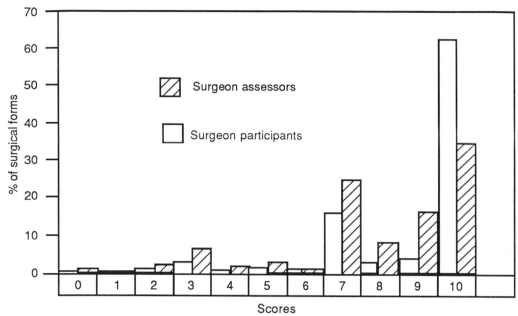

Figure 1.7 Comparison of scores (Surgeon)

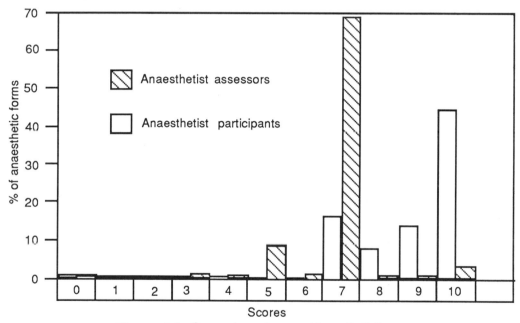

Figure 1.8 Comparison of scores (Anaesthetist)

assessors. There were very few cases recorded of total failure (*ie.* score zero for any phase); one hundred and thirty one surgical and thirty six anaesthetic cases had scores of zero.

Not too much emphasis should be placed on these scores since their variability determines that they may not be used in any precise manner. The scores were intended for use as a feedback mechanism and were not designed as an exact quality indicator. In general the anaesthetist participants scored themselves 10 for any phase in fewer cases (38%) than surgeon participants (58.3% of cases).

Figure 1.9 indicates the incidence of low assessors' scores *ie.* less than or equal to three, as given by the assessors. It suggests that, although the assessors score lower than clinicians in a majority of cases (see figs. 1.7,1.8), the surgeon assessors scored low in a greater proportion of cases than the anaesthetist assessors.

TABLE 1.5
Comparison of assessors and participants

	Anaesthetic forms %	Surgical forms%
Assessor scored lower than clinician	80.9	52.0
Assessor scored higher than clinician	3.7	12.3
Assessor scored same as clinician	15.4	35.6

NB Please see figures 1.7, 1.8 and 1.9.

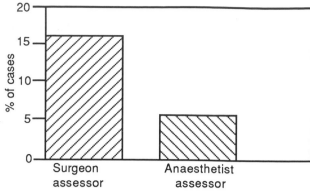

Figure 1.9 Incidence of low (less than 3) assessors scores

We found that the assessors tended to give low scores in cases where the assessors indicated that there were avoidable elements or that there were departures from ideal practice, with 48% and 47% of the anaesthetist and surgeon assessors respectively giving a score of 6 or less (less than adequate performance) compared to 6.7% and 3.6% respectively in other cases without avoidable elements or departures from ideal practice.

The assessors of each discipline were also given the opportunity to indicate if they considered surgery and/or anaesthesia as associated with the death. A validation programme ensured that where the assessors in each discipline disagreed with each others opinions, they were indicated for discussion by the coordinators. This did not happen frequently, but it is inevitable sometimes since these are clinical matters of judgement and different information was available to each discipline. Furthermore, in both disciplines, there was a reluctance to "blame" the other discipline as much as their own (see Part 4, table 4.151).

COMPARISONS WITH HAA (HOSPITAL ACTIVITY ANALYSIS) DATA.

The accuracy of statistical returns from the HAA system has far reaching effects on NHS resource management. It was used in this Enquiry as an independent external criterion for comparison of figures or for denominator data (*eg.* total numbers of operations). It became clear early in the Enquiry that in most cases whenever HAA was used as a checking device for the CEPOD figures obtained, the HAA data recorded larger numbers than CEPOD obtained figures. This first came to prominence during the pilot study when checks were done to estimate the coverage of CEPOD using HAA as the independent criterion for comparison (see table 1.6).

TABLE 1.6
Number of 30-day deaths

Pilot study area	HAA*	CEPOD
1	45	46
2	115	105
3	38	38

*HAA data supplied by regional statistics departments.

Individual cases were checked for completion of reporting by both HAA and CEPOD. We found that **both** HAA **and** CEPOD were deficient in containing all patients.

Some of the HAA patients not on the CEPOD list could be accounted for by the exclusions not applicable to CEPOD (*eg.* of the forty five HAA cases in area 1, seven were operations outside the CEPOD criteria). Further reasons for HAA patients not appearing on the CEPOD lists were, in area 2 particularly, those operated on in cottage hospitals where the methods for reporting back to the main hospital were not completely accurate. In fact, eight of the one hundred and fifteen HAA deaths in area 2 were at cottage hospitals. When these exclusions were accounted for, there were cases where CEPOD had not known about the deaths and they should have done; twenty five of the forty five HAA deaths in area 1 and seventeen of the thirty eight HAA deaths in area 3 were missed by CEPOD. The operations in those 30-day death cases missed by CEPOD but on HAA data in area 1 included; reduction with fixation ($\times$ 3), tracheostomy, oesophageal intubation, arthroplasty of hip ($\times$ 3), amputation, bronchoscopy ($\times$ 2), excision of rectum, anastomosis of intestine, colectomy, superficial drainage and laparotomy ($\times$ 2). In area 2, of the deaths missed by CEPOD, but on the HAA list, we found that the age profile was similar to that found in the subsequent main Enquiry.

Why did CEPOD miss cases?

Apart from the cottage hospital cases and the non-CEPOD cases, it is quite possible that further cases were not included because the consultants were not participating or the patient was in a private wing. Confusion existed over the differences between cardiac, and thoracic surgery, (the former being excluded); in area 3, seven of the seventeen HAA deaths unknown to CEPOD were admitted under a cardiothoracic surgeon. In some instances the local reporter knew the patient had died but could not obtain the patient's notes, or other mistakes were made on the exclusion criteria, (*eg.* local anaesthetics were not included by one local reporter). In addition, some HAA data included patients admitted under a surgeon, who visited the theatre, but who did not necessarily have any operation.

Why did HAA miss cases?

There were a number of cases reported to CEPOD of which the HAA had no record; twenty five of the forty six CEPOD deaths in area 1 and twenty of the thirty eight CEPOD deaths in area 3 were unknown to HAA. We found upon investigation that in some of these missing cases the patients' notes had either never been coded, or the coding forms had never reached the computer.

It is quite possible that within a medical records or coding department any notes of dead patients have a low priority and are therefore filed to be dealt with at a later date. We also investigated differences in the denominator rates we intended to use, *ie.* the number of operations carried out. Some local reporters were asked to provide details of the number of operations carried out in their hospitals from their theatre records. This was checked against the number of operations carried out according to Regional HAA data. Table 1.7 once again highlights the inconsistencies between HAA data and the data available in a hospital. It is possible that the HAA data recorded the same patient twice because they had more than one operation. Indeed, within the CEPOD system thirty four notifications were received which had already been reported and it is quite understandable that on a large scale many patients are coded twice.

Overall figures for the CEPOD main study and HAA 30-day deaths for the same period may be seen in table 1.8.

TABLE 1.7
Comparison of HAA and theatre records

Hospital	HAA*	Hospital theatre register
Hospital 1 Orthopaedic operations (1 year)	2709	2210
Hospital 1 All operations (1 year)	14359	11380
Hospital 2 All operations (2 months)	1368	1351
Hospital 3 General surgery (1 year)	4048	2734
Hospital 3 Fracture surgery (1 year)	732	670
Hospital 3 All operations (1 year)	12810	7140
Hospital 4 All operations (1 month)	513	562
Hospital 5 All operations(1 month)	912	846
Hospital 6 All operations (1 month)	1158	1038

* Supplied by statistics offices for the relevant regions.

TABLE 1.8
Comparison of HAA and CEPOD 30-day deaths

	Numbers	
Region	HAA 30-day deaths	CEPOD reported deaths
Northern	1469	1359
South Western	1853	1307
North East Thames	2485	1368

For a regional breakdown, see table 4.1.

CLUSTERING OF INFORMATION

It became clear almost as soon as the study began that pockets of "resistance to CEPOD" were beginning to emerge in each Region.

This first appeared in the consent to participate from each consultant. It was noticeable that in some hospitals, all the consultants were willing to participate. However, in other hospitals only a few were willing to consent. There were no hospitals, where all the surgeons or anaesthetists refused to cooperate, but there was one District where 45% of all the deaths reported to us could not be followed up because of just three non-participating consultants.

This type of clustering meant that 50% of the non-participating deaths reported to CEPOD originated in just three hospitals. The number of reports returned from individual hospitals showed considerable variations. Some Districts reported many deaths, some reported few. When compared with the HAA figures one can see (Part 4, table 4.1) that some hospitals' reporting systems were better than the HAA, whilst overall the HAA system contained more deaths. Some Districts were able to complete all the questionnaires and should be congratulated on the effort they put into this study. Unfortunately, some centres of comparable size, for one reason or another not always known to the Enquiry, returned less than 20% of the forms they were sent. The reasons varied from "The patient's notes have been lost for months", to "It's not in my job description to do this".

We had the agreement of seven consultant surgeons (who said they were too busy to complete our questionnaires), to peruse some of their deceased patients' hospital notes. A random sample was requested and nine out of ten requests were fulfilled. It is our overwhelming impression that it is not surprising that clinicians find retrospective completion of our questionnaires difficult, as the notes sampled were often dirty, ragged, disorganised, illegible, undated, unsigned and incomplete. If this is the standard with which all those who did complete forms coped, then we are even more grateful; but we think that good notes meant relatively easy cooperation and we believe that this matter speaks for itself. Of the nine records obtained, it was established that, in the assessors' opinion, seven looked "normal" but two cases would require more information, and could be classed as "of interest".

ERRORS

At each stage of data collection/collation, it was possible for errors to occur.

Local reporting

Omission errors. Table 1.8 shows that in comparison with HAA 30-day deaths data, the local reporters overall reported fewer deaths than those shown by HAA information. To some extent this was to be expected because of the inclusion in HAA data of cases CEPOD had excluded, for example, maternal mortality, cardiac operations, interventions by radiologists and physicians etc. (see supplementary notes in appendix 3).

Outside the protocol. The next most frequent errors in the actual reporting of deaths were those cases outside the CEPOD protocol, for example, cases with more than 30 days between operation and death, cases which did not have an operation, cases in private hospitals, cardiac surgery and operations carried out by non-surgeons accounted for 1.9% of all the reports we received.

Deaths at home. These were anticipated and two District Medical Officers in the Northern Region undertook to ensure that all deaths within 30 days of operation was reported. These two Districts reported 4.2% of the home deaths in the Northern Region. 1.5% of all CEPOD reports related to patients who died at home. Linkage Study data (Oxford) indicated that 6% of the 30-day post-operative deaths occur at home.

Errors of fact. Once the local reporters had reported a death, further errors of omission occurred when dates of death, birth or operation were missed or indeed names of anaesthetists were often unknown because the patient's notes had not yielded such information. (In these latter cases questionnaires were either sent back for clarification or on to the relevant chairman of division for his/her help).

Completion errors. The most frequent completion error on the part of the local reporter was double reporting. Some of these were explained by a change in local reporters, or support staff, midway through the Enquiry; others claimed logistical problems when hospitals moved or closed down, although all local reporters had a copy of each report for them to use as a check.

Miscellaneous exclusions. Twenty cases were notified before the study started and appeared to be in the study period but later had to be excluded when the true dates were known. One case was excluded because the local reporter later told us that the patient was fictitious!

Surgeons and anaesthetists

Failure to complete forms sent to clinicians varied from District to District (see Part 4, table 4.1). The failure to return forms was due to a number of factors.

It was a common feature of this Enquiry that, by the time some consultants were able to organise the completion of the form, or indeed when the patient's notes had been found, either the trainee operating surgeon or anaesthetising anaesthetist had moved from the hospital. We had one case where a trainee had moved away on rotation when the hospital received our forms but had returned by the time the patient's notes were found some six months later! Some consultants did complete forms in the absence of their juniors, others refused to do so and we found that sixty two forms were returned blank because the notes could not be found or the relevant person had left. In one case, the notes were lost when they were transferred from one hospital to another (they were put in the ambulance at one hospital but were not received at the other hospital!). Other cases existed where either the anaesthetist or surgeon completed and sent in their form to the CEPOD office, and shortly after that, the other of the pair wrote to say that he or she was unable to help at all in filling in their form because the patient's notes had "vanished for months".

Completion errors. Both the anaesthetic and surgical questionnaires requested the operation type for each case. The definitions of each type were reprinted in each questionnaire. However, these were not adhered to by the participants and all tables using operation type have been calculated from the dates given and **not** from the answers to the particular questions. We found that the participants indicated the wrong type in 46% of the cases with many clinicians (21%) indicating false emergency operations, whereas analysis of dates and times showed that only 1% of operations were true (by definition in the protocol) emergencies (table 1.9 below). We also found that there was a tendency to indicate urgent operations when the true (calculated) figure was lower. Consultants did seem able to indicate correctly when an elective operation took place. The large proportion of unknown operation types in table 1.9 are accounted for by cases where no questionnaires were returned and therefore no details were available.

TABLE 1.9
Operation types

Operation type**	Calculated from dates and times (%)	Given by anaesthetist (%)	Given by surgeon (%)
Emergency	1.2	21.0	21.0
Urgent	27.6	43.9	38.8
Scheduled	48.3	27.6	31.8
Elective	8.4	7.3	8.1
Unknown*	14.5	0.1	0.4

*Dates/times not given therefore unable to calculate
**Definitions as provided in both questionnaires:

Emergency: immediate operation, resuscitation simultaneous with surgical treatment (eg.ruptured aneurysm; head, chest and abdominal injuries). Operation usually within one hour.
Urgent: delayed operation as soon as possible after resuscitation (eg.intestinal obstruction, embolism, perforation, major fractures). Operation usually within 24 hours.
Scheduled: an early operation but not immediately life saving (eg.cancer, cardiovascular surgery). Operation usually between 1 and 3 weeks.
Elective: operation at a time to suit both patient and surgeon (eg.cholecystectomy).

Assessors

Omission errors. Some assessors did not complete all of the questions contained in their forms (see appendix 3). Some would not give scores and others only answered as far as question 9, despite the "and/or" placed next to the further parts of question 9. Cases of omission were dealt with by the clinical coordinators. A computer validation exercise identified those cases in which assessors had answered the question on "Were there avoidable elements?" positively, but had not specified these in question 9. Furthermore, any positive answers to question 9 had also to have positive answers to one or more of the subsets of factors, where applicable.

Completion errors. There was a check on the answers the assessors had given; this was a second opinion exercise where the cases were assessed by more than one assessor. The coordinators compared the answers given by surgeon assessors with those given by anaesthetist assessors and were able to rationalise and/or eliminate discrepancies. It was not always possible to pinpoint false replies to questions unless a second opinion was in conflict with the first, because implicit criteria were used.

AUTOPSIES AND CORONERS' REPORTS

There was some variation between the three Regions in the autopsy rate carried out on CEPOD patients (see table 1.10). We were able to establish which of the patients who died within 48 hours of an operation had an autopsy (see Part 4, table 4.6). In fact 43.8% of such patients had an autopsy. Variations between Regions also appeared in the attendance of a member of the surgical or anaesthetic teams at the post-mortem. Surgeons were much more likely to go to a post-mortem (see table 1.11). The reasons for non-attendance are unknown to CEPOD, however, one clinician entered the comment that his "priorities are with the living", and therefore did not attend.

TABLE 1.10
Autopsies

| Autopsy performed | SW | | N | | NET | |
	A	S	A	S	A	S
Yes	39.9	43.4	29.1	30.4	32.1	37.2
No	48.4	51.6	58.2	65.4	46.9	56.9
Not answered	11.7	5.0	12.7	4.2	21.0	5.9

A = Anaesthetists' answer. S = Surgeons' answer.
NB Anaesthetists & surgeons data not comparable because of cases with incomplete data.

TABLE 1.11
Attendance at autopsy

Autopsy	Anaesthetists	Surgeons
% attended	3.7	27.8

Autopsies may not take place at a convenient time and location, in some instances the clinician may not even be aware that an autopsy was to take place. In fact, the "blank" response to the question "Was there an autopsy?" of 14% may give an indication of the unawareness about autopsies. Coroners do not routinely notify clinicians of the date and time of an autopsy although the clinicians have a legitimate interest in cases that die soon after an operation.

REFERENCES

1. Six days to die. *The Lancet*, 1982;August,**21**:424.
2. Donabedian, A., *The definition of quality and approaches to its assessment.* Ann Arbor, Michigan: Health Administration Press, 1980.
3. Maxwell, R. J., Quality assessment in health. *British Medical Journal*, 1984;**288**:1470-2.
4. Lembcke, P. A., Evolution of the medical audit. *Journal of the American Medical Association*, 1967;**199**:543-50.
5. Codman, E. A., Report of a Committee on Hospital Standardisation. *Surgery, Gynecology and Obstetrics*, 1916;**22**:119-20.
6. Williamson, J. W., Improving medical practice and health care. *Journal of the American Medical Association*, 1977;**216**:1109.
7. Richardson, F. Mc D., Peer review of medical care. *Medical Care*, 1972;**10**:29-39.
8. Doyle, J. C., Unnecessary hysterectomies study of 6248 operations in 35 hospitals during 1948. *Journal of the American Medical Association*, 1953;**151**:360-5.
9. Fessel, W.V. & Van Brunt, E. R., Quality of care and medical record. *New England Journal of Medicine*, 1972;**286**:134-8.
10. Brook, R. H. & Appel, F. A., Quality of care assessment choosing a method for peer review. *New England Journal of Medicine*, 1973;**288**:1323-9.
11. Rosser, R. M., The reliability and application of clinical judgement in evaluating use of hospital beds. *Medical Care*, 1976;**14**:39-48.
12. Rutstein, D. D., Berenberg, W. et al., Measuring the quality of medical care. *New England Journal of Medicine*, 1976;**294**:582-588.
13. Beecher, H. K. & Todd D. P., A study of the deaths associated with anesthesia and surgery based on a study of 599,428 anesthesias in 10 institutions 1948-52, inclusive. *Annals of Surgery*, 1954;**140**:2-35.
14. Greene, N. M. et al., Survey of deaths associated with anesthesia in Conneticut; a review of 120,935 anaesthetics. *Connecticut Medicine*, 1959;**23**:512-8.
15. Phillips, O. C. et al., The Baltimore Anesthesia Study Committee: review of 1,024 postoperative deaths. *Journal of the American Medical Association*, 1960;**174**:2015-9.
16. Dripps, R. D. & Vandam, L. D., Long-term follow-up of patients who received 10,098 spinal anesthetics: failure to discover major neurological sequelae. *Journal of the American Medical Association*, 1954;**156**:1486-91.
17. Gaff, T. D. et al., Baltimore Anesthesia Study Committee: factors in pediatric anesthesia mortality. *Anaesthesia and Analgesia*, 1964;**43**:407-14.
18. Memery, H. N., Anaesthesia mortality in private practice: a 10 year study. *Journal of the American Medical Association*, 1965;**194**:1185-8.
19. Holland, R., Special committee investigating deaths under anaesthesia: report on 745 classified cases, 1960-68. *Medical Journal of Australia*, 1970;**1**:573-94.
20. Holland, R., Anaesthesia-related mortality in Australia. *International Anaesthesiology Clinics*, 1984;**22**:61-71.
21. Bodlander, F. M. S., Deaths associated with anaesthesia. *British Journal of Anaesthesia*, 1975;**47**:36-40.
22. Van't Hoff, W., 1981 Audit Reviewed: A report from the Regions. *Journal of the Royal College of Physicians of London*, 1981;**15**:135-6.
23. Gebbie, D., Anaesthesia and death. *Canadian Anaesthetists' Society Journal*, 1966;**13**:390-6.
24. Minuck, M., Death in the operating room. *Canadian Anaesthetists' Society Journal*, 1967;**14**:197-204.
25. Turnbull, K. W. et al., Death within 48 hours of anaesthesia at the Vancouver General Hospital. *Canadian Anaesthetists' Society Journal*, 1980;**27**:159-63.
26. *Proceedings of the European Academy of Anaesthesiology III*. Mortality in Anaesthesia. Vickers, M. D. and Lunn, J. N., Springer Verlag 1983.
27. Harrison, G. G., Anaesthetic contributory deaths – its incidence and causes. *South African Medical Journal*, 1968;**42**:514-18, 544-9.
28. Hovi-Viander, M., Death associated with anaesthesia in Finland. *British Journal of Anaesthesia*, 1980;**52**:483-9.

29. Wing, A. J., Why don't the British treat more patients with kidney failure? *British Medical Journal*, 1983;**287**:1157-9.
30. Swansea Physicians Audit Group. Audit reviewed: implementing audit in a division of medicine. *Journal of the Royal College of Physicians of London*, 1983;**17**:235-8.
31. Yates, J. M. & Davidge, M. G., Can you measure performance? *British Medical Journal*, 1984;**288**:1935-6.
32. Pollitt, C., MEASURING PERFORMANCE: A New System for the National Health Service. *Policy & Politics*, 1985;**13**:No 1,1-15.
33. *Guide to Hospital Waiting Lists 1985*; College of Health.
34. Office of Health Economics: Nov 1986, *'WHAT ARE MY CHANCES DOCTOR?' A review of clinical risks.*
35. Quality assurance; Yardsticks evolved for patient care. *Health and Social Service Journal*, 1984;June, 674.
36. Lee, J. A., Morrison, S. L. & Morris, J. N., Case fatality in teaching and non teaching hospitals. *The Lancet*, 1960;**1**:171-172.
37. Ashley, J. S. A., Howlett, A. & Morris, J., Case fatality of hyperplasia of the prostate in two teaching and three Regional board hospitals. *The Lancet*, 1971;**2**:1308.
38. Lipworth, L., Lee, J. A. H & Morris, J. N., Case fatality in teaching and non teaching hospitals. *Medical Care*, 1963;**1**:71.
39. Howie, J. G. R., Death from appendicitis and appendicectomy. *The Lancet*, 1966;**2**:1334-7.
40. Rosser, R. M. & Watts, V. C.,The measurement of hospital output, *International Journal of Epidemiology*, 1972;**1**:361.
41. Irving, M. & Temple, J., Surgical Audit: one year's experience in a teaching hospital. *British Medical Journal*, 1976;**2**:746-7.
42. Gough, M. H., Kettlewell, M. G. W., Mark, C. G. *et al.*, Audit: An annual assessment of the work and performance of a surgical firm in a regional teaching hospital. *British Medical Journal*, 1980;**281**:913-18.
43. Gilmore, O. J. A. *et al.*, Surgical Audit – comparisons of work load and results of two hospitals in the same District. *British Medical Journal*, 1980;**281**:1050-2.
44. Jeffreys, R. V. & James, J., Avoidable factors contributing to the death of head injury patients in a general hospital in Mersey Region. *The Lancet*, 1981;**2**:459-461.
45. Jennett, B. & Carlin, J., Preventable mortality and morbidity after head injury. *Injury*, 1979;**10**:31-9.
46. Mersey Region Working Party on perinatal mortality. Confidential inquiry into perinatal deaths in Mersey Region. *The Lancet*, 1982;**1**:491-3.
47. *Wales Perinatal Mortality Initiative* 1984-86 Report of the Perinatal Mortality Initiative Group.
48. Fielding, L. P., Stuart-Brown, S., Dudley, H. A. F., Surgeon related variables and the clinical trial. *The Lancet*, 1978;**2**:778-9.
49. *Epidemiology in Anaesthesia*. Edward Arnold, London. 1986. Ed. J. N. Lunn.
50. Edwards, G. *et al.*, Deaths associated with anaesthesia. *Anaesthesia*, 1956;**11**:194.
51. Dinnick, O. P., Anaesthetic deaths. *Anaesthesia*, 1964;**19**:125.
52. Lunn, J. N., Mushin, W. W., *Mortality associated with Anaesthesia*. London, Nuffield Provincial Hospitals Trust 1982.
53. Green, R. A. & Taylor, T. H., An analysis of anaesthesia medical liability claims in the United Kingdom, 1977-82. *International Anaesthesiology Clinics*, 1984;**22**:73-89.
54. Dripps, R. D., Lamont, A., Eckenhoff, J. E., The role of anesthesia in surgical mortality. *Journal of the American Medical Association*, 1961;**178**:261-6
55. Owens, W. D., Dykes, M. H. M. *et al.*, Development of two indices of post-operative morbidity. *Surgery*, 1975;**77**:586-92.
56. Soper, K. & McPeek, B., Predicting mortality for high risk surgery. In: *Health care delivery in anesthesia*, Philadelphia, George F. Stickley 1980,99-103.
57. Maxwell, R., Quality assessment in health, in: *NHS management perspectives for doctors*. King Edward's Hospital Fund for London, 1985.
58. Duncan, A., Quality assurance: What now and where next? *British Medical Journal*, 1980;**1**:300-2.
59. McQuillan, W. J., 1972-74 *Medical Audit* – Oxford Centre for Management Studies.
60. Preventable anaesthetic mortality and morbidity. *Anaesthesia*, 1985;**40**:79.
61. Vuori, H. Y., 1982 *Quality assessment of health services; concepts and methodologies*. Public Health in Europe; **16.** Regional Office for Europe, WHO, Copenhagen.
62. Hirschorn, N. Lamstein, J. H. McCormack, J. Klein, S. F., *Quality of care assessment and assurance*. G. K. Hall, 1978.

ACKNOWLEDGEMENTS

During the introduction of CEPOD throughout the three Regions it was necessary to visit and contact various bodies in order to inform and receive advice on its setting up and smooth running. We are indebted to the following groups not listed in the protocol, who helped and encouraged us to carry on:

Regional Medical Officers
District Medical Officers
Regional Nursing Officers
The Statistical Offices of the Northern, South Western and North East Thames Regional Health Authorities.

In particular, the Regional Medical Officers were unanimous in their support of the Enquiry and facilitated the payment of travelling expenses for assessors to attend seminars to discuss CEPOD.

In addition, we would like to particularly acknowledge the assistance of the following people:

Dr R D Jack
Mr G McLachlan
Dr M Ashley-Miller
Dr R Maxwell

The CEPOD office was at King Edward's Hospital Fund for London at first and then later (5 January 1987), moved to the Association of Anaesthetists of Great Britain and Ireland at 9 Bedford Square, London WC1.

HONORARIA

Local reporters were paid an honoraria of £2 *per* report for the pilot study, and £1 *per* death reported in the main study.

Assessors, clinical coordinators and participants involved in the CEPOD study did so on a voluntary basis, without renumeration, except for any travelling expenses incurred on CEPOD business.

part 2

surgery

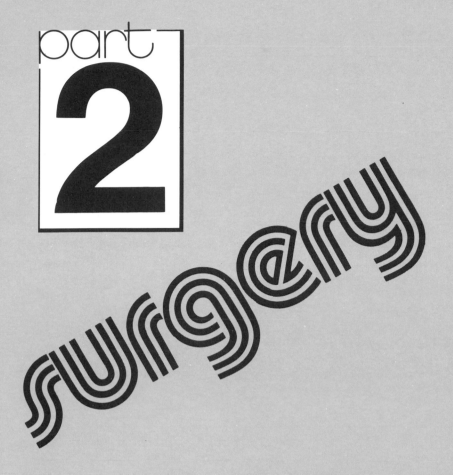

H. BRENDAN DEVLIN

M.A., M.D., M.Ch., F.R.C.S.

*Consultant surgeon, North Tees General Hospital,
Stockton on Tees, Cleveland TS19 8PE*

part 2 surgery

CONTENTS

INTRODUCTION

The assessment and analysis of the surgical data were undertaken in a different way from the anaesthetic data, the many surgical disciplines, orthopaedic, vascular surgery, gynaecology, neurosurgery etc., have necessitated this approach. As described in Part 1, the returned surgical forms were sent to appropriate assessors in the specialty concerned. When the assessments were completed and all the data collected, small groups of assessors in each specialty met together to discuss the data and draw conclusions. These are indicated (by an asterisk *) in the assessors' list in Part 4. For some very specialised topics further expert advice was sought. Particular attention has been given to upper intestinal surgery, colorectal, vascular, orthopaedic, urology, gynaecology, neurosurgery and paediatric surgery, as well as the management of multiple trauma. Both organisational and clinical features of the data were considered in this way.

Operations

The types and numbers of operations varied widely. The Office of Populations Censuses and Surveys (OPCS) classification of surgical operations (Third revision) was used to code each operation to three digits. There were two hundred and twenty four different types of operations coded in the CEPOD study, the five most common were; laparotomy (21.9%), dynamic hip screw (7.8%), hemiarthroplasty (4.8%), hemicolectomy (4.8%) and aortic aneurysm repair (4.6%).

Diagnoses

The working diagnoses made by the surgeons, using the International Classification of Diseases (ICD 9th revision) amounted to two hundred and eighteen different codes, the five most common were; fractured femur (12.1%), obstruction of the intestine (7.1%), aortic aneurysm (5.3%), peptic ulcer (5.0%) and cancer of the colon (4.7%).

Use of the ICD codes led to the recording of one hundred and twenty three different causes of death in the CEPOD study. The five most common clinical causes of death were; bronchopneumonia (13.5%), congestive cardiac failure (10.8%), myocardial infarction (8.4%), pulmonary embolism (7.8%) and respiratory failure (6.5%).

Background

The surgical practice in three Regions reviewed varied considerably. Each Region contains one or more university hospitals with the whole panoply of modern medicine available, equally each Region contains some very small, often relatively isolated Districts, with small hospitals and few consultants. However, equity of delivery of care, equity of standards of care and equity of access, are health service premises; CEPOD has set out to review the surgical and anaesthetic responses to these premises. In the university hospital detailed subspecialty differentiation of surgeons is commonplace, in the small Districts the undifferentiated surgeon is a necessity but, to be effective, the surgeon must have discriminative skills to decide on whom to operate and whom to refer elsewhere. He must also know what tertiary facilities are available and he must himself have the basic skills in his discipline to enable him to do his task locally. We have set out to discover how these objectives were being met.

In making our comments, we realise that this exercise depends on confidentiality and trust, trust particularly that an individual consultant or District will not be named. Although our data base is the individual consultant or District in order to maintain anonymity we publish no identifiable data broken down further than to Regional level.

Before reviewing the data received and the assessors' comments it must be emphasised that we are only reporting the management of patients who have died. Over the study period 555258 patients underwent surgical operations in the three study Regions, 4034 deaths were reported to CEPOD and our enquiries have been successful in recovering the surgical data on 2784 of these. 551224 patients had operations performed by the same surgeons, anaesthetised by the same anaesthetists, and survived. We know nothing about these patients other than that they had operations and survived. This lack of control data inhibits our drawing some conclusions from the data available, any conclusions we draw are based on the opinions of our assessors. Others may draw other conclusions based on their own opinions of these data. However, in the end these data must stand alone subject to the principle of *res ipsa loquitur*.

Whatever inferences are drawn from the surgical data it is important to realise that CEPOD is unique, the exercise was entirely voluntary, everyone involved in a self-audit of this nature knew that adverse criticism would emerge yet 93% of the consultant surgeons participated and when the letter box was closed to allow analysis to proceed 69% of all the surgical data had been returned. No other profession has successfully undertaken self-audit on this scale. Medical audit is concerned with the balance between personal responsibility and societal accountability on the one hand, or between professional judgement and the application of clinical science on the other. It is to be hoped that the data presented here will encourage surgeons to re-appraise and adjust these balances appropriately.

The enquiry is consultant based, we make no apology for this; the consultant should set the standards of quality and quantity for his team, he is vicariously responsible for his trainees and juniors. If he is responsible he needs to know what the action is, completing the forms for this enquiry has enabled surgeons to know that is happening on their own firms and, after an aggregation, how they compare to their peers.

THE OVERALL PICTURE

The surgical form was designed to be "user friendly" to **all** the surgical specialties. This has imposed constraints on the data collected. We set out to discover the important clinical and organisational aspects of surgical practice in three English Regions.

The majority of patients were elderly (see Part 1, fig. 1.1). The majority of these patients were urgent or emergency admissions (see table 2.1). These two facts must be appreciated when considering the data.

TABLE 2.1
Mode of admission for specific operations

Operation	Admission type*		
	Elective	Urgent	Emergency
Inguinal hernias	35.1	5.5	59.2
Peptic ulcers	0.0	7.6	89.4
Dynamic hip screws	0.6	21.7	76.4
Amputations	24.0	33.0	43.0

* For definitions see questionnaires in appendix 3.
NB Rows do not total 100% because of cases where the admission type was not answered.

REPLIES TO THE SURGICAL FORM

Specialty of consultant surgeon

Not unsurprisingly the specialties of consultants reporting the most deaths are general surgery, vascular surgery, and orthopaedic surgery, this distribution fits the principal causes of surgical intervention for critically ill patients, carcinoma, peripheral vascular disease and senile fractures (see Part 4, table 4.17).

Our assessors have commented on the lack of congruence between the specialty of the consultant surgeon and the operation undertaken, one consultant surgeon has claimed to be a specialist in five different categories, another in three, and so on; the claim to specialty was clearly made when the consultants were operating outside their known specialty. Equally worrying are instances of out-dated or inappropriate operations being performed by consultants (or their juniors) who are undertaking work for which they have no particular expertise.

There are always debates about turf among surgeons and the boundaries of surgical specialties are constantly changing. Our assessors understand and participate in these debates themselves but general surgeons undertaking non-urgent brain surgery or doing skilled urology, urologists doing skilled colorectal surgery, gynaecologists doing vascular surgery and orthopaedic surgeons doing bowel surgery, are examples that are difficult to defend.

Organisation, delegation and accountability

Assessors are most concerned by the lack of "control" some consultants seem to exercise over their trainees and junior staff. There are significant differences between the Regions and the specialties here (see Part 4, tables 4.7, 4.26, 4.24). For example (see Part 4, tables 4.25, 4.26), the consultant surgeon was consulted pre-operatively in 66.6% of the deaths where the operating surgeon was not a consultant reported in the Northern Region; the consultant surgeon took the history in 72% of the cases in the Northern Region; he was the most senior surgeon to examine the patient pre-operatively in 79% of the cases in the Northern Region (see Part 4, tables 4.15, 4.16). In contrast, while the consultant surgeon was consulted in 55% of instances in the North East Thames Region, he took the history himself in only 53% of instances and examined the patient himself in 58.5% of cases in North East Thames.

Similarly paediatric, cardiothoracic and neurological surgeons apparently exercise more "control" (measured by pre-operative consultation) than consultants in other disciplines.

General surgeons exercise more control than orthopaedic surgeons (when comparing the two specialties with the greatest burden of emergency admissions). This may be related to local staffing levels and workload but we are concerned that many of the cases referred to us (patients who were critically ill) were operated on by junior staff without prior consultation with the consultant surgeon in charge.

Inexperienced operators

Our assessors are similarly concerned that many operations were undertaken by surgeons too junior and too inexperienced to do the job. Assessors commented that mistakes were frequently made by these surgeons.

Two different "explanations" for these facts are advanced. Firstly, in some of the very small Districts where there are four or fewer consultant surgeons, the consultant surgeons may be so stretched with their regular service work in the daytime that they cannot exercise adequate supervision over critically ill emergency admissions out of hours, and there is some anecdotal evidence from the surgical forms to suggest that this may be the case. This is particularly true in the management of more specialised emergencies, particularly vascular emergencies, where in a small District only one surgeon may have expertise in vascular surgery and yet there is an Accident and Emergency (A&E) Department open which takes ruptured aortic aneurysms. If the surgeon with the expertise is not on duty that night somebody else has to perform the operation. On the other hand, we have found instances of grave failure of supervision in large District General and in large metropolitan teaching hospitals. There seems to be little excuse for large hospitals with large consultant surgical staff not being able to exercise complete consultant supervision at all times. This lack of supervision in many cases has led our assessors to recommend that no patient should undergo a surgical operation without prior consultation being obtained by the operating surgeon with the consultant on duty or his senior registrar.

Hours on duty

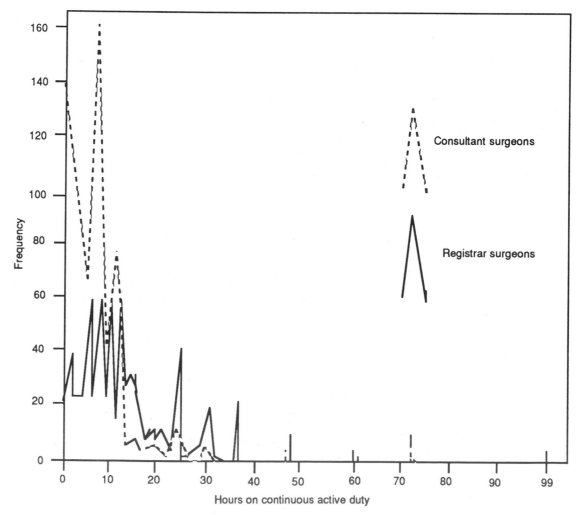

Figure 2.1 Hours on "continuous active duty" of operating surgeon

The questionnaire asked how many hours of continuous active duty had the surgeon undertaken prior to the surgical operation. The graph (see fig. 2.1) shows little evidence of excessive duty hours. The great majority of operating surgeons being on duty for less than 24 hours prior to undertaking the surgical intervention reported. A further group was on duty for up to 36 hours, but there are few examples of surgeons being on duty for excessive hours of duty longer than this. In the whole series there were only twenty examples where fatigue was cited by the consultant surgeons as a factor in the operative management of the patient, and of these all were investigated and only two of these cases were validated by the assessors who reviewed the cases. This is reassuring and, although the data are soft, and subject to digit number preference, at the moment, there seems to be little evidence that fatigue is a factor in operative failure, or that junior doctors or consultants who are operating are subjected to prolonged hours of duty leading to operative failure. Nonetheless, assessors cited possible fatigue as a factor in deaths associated with surgery in twenty six cases (see Part 4, table 4.59). We found (see Part 4, tables 4.8, 4.9, 4.13) that consultant surgeons do more of the operations which result in death during the working hours of the week and the junior staff tend to do more in the out of hours work and at the weekends. However, this was not as marked as assessors had expected it to be, and overall we found that the consultant surgeons carry a heavy burden of work both during the weekdays in office hours and out of hours too (see Part 1, figs. 1.5,1.6).

Regional variations in surgeons' behaviour

There are clear differences between the three Regions, both in their enthusiasm and ability to participate in the Confidential Enquiry into Perioperative Deaths, and in the accuracy of their reporting, and the avoidable factors reported in each Region. These are enumerated in Part 4, tables 4.1 and 4.54. Of the three Regions the Northern Region shows the highest degree of consultant involvement (see Part 4, tables 4.13, 4.25) and the greatest enthusiasm for this form of audit coupled with an ability to carry the enterprise through to the end. Between the Districts there are great differences in the involvement in the Confidential Enquiry into Perioperative Deaths. The percentage of avoidable factors in each Region is an average but there are marked differences in the rates reported in the different Districts (see fig. 2.2). The use of pre-operative investigations did not vary importantly between the three Regions (see Part 4, table 4.30).

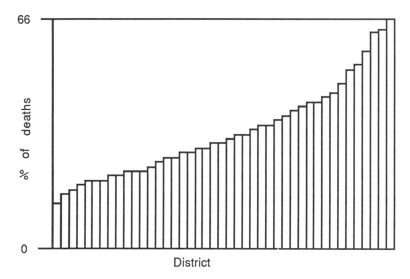

Figure 2.2 Percent of deaths assessed as "avoidable"
(Surgeon assessors' opinion)
NB Some districts reported few deaths (see table 4.1)

In house quality control

The question "Do you have mortality meetings?"* elicited very different responses across the specialties (see Part 4, table 4.19). There is concern with quality control in general surgery and in specialties such as urology and cardiothoracic surgery. However it is notable that one of the specialties with the most deaths reported in an age group with high co-morbidity, orthopaedic surgery, shows a very small percentage of consultants participating in local mortality meetings (see Part 4, table 4.20). This is disappointing.

There is a clear need here for all Districts in all Regions to review their in-house procedures and particularly to review their in-house quality control.

*Mortality and morbidity meetings are a structured meeting of all surgeons in a hospital reviewing all their poor outcomes corporately and non judgementally, and then adjusting their practice accordingly.

ASSESSORS' OPINIONS

Avoidable elements in surgical practice

The assessors were asked about avoidable elements in the management of patients which might, if corrected, have altered the outcome and were also asked were there departures from ideal practice which were worthy of comments (see Part 4, tables 4.54, 4.55). There are Regional differences in the responses to these opinion questions. These deficiencies may have been failure to consult with a consultant; they may have been an inappropriate operator; they may not have made any great difference to the outcome, nevertheless they do represent less than optimum surgical practice. This question of inappropriateness was pursued with the assessors who were asked would they themselves have agreed to operate on the patients, and in 5.6% of the surgical cases the assessors would not have operated (see Part 4, table 4.56). The assessors gave the opinion not to operate in cases of disseminated neoplasia when many felt that an operation was unjustified, the cause and the prognosis could have been settled using modern diagnostic techniques. In patients aged greater than 80 years old with ruptured aortic aneurysms and patients with fractured neck of femur with severe co-morbidity the assessors would have decided that there was little opportunity for the patient to survive an operation and therefore would not have operated. If a decision not to operate is to be made, it is essential that this be made jointly between the consultant surgeon and the consultant anaesthetist.

Deaths associated with surgery

In the opinion of the surgeon assessors the deaths were related to surgery in 30% of the cases (see Part 4, table 4.58), but it must be stressed that this relation to surgery does overlap with the consequences of the presenting surgical disease and the consequences of intercurrent co-disease. These are not mutually exclusive and indeed co-morbidity accounted for perhaps half of the deaths following surgical intervention reported.

Failure of surgery alone was given as the cause of death in 7% of patients (see Part 4, table 4.72). The assessors cited a whole range of overlapping factors that contributed to this surgical failure, the inappropriateness of the operation, the inappropriateness of the pre-operative management, an inappropriate grade of operating surgeon, and so on. It is, however, to be noted that inappropriate pre-operative management, inappropriate operation and deaths related to surgery are more marked when junior unsupervised surgeons are operating on their own (see Part 4, tables 4.66, 4.69, 4.70). When consultants operate their pre-operative and intra-operative management is generally considered good by their peers. Consultants usually undertake the most difficult cases though the assessors have expressed surprise on some occasions that these difficult cases were not referred to experts in that particular field.

Immediate pre-operative review of the patient

The failure of the surgeons to identify and check the patients pre-operatively in 1.2% of cases is recorded with regret (see Part 4, table 4.32). Similarly the failure of the operating surgeon to review the notes and working diagnosis immediately prior to surgery is also recorded in 6% of cases (see Part 4, table 4.33). In two instances the wrong side of a patient was operated on (one burr holes for extradural haemorrhage and one for a fractured neck of femur).

Problems with notes

The inadequacy of the patient's notes was a frequently mentioned cause of inability to complete the reply to us, and it is interesting to note that there are differences between the Regions here (see Part 4, table 4.48). The notes are apparently more complete in the Northern Region than they are in North East Thames, or perhaps they are more accessible in the Northern Region than they are in North East Thames. Clearly this is an area of anxiety. This adequacy of the notes to the surgeons correlates with the surgeon assessors' views of the replies furnished to CEPOD. The surgeon assessors find the information supplied to CEPOD adequate in 96.8% of cases (see Part 4, table 4.53), but again it is noticed that in 4.5% of the cases from North East Thames the data base supplied was inadequate for an assessment.

Shortage of trained personnel in the theatre (See Part 4, table 4.41)

Only a small percentage of surgeons claimed there was shortage of trained personnel in theatre. One of these indicated a shortage of nursing staff. We pursued this claim but our subsequent correspondence with the consultant concerned and the opinion of our assessors failed to validate this. This is a surprising finding, despite the widespread quoted shortage of nurses in theatre, this national shortage was not validated as contributing to deaths in our sample.

Lack or deficiency of surgical equipment according to the surgeon (See Part 4, table 4.43)

There is a small but worrying shortage of equipment as reported to us. In some cases the equipment shortage led directly to the mortality. The necessity of having all the instruments and prostheses for vascular, orthopaedic, neurosurgical and thoracic surgery available in each theatre receiving emergency admissions needs re-iteration. Ruptured aortic aneurysm patients died because vascular clamps were not available. One patient requiring an urgent thoracotomy died because the thoracotomy instruments had been discarded inadvertently and the general manager had refused to replace them immediately as a cost containment measure.

Available operating theatres

The general principle that one fully equipped theatre must be kept available to deal with emergencies is made over and over again in the reports to us. Failure to do this led to two patients with leaking aneurysms (two separate Districts) dying during transit from the one hospital's Accident and Emergency Department to another hospital with the available equipped operating theatre. In both these instances the surgeon reporting the death also informed us that previous complaints to the Health Authority had not resolved the issue.

Another patient bled to death from a chest wound. Consultants should not, and cannot, provide on call support to more than one hospital at once. An aneurysm patient died because the consultant was operating elsewhere and there are other examples.

Which hospital?

Another cause of concern is the practice of undertaking critical surgery at sites where no intensive therapy unit (ITU) facilities are available. Again this was cited as a contributory factor in some deaths. An example will make the point, a 58 year-old male underwent a straightforward abdomino-perineal resection of the rectum. This was performed in a satellite hospital without an ITU twenty five miles from the main District General Hospital. Seven days post-operatively the patient had a myocardial infarct. With no ITU care the patient's management was compromised and he died. The assessors questioned the wisdom of undertaking this major surgery in such a setting.

Other difficulties indicated by surgeons (see Part 4, tables 4.44, 4.45, 4.46)

These tables can be considered together since the factors listed in each overlap to some extent.

Continuity of care: Interdisciplinary transfers. Three clinical situations figure here, paediatric medicine to paediatric surgical units, general medicine to general surgical and geriatric to general surgical and othopaedic units. The diagnoses include neo-natal obstruction and diaphragmatic hernias, gastro-intestinal haemorrhage and fractured femoral necks.

Continuity of care: Surgical team and shift changes. These problems are related to failure to adequately brief the next on duty surgical team about the status of critically ill patients.

Summarising all these factors (see Part 4, tables 4.43, 4.44, 4.45, 4.46) our groups of assessors stress the importance in each District of having **only one** Accident and Emergency Department where all emergencies are brought, with one on site fully-equipped emergency operating theatre and with an on-site ITU. And consultants only being on call for one hospital (District) at one time.

Districts need to develop mandatory protocols for interdisciplinary transfers so these are accomplished rapidly with transfer of patient and appropriate clinical detail. Cross cover between surgical teams needs improving; in the CEPOD experience cross cover between different hospital sites was problematic (see Part 4, table 4.46).

Surgeons also have a responsibility not to admit patients for important surgery, particularly patients with significant co-morbidity (ASA Grades 4,5) to isolated hospitals where full recovery and ITU facilities are unavailable.

LOCAL ANAESTHETICS ADMINISTERED BY SURGEONS

Surgeons reported (on the surgical form) one hundred and eighty one cases in which the surgeon himself had administered anaesthetic agents. In ninety five of these cases the surgeon gave intravenous drugs to facilitate endoscopy; in eighty six the surgeon had administered a local or regional anaesthetic; only nineteen of these patients were weighed prior to the local anaesthetic administration; seventy seven operations and local anaesthetics were administered by non-consultant surgeons.

Anaesthetists (on their separate form) reported one hundred and seventy two cases where patients had died after a local anaesthetic administered by a surgeon. These data allow us a more complete picture of surgeons acting as anaesthetist and surgeon. Of these 172 deaths:

58 patients were given a local anaesthetic agent containing adrenaline.

47 patients were given another hypnotic/analgesic drug, usually diazepam, as well.

128 patients had intra-operative pulse monitoring.

114 patients had intra-operative blood pressure monitoring.

103 patients had intra-operative ECG monitoring.

10 patients had adverse reactions to the local anaesthetic agent.

86 patients required emergency intra-operative management by anaesthetists.

Some conclusions can be drawn from these data. The elementary management of patients undergoing local anaesthesia is often ill understood by surgeons, patients are not weighed prior to surgery, the maximum safe dose of anaesthetic agent is not known to the operator and frequently intra-operative monitoring is ignored. Surgeons frequently do not record the anaesthetic agent and/or the dose administered.

We make a clear appeal for improvement here; the surgeon/anaesthetist needs to employ the same rigours of pre-operative assessment and intra-operative monitoring as does an independent anaesthetist. The surgeon/anaesthetist must understand the emergency resuscitation of a patient who reacts adversely to a local anaesthetic.

SEDATION ADMINISTERED BY THE SURGEON

A 72 year-old woman was described as overweight, but had not been weighed, and was admitted for colonoscopy. She was on antibiotics, antidysrhythmics, and diuretics. The surgeon endoscopist (consultant) gave 10 mg diazepam, atropine 0.6 and pentazocine 30 mg intravenously. Twenty five minutes later she became "deeply sedated, moderately cyanosed, went into atrial fibrillation and was hypotensive". She did not respond to naloxone and the ECG, then applied, showed "increasing ischaemic changes". No further treatment appears to have been given. This death had nothing to do with the activities of anaesthetists because not one was involved. Nevertheless, it illustrates some of the misconceptions which still exist.

The consultant endoscopist had not been told that the patient had an ischaemic episode the day before, which he(she) considered to be a major failure in communication betwen staff. No autopsy was performed, although it was presumed by the consultant surgeon that myocardial infarction had occurred. The anaesthetist assessor comments, "it is reasonable to ask why was the ECG not monitored continuously and what was the reason to abandon resuscitation? Finally, why are general surgeons different from dentists who are advised not to be operator-anaesthetists?"

SPECIFIC OPERATIONS

Abdominal aortic aneurysm

One hundred and fifty surgical forms relating to surgery for abdominal aortic aneurysms were received. Of these, sixteen were emergency operations for leaking (ruptured) aneurysm. The grades of surgeon operating on these aneurysms may be seen in table 2.2.

TABLE 2.2 Grades of operating surgeons for patients with an aortic aneurysm		TABLE 2.3 Ages of CEPOD patients with aortic aneurysm	
Grade of surgeon	**Number of aortic aneurysm cases**	**Age group (years)**	**% of aortic aneurysm cases**
Senior House Officer	1	40-49	0.7
Registrar	16	50-59	8.0
Senior Registrar	30	60-69	29.3
Consultant	93	70-79	50.7
Others	10	80-89	11.3
Total	150	90+	0.0

Nearly half (seventy) of all these aneurysms were operated by surgeons with a special interest in vascular surgery but only 36% of the leaking aneurysms were operated by trained vascular surgeons. Assessors commented adversely on the one case operated by a senior house officer and the sixteen by registrars.

A male aged 65 with a leaking aneurysm was admitted to a teaching hospital, the senior house officer consulted the consultant on call and was told to do the operation. The senior house officer was assisted by a medical student. Our assessor comments, "I am shocked that a senior house officer was left to do the operation. The patient survived but died the following day from bilateral embolisation".

Another assessor comments on another case: "I do not think a surgical registrar should tackle a high leaking aneurysm unassisted".

Consultant failure is documented too; an elective aneurysm repair by a consultant on a male aged 70. "This is one of the least explicable bad outcomes of an elective case and raises questions to which answers are given". The operation was quickly completed in two and a half hours; there was an intra-operative error; the operating surgeon misinterpreted the anatomy believing the right common iliac artery to be the aorta. A graft was then placed between the main graft and the left common iliac. The patient developed gangrene of both lower limbs and died 24 hours after the operation. The consultant scored himself 7 (adequate) for the operation.

The age profile of patients dying after aortic aneurysm surgery showed they were in the second half of their lifespan.

The assessors opined that 25.6% of these deaths were avoidable and 29% were surgery related.

For the mortality for all abdominal aneurysm operations, using the HAA data as denominators, see Part 4, table 4.5.

Death rates. The unusual figure in this series (see Part 4, table 4.5) is the considerably higher death rate from aortic aneurysm in the Northern Region. Fewer aortic aneurysms come to surgery in the Northern Region than in the other two Regions – the law of supply and demand may be operating, there being fewer vascular trained surgeons in the Northern Region, and small Districts without a vascular trained surgeon always available.

Prostatectomy

Fifty five surgical forms relating to deaths following prostatectomy were received. Seven deaths followed open prostatectomy performed by general surgeons; two deaths after open prostatectomy by general surgeons with an interest in urology (though one of these surgeons was a frontiersman who claimed different interests in other deaths he reported to us). Twenty seven deaths followed transurethral prostatectomies (TURPs) by urologists and nine followed TURP by general surgeons with a special interest in urology. The remaining deaths followed TURP by other general surgeons. All of the patients were aged over 60 years old.

TABLE 2.4
Surgeon assessors' opinions
CEPOD patients who underwent a
prostatectomy

Surgeon assessors' opinions	Operation	
	Open prostatectomy	TURP
	(numbers)	
Death related to surgery	6	12
Inappropriate pre-operative management	2	3
Inappropriate operation	5	2
Avoidable elements in the death	5	11
Total number of cases	7	48

NB Multiple answers possible.

Of the TURPs the operating surgeon was a senior house officer in 4.2%, a registrar in 4.2%, a senior registrar in 12.5%, a consultant in 75% and of another grade in 4.1%. None of these TURPs was performed as an emergency operation.

These vignettes highlight the knowledge and skill differences urologists now have compared with non urologists in these fields:

A male aged 68 with retention of urine; our assessor comments "A man in hospital with chronic obstructive airways disease and congestive cardiac failure should not have a retropubic prostatectomy for a small gland performed by an inexperienced general surgical registrar." The consultant surgeon, with general and vascular specialty interests, comments on the form; "TURP safer?".

A male aged 70 with renal failure and retention of urine had a general surgeon attempt retrograde ureteric drainage for obstructive uropathy. The patient then had an open operation for his enlarged prostatic and bladder tumour obstructing the ureters.

Yet another elderly man had a partial cystectomy and transvesical prostatectomy without previous cystoscopy for a bladder base tumour causing uraemia and retention of urine. Our assessors questioned the advisability of open surgery rather than percutaneous nephrostomy in these circumstances

Oesophagectomy for carcinoma of oesophagus

Thirty six deaths followed oesophagectomy (see tables 2.5, 2.6).

TABLE 2.5
Grades of operating surgeons for
patients who underwent an
oesophagectomy

Grade of surgeon	nos. of oesophagectomy cases (n = 36)
Senior house officer	0
Registrar	3
Senior Registrar	2
Consultant	30
Others	1

TABLE 2.6
Ages of CEPOD patients who
underwent an oesophagectomy

Age group (years)	% of oesophagectomies (n = 36)
30-39	1.2
40-49	1.7
50-59	16.7
60-69	44.4
70-79	33.3
80-89	2.7
90+	0.0

The assessors reported that; 38% of the deaths were surgeon-related, 2.7% had inappropriate pre-operative management and 33% had avoidable factors.

The assessors comment that there are not many surgeons experienced in oesophagectomy. Some of these operations were done by occasional oesophageal surgeons and although we do not have control data, peer review suggests oesophagectomies would be best referred to consultants who regularly undertake this work and have the ITU support etc. Another plea for referral.

Orthopaedic surgery

Orthopaedic surgery contributed many deaths to the CEPOD total. The overwhelming number of deaths were elderly women with fractured neck of the femur. Comparing the sample of operations for fractured neck of the femur with entire CEPOD sample, orthopaedic consultants were the operating surgeon in 19% of the patients dying after an operation for a fracture of the femoral neck compared with the complete (all specialties and operations) sample in which consultant surgeons performed 47% of the operations (see tables 2.7, 4.7).

TABLE 2.7
Grades of operating surgeons for patients who underwent orthopaedic operations

| | % of operations | |
Grade of surgeon	Repair of fractured neck of femur (n = 336)	Hip hemiarthroplasty (n = 135)
Senior House Officer	10.1	9.7
Registrar	46.1	42.9
Senior registrar	6.2	5.9
Consultant	19.1	19.3
Others	18.5	22.2

The management of co-morbidity, particularly in the elderly, places a severe burden on orthopaedic surgeons. However, a smaller number of doctors on orthopaedic teams take histories and examine each patient pre-operatively than do general surgical teams (see table 2.8) and they perform fewer tests pre-operatively than general surgeons.

A commentary on one deceased lady, aged 91, with a fractured neck of the femur makes the point. The patient died 13 days after her hip was pinned by a registrar. There was no consultant involvement pre-operatively and no consultant saw her throughout her stay in

TABLE 2.8
Number of clinicians who took the pre-operative history

| | % of cases | | | |
Specialty of surgeon	1 clinician	2 clinicians	3 clinicians	Not Answered
Orthopaedic	20.0	45.0	35.0	0.0
General	7.8	25.9	65.5	0.8

NB See also table 4.15.

hospital. The registrar who completed the form wrote on it "Please note, in patients of this age with this condition, I consider filling in this extensive form a complete waste of time".

The assessors' observation deserves repetition, too; "The comment by the surgeon completing this form displays a lack of insight regarding the need for this assessment."

Pneumonectomy

Six surgical forms for deaths following pneumonectomy for malignant disease were received. Of the six deaths registrars operated unassisted on three cases, a senior registrar unassisted on one case, a consultant on the one case and a clinical assistant on the remaining case. In the three cases operated on by a registrar and the one operated on by a clinical assistant the consultant was consulted pre-operatively. However, the assessors took a less than optimistic view of the management of these patients. In four of the cases they thought that the death was avoidable; that there was inappropriate pre-operative management in one patient; that the operation was inappropriate in two patients and that in four patients there were surgeon related factors leading to the deaths of the patients. The question whether malignancies in the chests of some of these patients should have been operated on was raised by the assessors and finally the question of the appropriateness of the grade of the surgeon performing the surgery was raised by the assessors.

The question of pneumonectomy for malignant disease in the elderly needs to be be carefully reviewed. One male aged 76 had a pneumonectomy carried out for carcinoma of the bronchus and died 15 days post-operatively from a myocardial infarction. Our assessor comments "I would question the advisability of doing a pneumonectomy in a 76 year-old, especially one with angina. I would not have operated".

Exploratory thoracotomy for malignant disease

Twenty six surgical forms relating to death following exploratory thoracotomy at which no further procedure was carried out were received. Of these cases 3 were performed by registrars, 1 by a senior registrar, 20 by consultants and 2 by clinical assistants. For the patient age range see table 2.9.

TABLE 2.9
Ages of CEPOD patients who underwent an exploratory thoracotomy

Age group (years)	Number of thoracotomies
20-29	1
30-39	1
40-49	0
50-59	3
60-69	8
70-79	9
80-89	3
90+	2

In all these cases of thoracotomy the consultant had been consulted prior to the surgical intervention, 75% were performed by cardiothoracic surgeons.

Overall the assessors' opinions were that the deaths were surgeon related in 38%; that there was inappropriate pre-operative management in 3.8%; that the operation was inappropriate in 15.4%; that the death was avoidable in 26.9%.

Thoracic emergency surgery

One patient, a 30 year-old male who suffered a thoracic injury and required urgent thoracotomy, caused the assessors some anxiety. He was taken into a hospital and had to wait 45 minutes, bleeding severely from his chest, before a theatre could be made available to him. The assessors comments that although the operation was undertaken in a skillful manner by a general surgeon this was an avoidable death. There was another surgical form relating to an emergency thoracotomy performed for major trauma, again the operating surgeon was a general surgeon again delay is reported. These cases highlight the general point about theatre and surgeon availability.

Carcinoma of the pancreas

Sixty six surgical forms were received relating to operations for carcinoma of the pancreas (see table 2.10).

The age distribution of the patients is seen in table 2.11.

TABLE 2.10
Grades of operating surgeons for patients with carcinoma of the pancreas

Grade of surgeon	Nos. of operations for carcinoma of the pancreas (n = 66)
Registrar	11
Senior Registrar	7
Consultant	47
Others	1

TABLE 2.11
Ages of CEPOD patients with carcinoma of the pancreas

Age group (years)	% of patients with carcinoma of the pancreas (n = 66)
40-49	6.7
50-59	3.3
60-69	26.7
70-79	43.3
80-89	20.0
90+	0.0

Although none of these operations could be described as an emergency 8.3% were performed at night time and 76% of them were performed during working hours. In 97% of cases the consultant was consulted pre-operatively.

There were two serious errors of judgement reported among these cases. In one case a female aged 46 had a total pancreatectomy carried out for what proved to be benign pancreatitis. The assessor draws the attention of the importance of obtaining a histological diagnosis before proceeding to such a a vast operation.

A second assessor's comment does need repeating. "To perform a Whipple in a man aged over 70 with leukaemia and mitral valve disease must carry a near 100% predictive mortality".

Carcinoma of the ovary

Twenty four surgical forms of patients who died following operations for carcinoma of the ovary were received. All these operations were performed by gynaecologists and the majority, 83.3% were performed by consultant gynaecologists. None of these operations were emergency operations and in every case the consultant gynaecologist was consulted prior to surgery.

The age range of the patients may be seen in table 2.12.

The management of these patients was considered by the assessors to be generally good. However, in two cases the assessors did question the advisability of performing a laparotomy to make a diagnosis on a patient who was terminally ill.

TABLE 2.12
Ages of CEPOD patients with
carcinoma of the ovary

Age group (years)	Number of patients with carcinoma of the ovary
40-49	4
50-59	3
60-69	4
70-79	10
80-89	3
90+	0

Colorectal carcinoma

One hundred and ninety surgical forms were received relating to operations for colorectal cancer (see table 2.13), (134 hemicolectomy and 56 abdomino-perineal operations). We have not included the cases of carcinomatosis due to colorectal cancer in this sub-group.

The consultant concerned was consulted in 92% of cases. 66% of the operations were performed during working hours and 13% performed at night. However, reviewing the 13% performed at night there seems to be no reason why these should be regarded as emergency operations to be performed that urgently. Fifty six out of one hundred and ninety patients who had operations for colorectal cancer had abdomino-perineal resection of the rectum. The age of these patients may be seen in table 2.14.

TABLE 2.13
Grades of operating surgeons
for patients with colorectal cancer

Grade of surgeon	Nos. of cases with colorectal cancer (n=133)
Senior House Officer	2
Registrar	31
Senior Registrar	13
Consultant	86
Others	1

TABLE 2.14
Ages of CEPOD patients who
underwent an abdomino-perineal
resection of the rectum

Age group (years)	% of abdomino-perineal resection cases (n=56)
40-49	3.6
50-59	7.1
60-69	17.8
70-79	44.6
80-89	21.4
90+	5.5

Again although some of these cases were operated on outside working hours none of them could be described as a true emergency.

In the assessors' opinion; 39% of the deaths following abdomino-perineal resection were surgeon related; 5.3% had inadequate pre-operative management; 30% of the deaths were avoidable and 17% of these patients had inappropriate operations. Reviewing all the cases of colorectal carcinoma some general points are raised by assessors: There were cases of carcinomatosis where there was heavy loading of the liver with secondary deposits. In four such cases (4 out of 130) a pre-operative liver scan might well have avoided operation. These were in an 83 year-old male, a 91 year-old female, an 84 year-old male and a 65 year-old male. In each of these examples the assessor who reviewed the case would not have operated on account of the severely bad prognosis due to secondary deposits. Our assessors point out however, that sometimes resection of an obstructing colon malignancy may be the best option even in carcinomatosis.

Diverticulitis

There were twenty one surgical forms of deaths following operation for diverticulitis of the colon. The ages of the patients may be seen table 2.15.

TABLE 2.15
Ages of CEPOD patients with
diverticulitis

Age group (years)	Number of patients with diverticulitis
50-59	3
60-69	4
70-79	10
80-89	2
90+	2

The operating surgeon was a registrar in 42.8%, senior registrar in 4.7%, consultant in 47.6% and another grade in 4.9%. In 80% of cases consultants were consulted prior to surgical intervention in these cases.

Pseudo-obstruction of the colon

There were five surgical forms of deaths following operation for pseudo-obstruction of the colon. Two of these patients were not sigmoidoscoped prior to surgery and none had a water soluble contrast enema or colonoscopy prior to surgery.

A male aged 89 was admitted with abdominal distension, seen by a registrar and not sigmoidoscoped. Subjected to laparotomy and a colostomy, the patient died 11 days afterwards. There was no consultant involved in his case. The assessor comments, "Patients with pseudo-obstruction should not be operated on. The diagnosis can be made by contrast enema and treatment is colonoscopy".

Appendicectomy

There were five surgical forms received of deaths following appendicectomy operations. Over the study period more than twelve thousand appendicectomy operations were performed in the three Regions (see Part 4, table 4.5). Appendicectomy is a very common, neccessary and safe operation.

Each of these cases illustrates some aspect of surgical failure and will therefore be discussed in detail.

1. A female born in 1950. This patient was admitted with acute abdominal pain and a working diagnosis of acute cholecystitis or appendicitis was made by the house surgeon and the senior house officer. The patient also had congestive cardiac failure and a chronic chest infection. Resuscitation was commenced and the senior registrar contacted. The senior registrar told the senior house officer to get on and operate on the patient. The consultant reporting the case says he would have avoided operation and furthermore the senior registrar should have seen and assessed the patient himself pre-operatively before telling the senior house officer to get on with it. The patient died 24 hours after the operation from a cerebrovascular accident.

2. A female born in 1941. She had acute appendicitis. The consultant was consulted pre-operatively and the registrar performed the operation. At operation a perforated appendix was found. The patient was very obese and the operation very difficult. Despite the fact the patient had air boots, stockings and early ambulation and she stopped taking her contraceptive pill when she came into hospital, she died of a massive pulmonary embolism at 48 hours post-operatively. Should she have been heparinised?

3. A female born in 1921. She had had previous surgery for gastric carcinoma and was admitted to hospital with abdominal pain. The senior house officer examined her and immediately took her to theatre and operated on her. He removed a normal appendix and she was found to have carcinomatosis. She died 18 days after surgery with a pulmonary embolus. The question is whether or not she should have had an operation at all.

4. A male born in 1906. The senior registrar and senior house officer saw the patient pre-operatively. Despite the fact that he was ASA grade 4 with chronic obstructive airways disease and was dehydrated with a haemoglobin of 19.7 they proceeded to early operation. At operation they found a perforated appendix with peritonitis. The patient died 5 days post-operatively. The assessors raised the question of the management of his chronic obstructive airways disease and pre-operative resuscitation.

5. A female born in 1967. She was admitted to hospital and a working diagnosis of acute appendicitis was made by a locum senior house officer. The consultant was not consulted pre-operatively. The patient was an insulin dependent diabetic. The patient died three days after her surgical operation. We do not know whether she had acute appendicitis or not because the operation notes were very poor indeed and there was no histology done on the appendix. The assessors comment that this case illustrates many problems; there was no pre-operative consultation with the consultant on call or with a physician who could have advised about the diabetes; there were inadequate instructions given regarding her diabetic management; the operation notes are unclear; there was no diabetic management protocol being followed in the unit concerned and, lastly, the assessor comments "This is a very worrying case".

Hernia surgery

There were sixty surgical forms of deaths following hernia operations (see table 2.16).

TABLE 2.16
Grades of operating surgeons
for patients who underwent
hernia operations

Grade of surgeon	% of hernia operations (n = 60)
Senior House Officer	11.9 (7)
Registrar	49.1 (29)
Senior Registrar	8.5 (5)
Consultant	30.5 (19)

In all these cases the consultant was consulted in just over half (54%) of cases. The comments of the assessors are, however, worrying. In 52.5% they thought the death was attributable to surgery; in 30.5% there was inappropriate pre-operative management, in 27% there were avoidable factors or they would have avoided surgery, and lastly the operation was inappropriate in 18% of cases. The age of the patients who died with inguinal hernias are in table 2.17.

TABLE 2.17
Ages of CEPOD patients with
an inguinal hernia

Age group (years)	Number of inguinal hernia cases
50-59	1
60-69	3
70-79	12
80-89	18
90+	1

NB This includes 23 operations for obstructed/strangulated inguinal hernias, the remaining 12 elective operations include one operation performed by a consultant surgeon.

Of the inguinal hernias 35.1% were elective admissions, 5.5% urgent admissions and 59.2% emergency admissions (see table 2.1).

Inguinal hernias

Out of the total of thirty three deaths following surgery for inguinal hernia sixteen of these cases are of particular interest. Particular problems with strangulated inguinal hernia were the failure to resuscitate patients or hastily taking the patients to the operating room before resuscitation was adequate. An example of this is an 82 year-old male with a strangulated right inguinal hernia who was operated on by an senior house officer one-and-a-half hours following admission to hospital. The patient was dehydrated, the consultant was not consulted prior to surgery and the patient had an on-table cardiac arrest. The patient died three days later and at that stage a consultant had still not seen the patient at all. Our assessor comments "This form is filled in in a careless manner. The senior house officer gives the impression that this was an old man that died – so what?" There is no record that a consultant saw the patient at any time between admission and death. "It would be interesting to know about the senior house officer; I suspect he may have done more than twenty five hernias but not more than twenty five strangulated hernias. And why, in an old man, did he remove the Meckel's diverticulum unless it was strangulated?". The senior house officer gives himself 10, 10, 10 for this case.

A further example will illustrate the problems of patients with strangulated herniae. This time the patient was female and aged 78 years. She was admitted with a strangulated right femoral hernia and pre-operatively seen by a senior house officer. There was no consultant involvement and the senior house officer operated. At operation he found strangulated omentum and strangulated ileum in the right femoral hernia. He removed the strangulated omentum and constructed an ileum to right transverse colon anastomosis leaving the strangulated ileum *in situ* in the hernial sac. He gave himself 10, 10, 10 for this. The patient died some days later with gas gangrene.

Peptic ulcers

There were one hundred and fifty one surgical forms received of deaths following surgery for peptic ulcers. 9.2% of these operations were performed by senior house officers, 44.4% by registrars, 14.3% by senior registrars, 31.1% by consultants and 1.0% by others. Most of these operations were performed out of hours or at night, only 30% were performed during regular day time operating sessions. The consultant surgeon was informed or consulted in 56% of the cases.

Our assessors found that the deaths were surgeon related in 31.2%; that there was inappropriate pre-operative management in 8.6% of cases; that in 11.2% the death was avoidable and that in 1.9% the operation was inappropriate.

Two particular problems are highlighted in this series of deaths. Firstly the problem of resuscitation prior to surgery, either adequate fluid replacement or adequate transfusion if the patients are bleeding. If the patients are bleeding adequate resuscitation depends on good collaboration with the medical team. And the second problem is the status of the surgeon who performs the operation. An example of this is an 84 year-old male patient who had had a previous gastrectomy and who had been admitted with a haematemesis under the care of physicians. The patient was bleeding severely and was seen by a surgical registrar who proceeded to operate without any consultation with a consultant. Our assessor comments on this case "I am amazed that an operation as difficult as this was done by a registrar who at no time contacted his consultant. The operation shows unnecessary resection of small bowel. This should have been done by a consultant in view of the patient's age and previous operation. These operations are difficult even for an experienced surgeon. The system in this hospital that allows a registrar to take on such cases is regrettable."

Biliary tract surgery

Forty two surgical forms were received of deaths after biliary tract surgery. Only five of these deaths were after elective cholecystectomy:

TABLE 2.19
Deaths after elective cholecystectomy

Age	Sex	Clinical cause of death	Surgeon assessors' comments
78	Male	Myocardial infarct	----
74	Female	Myocardial infarct	"Unnecessary operation"
90	Male	Pneumonia	---
70	Male	Pulmonary embolism	No prophylaxis given
76	Female	Pulmonary embolism	Prophylaxis given

The decision to perform elective cholecystectomy in these elderly patients was questioned by some assessors, the surgeon respondents in three of these cases did stress they had expressed doubts to the patients who had insisted operation was a worthwhile option for their symptoms. In one patient the responding consultant with hindsight volunteered that the operation was probably "unnecessary" and symptomatic care would have sufficed. All these patients were elderly high risk cases, all were elective operations and all were performed by consultant surgeons.

Nine deaths were reported after operations for obstructive jaundice due to stones (one patient had acute pancreatitis too).

Acute biliary tract operations

Nineteen patients died following operations on acute phase cholecystitis. Five patients (including one already mentioned with jaundice) with acute pancreatitis underwent emergency open exploration of the common bile duct.

TABLE 2.20
Emergency and urgent biliary tract operations

Operation	Number	Grade of surgeon	
		Consultant	Registrar
Cholecystectomy	9	1	8
Exploration C.B.D.	9	3	6
Cholecystectomy & Sigmoid colectomy	1		1
Total	19	4	15

Assessors commented on the failure to resuscitate many of these patients, the failure to administer suitable antibiotic prophylaxis and the inappropriateness of the surgeon's grade to the difficulty of the task.

Other issues raised in the biliary tract surgery sample were the advisability of second simultaneous, "encore" operations, for example the registrar who operated on a 77 year-old female, who underwent a cholecystectomy, a hiatus hernia repair, an incisional hernia repair and suffered a damaged jejunum to die 31 days post-operatively (included in study because she needed subsequent surgery to place a feeding line).

The excision of a sigmoid mass, histologically shown to be diverticular disease, with no pre-operative bowel preparation, already mentioned is another example of dangerous "encore" surgery.

Lastly the employment of open surgery, exploration of the common bile duct in acute pancreatitis was adversely commented on in five cases; no attempt at endoscopic drainage of the biliary tree was made in these cases.

Head injury

Twelve surgical forms were received which related to patients with head injuries. The grade of operating surgeon was a registrar in ten cases, a senior registrar in one case and the remaining case was operated on by an associate specialist. One-third of the operations were during the night and the consultant was consulted on ten occasions.

Within the framework of the surgical form it was not always possible to decide why these patients died. The data on clinical status prior to operation was unavailable. Assessors recommended more consultant involvement in the pre-operative assessment and earlier transfer to the appropriate neurosurgical unit.

A vignette will highlight the issue; a 53 year-old male was admitted with a head injury. He was seen by a general surgical registrar who did not contact his consultant, forty minutes after admission this registrar carried out bilateral burr holes. The patient died 2.5 hours later. Our assessors commented that this was unnecessary surgery. The patient had not had a C.T. scan, no consultant had seen him. The Regional neurosurgical unit was only thirty miles away.

Multiple trauma deaths

There were ten surgical forms of patients dying after multiple trauma reported to us. In six instances consultants were consulted before the operation was commenced; five patients were operated on by registrars; one by a senior registrar and four by consultants.

The small number of deaths reported highlights the problem which confronts the NHS, these ten patients were taken into Accident and Emergency Departments which were not geared to the instant management of major trauma. Few such departments have fully trained consultants always on tap.

Although at least five of these patients were salvageable, the management of the severely injured requires many resources which cannot easily be mobilised in all A&E departments. Assessors did comment that five of the ten cases reported would probably have survived in an American or Continental Trauma centre. A review of the workload and siting of major trauma centres is required to resolve these problems.

DAY-CASES

Twenty surgical forms of deaths following day-case surgery were received from the consultants. However, it must be clearly stated at the beginning that there is confusion over the definition of a day-case, not all these patients who were marked up as day cases would have fitted the NHS criteria of a day-case.

For instance eleven of the twenty patients were transfers on a day basis from one department to another within a District to allow a technical or surgical procedure to be carried through. These included orthopaedic patients transferred from medical units to have pins put in and neurological patients transferred from medical units to neurosurgical units to have urgent neurosurgical intervention, for example a child having an urgent shunt for hydrocephalus and, another example, a man having an emergency craniotomy for a frontal tumour.

Therefore of the twenty day-cases reported by consultant surgeons only nine are truly day-cases. These nine do require some further consideration from the CEPOD perspective. Of these nine cases three were elderly men aged 64, 75 and 77 each having day-case cystoscopies carried out for bladder tumours. All three died (at 2 days, 10 days and 12 days) post-operatively of myocardial infarcts. The assessors had no criticisms of the management of any of these cases. Five patients had endoscopies carried out on a day-case basis and were found to have advanced malignant disease and went home and died subsequently at home. Again the assessors had no adverse comments on these cases.

One patient had an inguinal hernia repaired under local anaesthetic and died at home 14 days later with a myocardial infarct. Apart from the fact that details of the dose of local anaesthetic were not adequately recorded in this case, the assessors had no adverse comments.

It can therefore be said quite categorically that there have been no deaths related directly to day-case surgery.

AVOIDABLE DEATHS IN DIFFERENT AGE GROUPS

In each age group there are some deaths which the assessors found were avoidable. Surprisingly the percentage of avoidable deaths in each age group seems to be distributed right across the age range. No age being immune to this phenomenon.

TABLE 2.21
**Surgeon assessors'
opinions**
Ages of CEPOD patients
and avoidable deaths

Age group (years)	% of avoidable deaths
0-10	17.2
11-20	22.7
21-30	19.3
31-40	8.0
41-50	25.0
51-60	11.0
61-70	18.3
71-80	16.9
81-90	17.6
91+	13.2

NB Each cell has its own denominator.

CARCINOMATOSIS

There were two hundred and twelve cases where carcinomatosis was given as the cause of death. In twenty nine of these cases in the assessors' opinion the operation was unnecessary, the diagnosis of carcinomatosis could have been made and the patient not subjected to a further operation. A particular example of an unnecessary major operation being performed in a patient with carcinomatosis is the example of a 40 year-old female who had severe back ache and a pleural effusion due to disseminated malignancy from carcinoma of the breast. She was admitted to hospital and subjected to a Halsted mastectomy by a surgical registrar. There was no consultant involvement pre, during or post-operatively. There was no further discussion of the death when she died some nine days post-operatively. The registrar scores himself 10, 10, 10 for this case. Our assessors are of the opinion that this operation was unnecessary and inhumane.

Pulmonary embolism

Concern was expressed by surgeon assessors about prophylaxis against pulmonary embolism. There are different opinions regarding this prophylaxis especially amongst the orthopaedic surgeons, however our general surgeon assessors seemed to support a consensus that prophylaxis was valuable. One hundred and eighty nine deaths from pulmonary embolism were reported, forty two of these had prophylaxis administered, the remainder did not.

TABLE 2.18
Anticoagulation therapy

| Use of anticoagulation therapy* | Number of cases | |
	Pulmonary embolism as clinical cause of death (assessors' opinion)	All other causes
Yes	42	1090
No	157	1939

Anticoagulant therapy is defined as the use of anticoagulant drugs (*Heparin, Warfarin* etc.) before, during or after operation, the use of intravenous dextran, the use of compression stockings and (or) automatic mobilization devices.

There is a significant difference between those given and those not given antipulmonary embolism prophylaxis. We therefore, on the recommendation of our assessors, would draw surgeons' attention to anti-embolism prophylaxis; we would however remind surgeons in some specialties, *eg.* urologists doing TURP and neurosurgeons operating for intra-cranial haemorrhage, that anticoagulants can be contra-indicated.

CLINICAL SUB-GROUP RECOMMENDATIONS

Colorectal surgery

Colorectal assessors in general considered that much more of the colorectal surgery must be performed by specialists with a particular interest and expertise in this field. The particular clinical problems in the cases reported to CEPOD included inadequate pre-operative investigation, for instance the failure to sigmoidoscope patients with intestinal obstruction or intestinal pseudo-obstruction, the failure to use water soluble contrast enemas and colonoscopy to investigate emergency admissions with intestinal obstruction. This failure indeed led to five patients with pseudo-obstruction of the colon undergoing surgical operations and subsequently dying and being reported to CEPOD. The management of septicaemia and in particular the failure to use intra-operative prophylactic antibiotics. The failure to give anticoagulants leading to the development of post-operative pulmonary embolisation with a fatal result. Lastly, the management of carcinomatosis and subacute intestinal obstruction particularly following previous surgical intervention for carcinoma of the colon. Many assessors felt such patients should not be subjected to further surgical intervention.

Gastro-intestinal surgery

Of particular concern is the failure to resuscitate patients with abdominal crises pre-operatively. In particular the point was well made that strangulated hernias should not be rushed to theatre. It was felt surprising that so many cases of strangulated hernias subsequently died. Clearly there had been a failure to manage them adequately pre-operatively and in particular to manage their electrolyte and fluid balance, their renal function and their cardiorespiratory function. In biliary tract surgery many comments were made about the role of inexperienced surgeons operating on patients with acute infection in the biliary tree.

Thoracic surgery

The problems of thoracic surgery, thoracotomies and oesophagectomies, do raise questions. With most thoracic surgery now concentrated in Regional cardiothoracic units which specialise in cardiac surgery there is an urgent need for general surgeons with experience of non-cardiac thoracic surgery to be trained and available in District hospitals. It is clearly impractical to concentrate all non-cardiac thoracic surgery including emergencies in one Regional centre and the profession should look again at the possibility of training general surgeons with thoracic skills to work in District general hospitals. There these consultants could provide a focus for non-cardiac thoracic surgery and undertake the oesophageal, trauma and other occasional thoracic surgery that needs to be done.

There is a necessity for general surgeons in peripheral units to gain experience in thoracic surgery throughout their training so that they could deal with multiple injuries and particularly open wounds in the thorax. Thoracic surgery assessors expressed the view that there was relatively little indication for night time thoracic surgery and in particular one surgeon in the District who was suitably trained could deal with the non-cardiac surgery on a day-time basis.

Neurosurgery

The neurosurgical assessors were strongly of the opinion that head injuries which require surgical intervention should be expeditiously transferred to neurosurgical units and that other neurological surgery should not be undertaken outside these units. There is certainly no reason why non-emergency craniotomy should be undertaken out of hours and undertaken by non-neurological trained surgeons.

Paediatric surgery

The paediatric surgeons were of the opinion that neo-nates should not be operated on by general surgeons but should all be transferred to Regional paediatric units. And perhaps these paediatric units should review their mortalities and in particular publish guidelines for the referral of neo-natal cases. The failure to transfer neo-natal cases to neo-natal surgical units was influenced by the lack of availability of space in Regional units on two occasions.

Orthopaedic surgery

The orthopaedic deaths reported to CEPOD showed the present almost overwhelming tide of elderly patients suffering from fractured neck of femur. The management of these patients demands many more resources should be made available in orthopaedic surgery. There was a feeling in many cases that the management of these patients was dictated more by the available facilities in the District hospital rather than by the clinical exigencies of the situation. The shortage of orthopaedic consultants was perhaps illustrated by the fact that of the fractured neck of femurs reported to CEPOD only 19% had their operations carried out by consultant surgeons whereas of all the remaining deaths reported to CEPOD in all disciplines 47% of the operations were performed by consultant surgeons. This shortage of orthopaedic consultants is reflected by noting that orthopaedic patients were examined by fewer doctors pre-operatively than were general surgical patients. Orthopaedic surgeons ordered fewer pre-operative tests than did general surgeons pre-operatively suggesting that the management of co-morbidity in the elderly could be improved.

There were instances of parts of orthopaedic appliances not being available in operating rooms and of junior staff being unable to use different orthopaedic appliances. The standardisation of nails and screws is urgent and does need review on a national basis.

Vascular surgery

Almost half the vascular surgical operations were undertaken by, or overseen by, consultant surgeons who did not indicate vascular surgery as their special interest. The assessors stress the need for vascular surgeons to be available to operate on these patients. The assessors suggest that in many Districts two or more vascular consultants are needed to provide this care. In smaller Districts sub-regional units on consortium arrangements could improve the prognosis for these patients.

Vascular assessors commented adversely on operations for ruptured aortic aneurysm in patients aged over 80 and on elderly patients with known co-morbidity.

Accident and emergency/trauma patients

In trauma the twin problems of the siting of the admission hospital with the availability of all the services at that admission hospital and the availability of consultants on site to make the initial assessment and management decisions were highlighted in all the cases reported. Organisationally the principle problem is the availability of an emergency fully staffed theatre and an experienced surgeon and anaesthetist. Examples of this occurred in Districts with more than one Accident and Emergency Department receiving cases and there being no consultants available at one or other site to deal with multiple trauma patients. Secondly, examples occurred in small Districts who only occasionally receive multiple trauma and anyway find their resources stretched so that no consultant can be immediately available to involve themselves in trauma management. There is need to review and concentrate services for acute emergency admissions and for trauma.

Urology

The urology assessors were perturbed by examples of urological surgeons undertaking abdominal or other surgery outside their main field of expertise and not doing it very well. They were also concerned by the number of open urological operations still performed by general surgeons without special experience in urology.

part 3

anaesthesia

JOHN N. LUNN

M.D., F.F.A.R.C.S.

Reader, Department of Anaesthetics,
University of Wales, College of Medicine, Cardiff CF4 4XW

part **3** anaesthesia

CONTENTS

DATA FROM THE QUESTIONNAIRES

The tables which follow are derived from all the information supplied by anaesthetists. There are few differences between Regions but, where they seem to be important, there is a brief commentary. All other tables on which there is little comment but which do reflect, in a limited manner, the practice of anaesthesia in the three Regions are in Part 4, appendix 1.

Grade of anaesthetist

TABLE 3.1
Grade of anaesthetist undertaking the operation by region

Grade of Anaesthetist	SW	% by region N	NET	Total
Senior House Officer	22.8	15.5	25.0	20.8
Registrar	20.8	14.4	26.7	20.2
Senior Registrar	11.5	6.8	9.4	9.1
Consultant	39.3	49.2	34.3	41.5
Associate Specialist	1.1	8.5	0.9	3.8
General Practitioner	0.5	0.6	0.0	0.4
Clinical Assistant	3.0	4.7	2.5	3.5
Other	0.6	0.0	0.2	0.3
Not answered	0.4	0.3	1.0	0.4
Number of cases	984	1081	863	2928

There are substantial differences between the Regions in the grades of staff in CEPOD cases. 15.5% of cases in the North were managed by senior house officers or registrars but 25.0% were so managed in North East Thames. The number of cases in both the South West and North who were reported to have three anaesthetists *per* patient was half that in North East Thames.

It is important to note that, owing to the peripatetic nature of employment of junior staff and the necessity for locum (temporary) appointments, it was often impossible for local staff to complete questionnaires fully, about 10% were completed by consultants (divisional chairmen or consultant on-call) who may not have been directly involved in the management of the case.

Location at death

TABLE 3.2
Location of patient at death

| Location | % by region | | | |
	SW	N	NET	Total
Theatre	5.0	3.3	4.5	4.2
Recovery	2.1	0.6	0.5	1.1
ITU	16.4	20.3	20.4	19.0
HDA	0.3	1.0	0.2	0.5
Ward	73.0	71.0	71.5	71.8
Home	1.4	2.2	0.8	1.5
Not answered	1.8	1.6	2.1	1.9

ITU = Intensive Therapy Unit
HDA = High Dependency Area.

There are apparently Regional differences in the location of the patient at death. However, there are also Regional differences in terminology. It is therefore unlikely that the differences are real.

Ethnic group

TABLE 3.3
Ethnic group of the patient

| Ethnic group | % by region | | | |
	SW	N	NET	Total
Europid	99.3	98.4	97.2	98.4
African	0.2	0.0	0.7	0.3
Asian	0.1	0.3	1.6	0.6
Oriental	0.0	0.0	0.1	0.1
Not answered	0.4	1.3	0.4	0.6

The Confidential Enquiry into Maternal Deaths has regularly drawn attention to the fact that avoidable anaesthetic deaths from undiagnosed airway obstruction or unrecognised cyanosis are associated with patients with pigmented skin. There were twenty eight deaths reported to the enquiry which happened to non-Europid patients. (There were none in these ethnic groups which were solely due to anaesthesia and three in the four hundred and ten anaesthesia-associated group.)

Consultation between anaesthetist and surgeon

This occurred in about 50% cases, whilst this cannot be regarded as totally satisfactory it is a considerably more frequent event than the clinical coordinators expected.

Anaesthetist's visit before operation

TABLE 3.4
Pre-operative visit by anaesthetist

| Patient visited | % by region | | | |
	SW	N	NET	Total
Yes	82.2	88.7	74.5	82.3
No	15.0	9.9	21.4	15.0
Not answered	2.8	1.4	4.1	2.7

It is gratifying that overall 82% of CEPOD patients were visited by an anaesthetist before operation. There are differences in Regional practice: more than 20% of patients were not seen in the ward before operation in North East Thames, whereas less than 10% were not seen in the North.

The role of the anaesthetist in pre-operative assessment of fitness for surgery is not yet uniformly accepted. For instance, in one District General Hospital 20% of the patients were visited pre-operatively, whereas in another District General Hospital in the same Region this figure was 60%.

If one assumes that pre-operative assessment fulfils a useful function in the practice of some anaesthetists, it is still surprising to discover such wide discrepancies between hospitals. Even if the reader believes the opposite, that a visit before operation has no importance, then why is it so important in one hospital and not in the other?

Investigations

TABLE 3.5
Pre-operative investigations by the
anaesthetic team
No regional differences

Investigation	% yes
Chest X-Ray	84.3
Haemoglobin	96.5
Blood urea	93.6
Plasma electrolytes	94.1
Electrocardiograph	82.7
Respiratory function tests	5.8
Blood gas analysis	11.3
Sickle test	0.6

With regional differences

| | % by region | | | |
	SW	N	NET	Total
Liver function	46.8	50.2	43.1	47.0
Urinalysis	57.2	61.1	65.9	61.2
Blood glucose	40.8	47.4	46.2	44.8
Other	23.3	28.0	27.0	26.1

Haemoglobin estimation

Most (96.5%) patients had at least one haemoglobin measurement made before anaesthesia and surgery. Other indications suggest that the information from this simple laboratory test were sometimes misinterpreted.

ASA grade

TABLE 3.6
ASA grade and operation type

Operation	% of ASA grade				
type	1	2	3	4	5
Emergency	3.0	0.2	0.5	0.4	7.6
Urgent	40.9	47.5	39.0	40.5	59.9
Scheduled	50.0	47.3	51.5	47.8	28.1
Elective	6.1	5.0	8.6	10.7	4.1
Not known	0.0	0.0	0.4	0.6	0.3
Total	100.0	100.0	100.0	100.0	100.0

NB See definitions in tables 3.8 and 1.9.

TABLE 3.7
Operation type and ASA grade

ASA grade	% of operation type			
	Emergency	Urgent	Scheduled	Elective
1	4.8	2.0	2.5	1.7
2	2.4	24.1	23.2	14.1
3	9.5	24.1	30.7	29.5
4	9.5	29.3	33.4	43.2
5	73.8	18.7	8.5	7.3
Not answered	0.0	1.8	1.7	4.2
Total	100.0	100.0	100.0	100.0

NB See definitions in tables 1.9 and 3.8.

Most (67.5%) ASA 5 were urgent or emergency cases and 73.8% of emergency operations were ASA 5. Half (50.5%) the elective procedures were classified as ASA 4 or 5; this seems an extraordinary figure and indicates that some very poor risk patients are being subjected to elective surgery. It seems unlikely that any ASA 5 patients (moribund) should have an **elective** operation and thus it is at least possible that these are the result of faulty records.

The other source of error which has been noted before in a previous report is that, not unnaturally, the anaesthetist is inclined to downgrade a patient whom he knows subsequently to have died.

Deaths among ASA 1 patients. There were four deaths amongst patients who had elective procedures who were classed as ASA 1. Three of them were not attributable to anaesthesia; one was attributable, in part, to surgery. A man died within two weeks of operation as a result, in the opinion of the surgeon assessors, of a leak at the intestinal anastomosis. Nevertheless,

TABLE 3.8
* A.S.A. Status

Class	SW	% by region N	NET	Total
1	2.1	2.0	2.7	2.3
2	21.8	23.4	22.1	22.5
3	28.7	27.9	25.3	27.4
4	31.1	31.4	34.2	32.1
5	15.0	12.6	14.1	13.9
Not answered	1.3	2.7	1.6	1.8

*A.S.A. (American Society of Anesthesiologists) classification of physical status.

Class 1 The patient has no organic, physiological, biochemical, or psychiatric disturbance. The pathological process for which operation is to be performed is localized and does not entail a systemic disturbance. Examples: a fit patient with inguinal hernia; fibroid uterus in an otherwise healthy woman.

Class 2 Mild to moderate systemic disturbance caused either by the condition to be treated surgically or by other pathophysiological processes. Examples: non-or only slightly limiting organic heart disease, mild diabetes, essential hypertension, or anaemia. Some might choose to list the extremes of age here, either the neonate or the octogenerian, even though no discernible systemic disease is present. Extreme obesity and chronic bronchitis may be included in this category.

Class 3 Severe systemic disturbance or disease from what ever cause, even though it may not be possible to define the degree of disability with finality. Examples: severely limiting organic heart disease; severe diabetes with vascular complications; moderate to severe degrees of pulmonary insufficiency; angina pectoris or healed myocardial infarction.

Class 4 Severe systemic disorders that are already life threatening, not always correctable by operation. Examples: patients with organic heart disease showing marked signs of cardiac insufficiency, persistent angina, or active myocarditis; advanced degrees of pulmonary, hepatic, renal or endocrine insufficiency.

Class 5 The moribund patient who has little chance of survival but is submitted to operation in desperation. Examples: the burst abdominal aneurysm with profound shock; major cerebral trauma with rapidly increasing intracranial pressure; massive pulmonary embolus. Most of these patients require operation as a resuscitative measure with little if any anaesthesia.

the anaesthetist assessors noted that the clinical monitoring was inadequate. Two deaths followed pulmonary embolism; one in a lady who had a surgical operation on her varicose veins and did receive anticoagulant prophylaxis. The fourth death occurred after a hurriedly planned, albeit elective, operation; the consultant anaesthetist was unable to see the patient beforehand. Blood stained vomit was found in the trachea and bronchi at post-mortem and there was a small perforation of the urinary bladder. No surgical questionnaire was returned.

Pre-operative precautions

TABLE 3.9
Pre-operative precautions taken by the anaesthetist
to minimise the risk of pulmonary aspiration

| Precaution | % by region | | | |
	SW	N	NET	Total
Antacids	0.9	0.9	1.4	1.1
H_2 antagonists	6.4	7.5	5.3	6.5
Metoclopramide	3.2	8.5	2.9	5.1
Stomach tube	12.5	19.6	14.8	15.8

The use of both metoclopramide and a stomach tube is much greater in the North than in the South West or North East Thames. It is probably coincidental that no case of aspiration of vomit as a clinical cause of death was recorded in the North.

Visit after operation

The differences between the Regions are not only substantial but very surprising in view of the fact that many of the patients were graded as ASA 4 or 5.

TABLE 3.10
Post-operative visit by the anaesthetist

| Patient visited | % by region | | | |
	SW	N	NET	Total
Yes	42.5	64.5	36.2	48.7
No	40.3	19.3	45.1	34.0
Not answered	17.2	16.2	18.7	17.3

TABLE 3.11
Percentage of consultant anaesthetists
visiting patients

| Post-operative visit | Pre-operative visit | | |
	Yes	No	N/A
Yes	47.7	22.9	13.2
No	4.9	6.4	3.4
N/A	0.4	0.5	0.6

NB Each cell's denominator is 1215.

Ward visits

In 47.7% of cases consultants visited patients before and after operations but in 22.8% the consultant visited before operations but not afterwards. This behaviour was similar for all the grades except clinical assistants and general practitioners who, if they saw patients before operation, were likely to see them also afterwards.

Numbers of monitoring devices

TABLE 3.12
Monitors used/measured/displayed by anaesthetist
during the operation
No regional differences

Monitors	% used
Indirect B.P.	89.9
E.C.G	96.8
Urine output	38.3
Core thermometry	6.9
Pulmonary arterial pressure	0.7
Other	3.6

With regional differences

| Monitors | % by region | | | |
	SW	N	NET	Total
Pulse - manual	60.3	68.8	68.5	65.8
Pulse - meter	43.0	32.8	26.8	34.5
C.V.P	25.6	19.0	22.4	22.2
Stethoscope	25.1	32.4	26.3	28.1
Ventilation volume	54.0	60.6	67.2	60.3
Airway pressure	61.7	64.5	70.7	65.4
Expired carbon dioxide analysis	26.3	16.9	12.9	18.9
Direct arterial pressure (invasive)	14.4	6.1	12.9	10.9
Inspired oxygen analysis	16.8	20.7	10.0	16.2
Peripheral nerve Stimulator	14.5	15.9	10.7	13.9
Ventilator alarm	39.6	47.9	26.9	38.9

The list of monitoring devices which could have been used, whilst neither exhaustive nor prescriptive, does indicate clinical practice in relation to CEPOD cases. More than half the cases had between five and eight devices used. Five percent of cases had two or fewer monitors.

Number of monitors and grade of anaesthetist. Analysis of the data shows that senior registrars use a few more monitors than other grades, and registrars use the least.

ANALYSIS OF SOME SPECIFIC QUESTIONS

Was there a lack of equipment?

There were fifty four positive answers, however in seventeen, there was no indication of the supposed deficiency. There were twenty three complaints about unavailable monitors (oxygen analysers, carbon dioxide analysers, ventilator alarms, neuromuscular stimulators were specified). Failures of automatic non invasive blood pressure machines, blood pressure transducers and electrocardiographic monitors were reported on eleven occasions. The vaporizer was wrongly sited on one occasion and the tracheal tube failed on two occasions.

Did you have adequate trained help?

A total of fifty four negative answers were received (not the same fifty four cases as above) but there was no explanation for thirty one of these and the coordinators are forced to conclude that the question was misunderstood and(or) completed in error. Six stated that there was no junior anaesthetist present to help and three stated that the help was adequate at induction but not for the remainder of the anaesthetic. In fourteen cases there was neither an ODA (operating department assistant) nor an anaesthetic nurse. These fourteen cases included several which reported that ODA's were not available at night or weekends and one reported that it was customary for an anaesthetist to work alone in the X-Ray department without help.

Was there any misadventure during anaesthesia?

There were one hundred and thirty two positive answers to this question. There were twenty instances of miscellaneous events which were not considered to be very important in the context of the particular patient (difficult veins, broken teeth, ischaemia from radial artery cannula, temporary oliguria, transient hypertension). The other noted reasons are listed:

Aspiration of vomit	9	Failure to recover consciousness	
Dysrhythmia	25	promptly	2
Dysrhythmia resulting in cardiac		Myocardial infarction	1
arrest	6	Cardiac arrest	8
Uncontrolled haemorrhage	17	Vaporizer wrongly sited	1
Unexplained cardiac arrest	4	Bronchospasm	2
Difficult tracheal intubation	6	Pneumothorax	3
Hypotension – drug induced	22	Wrong drug	1
Hypotension – spinal/epidural	4	Air embolus	1

Were adequate recovery facilities available for this patient?

Amongst the one hundred and sixteen negative answers, which came from thirty four hospitals, there were twenty two which gave no reason. Forty eight reports stated that facilities were not available, twenty one reported early closing, eight closed at weekends and six had no staff. Seven patients were moved directly to the intensive therapy unit (ITU), presumably because no recovery facilities were available. Two answers confused recovery rooms with high dependency units; two reports stated that there were no ECG monitors in the recovery room and that therefore the patient had to be moved to the ITU for monitoring.

Did any organizational aspects, lack of resources or any other non-clinical factors contribute to the fatal outcome?

There were ninety two positive answers to this question; thirty six were in fact, clinical failures or they were unexplained. Twenty two commented again (see table 4.104) on the absence of an high dependency or intensive therapy unit. There were twelve instances of problems which resulted directly from the involvement of two or more hospitals in the management of one patient; this often involved the transfer of a patient after surgery to another hospital for intensive care. There were seven instances of delay in surgery due to organisational problems (late referral, non-availability of surgeons or anaesthetists). There were fourteen other miscellaneous problems of an organisational nature (precipitate operation, poor supervision of house and junior staff).

ANAESTHESIA-ASSOCIATED DEATHS (AA)

There are some differences between the main set of CEPOD deaths (2928 cases) and those in which anaesthesia was associated (410 cases) and there are some noteworthy similarities.

TABLE 3.13
Anaesthesia associated deaths
Patients visited pre-operatively by anaesthetist

Patient visited pre-operatively	SW	% of deaths N	NET	Total
Yes	84.1	87.1	76.9	83.1
No	12.4	12.9	20.5	15.1
Not answered	3.5	0.0	2.6	1.8

For other deaths see table 3.4.

Visit before operation

The figures are similar to the overall figure.

Age

The age distribution in the two columns in the table 3.14 indicate that assessors were more likely (approximately 10 times) to consider a death to be associated with anaesthesia in patients less than 50 years of age.

TABLE 3.14
Ages of patients

Age group (years)	% of age group AA deaths	All CEPOD
0-9	10.3	0.67
10-19	4.5	0.49
20-29	9.6	0.7
30-39	6.0	1.3
40-49	12.0	2.7
50-59	7.6	7.0
60-69	10.5	19.2
70-79	9.9	35.5
80-89	14.5	26.6
90+	12.7	5.6
(1 case age not known)		

Preparation of the patient

Anaesthetists stated that in about a quarter of the cases they were not satisfied with the preparation of patients for anaesthesia and surgery. This is **twice** the rate recorded amongst all the CEPOD cases.

Intercurrent disease

The table below shows that the incidence of different medical diseases in all the CEPOD cases was not very different from that of the anaesthesia-associated deaths.

TABLE 3.15
Intercurrent medical diagnoses in anaesthesia-associated deaths

Number of cases in which these diagnoses were recorded
(All CEPOD cases)

Chronic bronchitis, emphysema and chronic respiratory disease, 65 (207)
Congestive cardiac failure, 50 (290)
Hypertension, 39 (273)
Diabetes mellitus, 34 (215)
Ischaemic heart disease, 34 (242)
Atrial fibrillation, 34 (183)
Renal disease and failure, 28 (131)
Anaemia, 30 (235)
Depression, 24 (29)
Cerebrovascular accident, 19 (139)
Myocardial infarction, 14 (130)
Rheumatoid arthritis, 20 (129)
Dehydration and electrolyte imbalance, 13 (34)
Bronchopneumonia, 10 (38)

There were 850 (5760) different disease processes amongst the 410 (2928) cases; table 3.15 lists some of these in order of frequency of occurrence. It is noteworthy that there are a similar number of disease processes amongst anaesthesia-associated deaths as among all CEPOD cases.

The table 3.16 confirms that ASA grade is not a good predictor of death associated with anaesthesia; the distribution of grades is no different from that in any general hospital practice.

TABLE 3.16
ASA grade/anaesthesia-associated deaths

	1	2	A.S.A. grade 3	4	5	n
Anaesthesia associated %	2.7	21.2	27.6	36.3	11.7	410
All cases %	2.2	22.5	27.4	32.1	13.9	2928

Rows do not total 100% because of cases where ASA grades not known.

Consultation

There was no consultation between trainees and consultants in 60.6% of their anaesthesia-associated cases in contrast to 57.9% of all CEPOD cases. Similarly, the amount of consultation in relation to the ASA grade of the patient was not very different in the anaesthesia-associated deaths and all the CEPOD cases.

Consultant assistance for trainees in the operating room

This was neither available in the 17.6% of trainees' anaesthesia-associated cases nor in 78% of those cases in which anaesthesia was not so associated. This may suggest that both trainee and consultant perceive the need for help quite well. (The consultant came in to help in 11% of all cases).

Assistance for the anaesthetist

The figures for inadequate assistance in all CEPOD cases (1.8%) and anaesthesia-associated cases (2.9%) do not suggest gross deficiency.

TABLE 3.17
Anaesthetist assessors' opinions
Was adequate monitoring used?

Answer	SW	% by region N	NET	Total
Yes	78.7	79.6	76.0	78.2
No	20.9	19.8	23.4	21.2
Not answered	0.4	0.6	0.6	0.6

Was the monitoring adequate?

Table 3.17 shows the assessors' opinions about the adequacy of monitoring for particular cases. 21.2% cases were regarded as inadequately monitored. Table 3.18 shows this in relation to the grade of the anaesthetist.

TABLE 3.18
Anaesthetist assessors' opinions
Monitoring inadequate by grade

Grade of anaesthetist	SW	% by region N	NET	Total
Senior House Officer	20.5	24.4	24.1	22.9
Registrar	15.5	20.5	26.5	22.5
Senior Registrar	16.8	12.3	9.9	13.5
Consultant	20.7	16.9	22.3	19.4
Associate Specialist	54.5	27.0	50.0	31.5
General Practitioner	40.0	33.3	0.0	36.4
Clinical Assistant	26.7	29.4	36.4	30.1
Other	83.3	0.0	100.0	87.5
Not answered	0.0	0.0	12.5	7.1

NB Each cell has its own denominator.
There are quite substantial regional differences for use of monitors by registrars and senior registrars; these are not in the same direction in the two grades.

Misadventure

The overall rate of misadventure was 4.5%. It was 9.8% when death was associated with anaesthesia and 3.6% in the remainder.

ASSESSORS' OPINIONS

The arrangements for selection and choice of assessors for particular cases are described in Part 1 of this report. An assessor's form (see appendix 3) was completed on each death and in cases of difficulty or widely disparate views, the anaesthetist coordinator derived a consensus view.

TABLE 3.19
Anaesthetist assessors' opinions
Were there avoidable elements in the entire management of the patient, which, if corrected, would have altered the outcome, or might have reduced the chance of death at that time? *ie.* Was the death avoidable?

| Answer | % by region | | | |
	SW	N	NET	Total
Yes	19.5	16.3	18.1	17.9
No	79.0	82.2	80.2	80.5
Not answered	1.5	1.5	1.7	1.6

Figure 3.1 Percent of deaths assessed as "avoidable"
(Anaesthetist assessors' opinion)
NB Some districts reported few deaths (see table 4.1)

Avoidable factors

This question was answered by anaesthetist assessors in relation to the entire management of the case. Thus there are more cases with avoidable factors than there are **anaesthesia-associated** deaths. There are, on average, no Regional differences but the ranges for Districts within the Regions do differ quite markedly. (See fig. 3.1; the location of each District is not the same as that in figure 2.2, Part 2.).

The actual Districts for these extreme figures were not usually the same for the surgeon assessors' opinions on avoidability, although two were.

TABLE 3.20	
Avoidable elements range :	
Anaesthetic data	

Region	% range		
North	8.6	-	26.2
South West	9.6	-	35.7
North East Thames	5.7	-	27.0

2391 cases (where data from both disciplines was available)

TABLE 3.21

Anaesthetist assessors' opinions
Were there departures from ideal practice which are worthy of record?

Answer	% by region			Total
	SW	N	NET	
Yes	39.9	38.9	43.9	40.7
No	59.2	60.4	55.2	58.5
Not answered	0.9	0.7	0.9	0.8

Departures from ideal clinical practice

This section dealt with the perceived practice of anaesthesia without the implication that less-than-ideal was causative of the death. For example, assessors commented freely about the completion of the questionnaire when this was casual or illegible and assessors seemed to infer that this indicated the standard of clinical practice.

In addition, when assessors considered that the choice of method of anaesthesia, the use of particular monitoring, the grade of anaesthetist, the inevitable absence of facilities, the absence of a reliable anaesthetic record, or other detailed criticisms, could, **in their view** have been improved, they indicated this here. It must be emphasised again that clinically suboptimal care does not by itself indicate avoidability of death at that time and that, notwithstanding this, the same deficiencies were mentioned amongst the reasons for avoidable deaths. Thus the assessors expressed **opinions** about clinical matters.

There were three **clinical** conditions which occur commonly and they each featured in this section of the assessors' reports.

Prophylaxis against pulmonary embolus. The clinical coordinators recognise that clinical opinion is not uniform on this matter and, in particular, practice amongst orthopaedic surgeons varies. However, when prophylaxis was not arranged, and the patient succumbed from autopsy-verified pulmonary embolus, and when the risk of thromboembolism is generally accepted to be high (obesity, varicose veins, abdominal cancer) then avoidable elements for both surgeon and anaesthetist would be recorded and "failure to apply knowledge" indicated. Assessors commonly drew attention to the absence of prophylaxis in orthopaedic cases (see Part 2) and sometimes on other occasions, even though the patient may have died from another cause, they seemed to consider this suboptimal care.

Control of diabetes mellitus. Evidence of careful management during and immediately after surgery, indicated by the presence of results of laboratory or clinical tests during the recovery period, was often missing.

Atrial fibrillation. This was a common finding before operation. It is often apparently ignored and elderly patients die subsequently in cardiac failure. The assessors do not suggest that death might have been avoided in these cases but they sought evidence that the matter had been appropriately considered.

Pre-operative evaluation and preparation. A very substantial proportion of these reports (approximately 33%) received the comment that the assessment and preparation of the patient before operation was inadequate. Precipitate operation without proper fluid replacement still happens. The responsibility for this is shared between the two disciplines and surgeons were more inclined to be critical of this, to the extent that the death was then classified as avoidable, than were anaesthetist assessors.

Consultation. The absence of consultation between anaesthetists was frequently noted (25%) and the assessors noted particularly that where this was absent between disciplines it resulted in poor management, if not poor outcome.

Anaesthetic records. These were often of very poor quality. The amount of information was sparse and often difficult to read. Most (95%) reports claimed that there was a record in the notes but only 90% were actually sent. Discrepancies between the questionnaire and the anaesthetic record were noted but the most frequent occurrence was that the questionnaire was itself illegible or incomplete. Assessors drew conclusions which might not be justified.

Monitoring. One of the commonest (about 45% of these records) reasons for suboptimal care to be noted by assessors was the failure to use appropriate monitoring. Central venous pressure was commonly omitted but the absence of other monitors, particularly of the anaesthetic machine, were also noted.

PART OR TOTAL CONTRIBUTION TO DEATH

TABLE 3.22
Anaesthetist assessors' opinions
Death partly or wholly associated with
each factor

Factor	% of all cases	
	Partly associated*	Associated **only** with factor indicated
Surgery	14.1	0.5
Anaesthesia	14.0	0.1
Presenting surgical disease	65.1	34.5
Intercurrent disease	51.6	21.8
Unknown	0.8	1.6
Not assessable	1.3	-

* More than one factor could be recorded by assessors.

There were four categories causative of contribution of which a single one, or a combination was possible (excluding unknown or not assessable). Anaesthetist assessors differed from surgeon assessors in their readiness to incriminate surgery because their questionnaire often contained more clinical information about the surgery than the surgeons had information about anaesthesia.

The great majority of the patients died because of the disease process.

Anaesthesia-associated deaths

There were four hundred and ten deaths in which anaesthesia had some part. This is 14.1% of all CEPOD deaths, **but in only three cases was anaesthesia the only factor recorded by anaesthetist assessors.**

Anaesthesia. These three cases are reported in merest outline to illustrate the principles on which it is presumed the assessors formed their opinions. Two of the three patients had fatal conditions but their deaths took place earlier as a result of the delivery of anaesthesia than they would otherwise have done.

One followed within one hour of anaesthesia before which the consultant had expressed dissatisfaction with the preparation of the patient, but nevertheless had proceeded. One was in a patient anaesthetised by an associate specialist who failed to intubate the trachea in the presence of intestinal obstruction. The third death occurred in a young man, entirely because of relative deficiency in a particular tracheal tube about which the particular department has now reconsidered its view. (There were many other details in each of these cases to justify the assessors' opinions).

Readers might be tempted to compare these results with the customary figure determined by other studies that anaesthesia is totally responsible for one death after 10000 operations. There are many advances in the design of this current study of which the inclusion of surgeons, and therefore of surgery as a factor, seems to be the most important. The use of 80 anaesthetist assessors (as distinct from 3 pairs of anaesthetists) who had the opportunity to select, on this occasion, surgery (the delivery of surgical care) as a cause of death. The result of this option is that very few cases have been attributed solely to anaesthesia.

Anaesthesia and intercurrent disease. Assessors placed cases in this category when the process of anaesthesia, which could itself be criticized, caused, in their view, the death earlier than the disease process would have done. They noted, for example, the failure by a trainee to treat a patient in heart failure with atrial fibrillation and hypertension and an active chest infection. No consultant anaesthetist or surgeon was involved and the patient died three hours after operation.

Anaesthesia, surgical and intercurrent disease. For example, cardiac arrest 30 minutes after the start of an operation was followed by death 9 hours later. The absence of a visit before and after operation by the consultant anaesthetist, the absence of pre-oxygenation and a relative overdose of thiopentone all contributed to the assessors' decision to include anaesthesia as a causative factor.

Surgery, anaesthesia and surgical disease. There was always discussion between the surgeon and anaesthetist coordinator, when the anaesthetist assessor indicated surgery to be a causative factor and *vice versa*.

An 80 year-old patient had an emergency operation performed by a surgical registrar who did not consult his consultant. The anaesthetic was started by a senior house officer supervised directly by a senior registrar. The operation lasted three hours and fifty minutes; it was a laparotomy for peritonitis and a Hartman's procedure was done. It was necessary also to remove some small bowel, to perform a uretero-ureteric anastomosis and to repair bilateral femoral and incisional hernias. The patient was dehydrated before operation and attempts to insert a central line failed. Progressive hypotension developed (for about 3.5 hours the heart rate was 100–120 *per* minute and the systolic blood pressure 80 mmHg). Fifteen minutes before discharge to the ward at 0325 hours the systolic blood pressure was 60 mmHg.

The assessors, both anaesthetist and surgeon, considered that the delivery of surgical and anaesthetic care to be suboptimal. One anaesthetist assessor wrote: "The senior house officer did his best and obtained help, but that help proved a broken reed. If I had been the senior registrar I would have called my consultant. If I had been that consultant, I would have called in the surgical consultant and stopped all proceedings until he arrived".

Anaesthesia and surgical disease. This category is similar to that of anaesthesia and intercurrent disease. There were cases in which the surgical condition was already very serious, if not mortal, but the process of anaesthesia accelerated the moment of death. One example included a disconnection which was not noticed (there was no ventilator alarm and no carbon dioxide analyser, – both of which would have helped) and the patient eventually succumbed two weeks later.

Surgical and intercurrent disease. The assessors so classified one death despite the failure of a hospital practitioner to visit the patient before operation; despite an unsuitable general anaesthetic and despite the absence of treatment for diabetes mellitus, with the words "although the anaesthetic management was open to considerable criticism, it could not have been responsible for the death one month later".

Factors included in anaesthesia-associated deaths

The assessors were asked to indicate, for the four hundred and ten deaths in which anaesthesia played a part, those general features which they noted when they reached their conclusions.

In 75% of the four hundred and ten deaths the assessors considered that there had been a **failure to apply knowledge** (table 3.23). This was fairly evenly split by grades; senior house officer, 11.0%; registrar, 13.0%; senior registrar, 7.5%; and consultant 9.8% of the total number of cases for which that grade was responsible. However, in the four hundred and ten deaths, consultants failed to apply knowledge in 29.0%; presumably the assessors considered that this was the only appropriate category of human failure which was appropriate, senior house officer, 16.3%; registrar, 18.7%; and senior registrar, 4.9% were similarly categorised.

TABLE 3.23
Anaesthetist assessors' opinions
When death was associated with anaesthesia which factors were involved?

Answer	SW	% by region N	NET	Total (n=2928)	% of cases where death associated with anaesthesia (n=410)
Failure of organisation	4.0	3.2	3.2	3.5	24.9
Failure of equipment	0.1	0.3	0.3	0.2	1.7
Drug effect	1.5	1.3	1.2	1.3	9.5
Lack of knowledge	1.6	1.6	3.4	2.1	15.1
Failure to apply knowledge	11.6	10.5	9.3	10.5	75.1
Lack of care	4.5	4.2	3.9	3.3	30.0
Lack of experience	3.7	2.5	3.9	3.3	23.7
Fatigue	0.1	0.0	0.0	0.1	1 case
Impairment	0.0	0.0	0.0	0.0	0.0
Other	0.6	0.3	0.2	0.4	2.7

Failure to apply knowledge included the absence of prophylaxis for pulmonary thromboembolism in patients who were at risk. Thirty percent of these deaths were categorised as due, at least partly to, **lack of care.** This included failure of a trainee to consult, grossly inadequate monitoring, use of inappropriate doses of drugs or other fairly clear indications of a poor standard of practice. 24.9% of cases were included in the category of **failure of organisation**; this, referred to the availability of appropriate staff. **Drug effect** was, however, relative overdose as judged from the information in the questionnaire; twelve of these closely followed intravenous induction of anaesthesia and twelve were associated with narcotic administration before, during or after anaesthesia.

Human failure – other (2.7%). There were eleven instances. These were always supplementary to other factors and on ten occasions referred to failure to refuse to anaesthetise.

Equipment failure (1.75%). There were seven cases categorized under this heading. There were two cases of disconnection, two in which essential equipment was not available, two of misuse of equipment and one potentially very serious failure to test the anaesthetic machine beforehand.

DATA FROM BOTH DISCIPLINES

The original plan for the study was that a single form would be examined by both surgeon and anaesthetist assessor. A number of practical problems prevented the realisation of this aim and we had to design two forms. This resulted in receipt of some data from the two disciplines which emanated from different cases. We have not examined the matter exhaustively but are convinced that no serious error is introduced by analysis of 2784 surgical forms and 2928 anaesthetic forms separately. For 2391 cases complete data was received for both disciplines and the assessors' opinions, listed here, are not importantly different from any other tables; and in addition the age distribution and date of death after operation are, overall, similar. Thus no error is introduced by consideration of all the forms received from the two disciplines, although they come from different cases. (There are fewer surgical forms than anaesthetic forms and there are fewer surgical forms without anaesthetic forms than there are anaesthetic forms without surgical forms).

DISCUSSION

In the section of the report which follows, several subjects are discussed in the light of the specific opinions expressed by several assessors. These assessors were all presented visually with some general results of the study and then with some of the specific information about a particular topic, at small meetings. These assessors★ were intentionally chosen to represent disparate views (as perceived by the author from their assessments, all of which had been studied) and also because they did not currently work in hospitals within the Regions of study. The opinions which follow remain those of the author, but they are also significantly influenced by the discussions. (It should also be recalled in addition that opinions of many assessors are reflected in the totality of assessments).

Old age

The distribution of age at death in the patients (4034) studied indicates (Part 1, fig. 1.1) that most patients (75%) in the study were over 70 years of age. Thus any observations on the whole population in general apply, in particular, also to the older age group.

Decision to operate. This is properly a matter for interdisciplinary discussion. There is evidence that insufficient discussion takes place at the appropriate time between consultants and that a large proportion of the operations, for example, those for fractured neck of femur are carried out by non-consultant grades of surgeon and anaesthetised by non-consultant grade anaesthetists. Table 3.24 shows the proportions of the deaths in patients with fractured

★The names of the assessors involved are marked with an asterisk in Part 4, appendix 2.

hips anaesthetised by senior house officers and registrars who did not consider it necessary to consult with a senior colleague. There may be many understandable reasons for this reluctance (fear of seniority, absence of spontaneous help, overconfidence, unwillingness to disturb seniors at night) to name but a few.

TABLE 3.24
Consultation by trainee anaesthetist

| Grade of anaesthetist | Consultant **not** consulted | | |
	% of all cases	% anaesthesia attributable cases	% cases with fractured femur diagnosis
Senior House Officer	53.8	64.6	50.0
Registrar	58.9	52.5	70.9

The figures in table 3.24 compare the failure to consult for all operations with those for anaesthesia attributable deaths. It is at least possible that assessors were more inclined to attribute a death to anaesthesia when no senior anaesthetist was involved in the decision to operate and the anaesthetist was a senior house officer.

For example, if a junior anaesthetist agrees to anaesthetise a very sick elderly patient for a non-urgent operation on Saturday at midnight when there is no recovery room and no operating department assistant, it is that decision which must be questioned. The assessors noted that this junior team did well in the circumstances, but one commented "It is not satisfactory in 1986 that the best which can be offered is to be provided by such an inexperienced team." The group of anaesthetist assessors wondered why such an operation needed to be performed at that time. It is possible that no operating time was to be available for the next few days and thus there was this precipitate rush into surgery.

Physical facilities. It is sometimes asserted that, since there are no facilities for high dependency or intensive care for particular elderly patients, no operation should be undertaken at all. This assertion ignores the possible reality, of which we do not have evidence from this enquiry, that many elderly patients recover satisfactorily without the use of these facilities. Thus, the denial of anaesthesia and surgery because a patient is old, and some facilities are unavailable, cannot be supported. Nevertheless, it is clear that the facilities for the elderly should not be less than those available for anyone younger and the overall care of patients, particularly after operation in this context, will be improved when recovery rooms and high dependency areas are available always.

Clinical aspects. Imagine an (all-too-common) clinical scenario. There is an elderly patient with a chest infection, mild (treated) congestive cardiac failure with atrial fibrillation who needs an urgent operation (see classification). Suppose that this operation is undertaken with anaesthesia provided, without consultation, by a registrar as an emergency procedure early in the evening. The patient dies two days later without any additional therapy directed by senior staff.

Contrast the situation in which the same sequence is followed except that the decision to operate is deferred until, say 36 hours of appropriate antibiotic therapy and physiotherapy together with diuretics, after appropriate consultation, have had time to be effective. If this patient then dies, no-one can assert that either anaesthesia or surgery were specifically suboptimal; all that could reasonably be attempted had been, nevertheless, despite the best care, the patient died. The assessors do not have the evidence for this, nevertheless the assessors are quite clear that there are sufficient grounds to suspect (no more) that much more consideration needs to be given before the decision to operate is made.

Sometimes the argument of easier nursing and earlier mobilisation of elderly patients, is advanced as a reason for early operation. Again, because we do not have denominators for operations, it is not possible to be certain about this matter. The assessors consider *a priori* that the better the condition of patients before operations the better they are likely to withstand anaesthesia and surgery. Nowhere is this more true than in the care of the elderly.

The data from all CEPOD deaths, but in particular from anaesthesia-associated ones, serves to emphasise that the margins for error are considerably narrowed in old patients. The effect of a poor clinical decision may be averted in a young patient but is often fatal in an old one.

Grades of staff

Assessors are concerned at the numbers of very sick patients who are anaesthetised as **urgent** or **emergency** cases by trainees without reference to consultants. Similar concern was expressed by surgeon assessors about surgical trainees. It is appreciated that there may be many reasons for this reluctance to consult, apart from non-availability. Experience may have led a trainee to believe that he would not receive the guidance or help which he sought or he may have previously been insulted. He may have been unwilling to disturb a consultant in bed. Assessors considered that trainees should be instructed to inform their consultants whenever any ASA 4 or 5 category patient is to have an operation.

Consultation between career non-consultant grades and consultants may also require to be reviewed, and on several occasions, it was also obvious that discussion between surgical specialists and anaesthetists might have averted trouble.

TABLE 3.25
Anaesthetist assessors' opinions
Deaths associated with anaesthesia and grades

Grade of Anaesthetist	SW	% by region N	NET	Total
Senior House Officer	16.9	19.1	19.9	18.6
Registrar	17.6	15.4	14.3	16.4
Senior Registrar	11.5	8.2	6.2	8.9
Consultant	12.9	12.0	10.1	11.8
Associate Specialist	18.2	8.7	12.5	9.9
General Practitioner	0.0	33.3	0.0	1.8
Clinical Assistant	13.3	15.7	22.7	16.5
Other	33.3	0.0	0.0	25.0
Not answered	0.0	0.0	0.0	0.0

NB Each cell has its own denominator.

Table 3.25 shows that senior house officers head the list of trainees in the anaesthesia attributable deaths, when these are classified by grade of most senior anaesthetist present. There may be an element of bias here because assessors may (justifiably) consider that senior house officers should not deal with moribund patients by themselves. Note that of the six hundred and eight anaesthetics given by senior house officer anaesthetists, one hundred and thirteen were believed by the assessors to be deaths attributable to anaesthesia. On several occasions trainees did superlatively well, but they should not according to the assessors, have been left by themselves in the particular circumstances.

Two forms contained the surprising reply in relation to **elective** lists: "no consultant directly responsible". The assessors noted that a senior registrar had been consulted but they commented that it is "rubbish" to state that no-one is responsible for what trainees do, although in the strict legal sense each doctor is responsible for his own actions.

Out-of-hours and weekend work seems mainly to be undertaken by trainee anaesthetists. When this observation is linked with the observation in the first paragraph of this section the assessors were emphatic that some changes in the working practices of consultant staff may be required. The fact that a higher proportion of consultant surgeons appear to come into hospital to supervise their trainees, requires careful interpretation. There is usually one single consultant anaesthetist on call and he may cover three or four surgical specialties. The apparently lower attendance rate by consultant anaesthetists may be thus explained. The function of this report is not to advise how changes should be implemented but on this occasion to suggest that the profession should at least consider whether a change is required.

Junior staff. The assessors were disturbed to read that one registrar had declined to complete a form "because it is not in my job description". This young doctor worked in a centre of excellence in the North East Thames Region; the consultant surgeon had withdrawn from the study after it began; three operations were necessary in three weeks at one operative site; no morbidity meetings are held at this hospital so how are the trainees to learn about **their (and others') errors and thus improve?**

Another trainee described his disinterest in learning how the assessors scored his management with the words "No, certainly not, I am perfect". The tragedy of this story was that an 82-year-old patient had died no more than twenty seven hours after surgery, and the anaesthetist had not seen her after operation at all.

Monitoring

The use of devices to monitor anaesthetised patients is a controversial matter and this fact is amply demonstrated in the variety of opinions which are expressed about it. The results of this study cannot, and do not, support any particular view since it is quite clear that practice also varies widely in the country. The extent to which monitoring devices were used amongst the patients whose deaths were reported, may or may not reflect their usage in the rest of the country and in patients who survive.

Indirect blood pressure(BP) and ECG. These are not yet used in every case, but the assessors agreed that for almost every procedure both should be attached to the patient, although it was accepted that in very brief operations the BP might be taken before induction only since there might not be time during the procedure.

Pulse palpation. Table 3.12 seems to indicate that palpation of the pulse is less frequently used since pulse monitors, ECGs with displays, and automatic blood pressure measurements have been available.

Urinary catheter. Urine flow measurements are useful in the detection of decreased peripheral perfusion and it was surprising to find use of this relatively simple manoeuvre is not more widespread. However, during operations for abdominal aortic aneurysm it was used much more frequently (94.8%).

TABLE 3.26
Monitoring of specific operations

| Operation | Number | Monitors used | | | |
		Indirect BP	Direct BP	CVP	Urine output
Thoracotomy	29	72.0%	31.0%	34.0%	34.0%
Aortic aneurysm	134	74.6%	59.7%	88.0%	94.8%

Monitoring for specific operations

Central venous pressure. Central venous pressure measurement was used in major surgery, but by no means as frequently as might be expected, particularly, for instance when fluid replacement in a dehydrated patient was undertaken prior to orthopaedic surgery. The assessors recognised that whilst experienced clinicians might themselves not always use the method, it does enable less experienced anaesthetists to avoid overload of the circulation. It is important to emphasise that the technique of insertion itself carries real risks and there must be a balance between that risk and the advantages gained. Its value during transfusion and or after brisk haemorrhage is undisputed.

TABLE 3.27
Use of muscle relaxants

| Relaxants | % by region | | | |
	SW	N	NET	Total
Alcuronium	17.4	2.6	11.5	10.2
Atracurium	33.5	27.1	39.0	32.8
Pancuronium	12.2	17.4	12.7	14.2
Suxamethonium	48.0	36.9	43.3	42.5
Tubocurarine	1.5	1.7	3.9	2.3
Vecuronium	14.3	25.7	15.6	18.9
Other non-depolarising	0.2	0.8	0.7	0.6

Peripheral nerve stimulator. (See table 3.12) The increased need for this type of monitoring has become obvious with the widespread use of vecuronium and atracurium. Despite considerable use (51.7% of all cases) of these drugs table 3.27, table 3.12 shows that appropriate neuromuscular monitors are not commonly employed. Assessors noted the predominance of early deaths in those attributed to anaesthesia and questioned whether there was any evidence of failure of adequate reversal of relaxant drugs; in no case was this claimed by assessors as a cause of death, and the numbers of patients, amongst those who died from bronchopneumonia within five days (105 cases) and had monitoring of neuromuscular function, was too small for satisfactory analysis.

Machine/ventilator monitors. *(pressure, inspired oxygen, ventilator alarms).* This is a different category of monitors which, although they may be built-in to some anaesthetic machines and ventilators, they are not available on all. Thus the high proportion of cases (21.2%) in which the assessors opined that monitoring was inadequate (table 3.17) may need to be carefully interpreted in the light of the pattern of provision of these devices about which we do not have data.

Airway pressure monitors are used in most automatic ventilators and may be assumed by some anaesthetists as integral parts of machines for lung ventilation and thus not to require special note. This does not seem to the writer to be a tenable view of optimal practice but it was so expressed by some assessors.

Ventilation alarms (disconnect or overpressure) were considered to be essential by the assessors although inspired gas analysis for oxygen was thought to be less important, provided that Rotameters were known to be functional. The fact that leaks and other sources of inaccuracy in the delivery of gas mixtures are well known to cause disasters did not persuade this group of assessors. The disadvantages of oxygen sensors (effect of nitrous oxide and water vapour) and their consequent and usual location in the fresh gas flow outweighed their potential advantages.

Expired carbon dioxide analysis is still not used frequently. It is recognised to be appropriate in the practice of neurosurgical anaesthesia. The amount of information which can be gleaned, (increased CO_2 output, decreased cardiac output, under- or over-ventilation) seems sufficient however for this author to advocate more, rather than less, use of this device. The assertion that anaesthetists should measure ventilation with a spirometer is not helpful since there is overwhelming evidence that they do not and (presumably) will not. Expired air analysis provides them with information which otherwise they would not seek actively; it is at least possible that the warning effect of a display which showed that the inspired CO_2 was four percent might alert them.

part 4

appendices

part 4 appendices

CONTENTS

APPENDIX 1 Tables and Figures

Tables

TABLE 4.1
Regional profile

Region	HAA* 30-day deaths	Cases reported to CEPOD		CEPOD cases consultant(s) withdrawn		CEPOD surgical forms returned		CEPOD anaesthetic forms returned	
		Nos	% of HAA**	Nos	% of CEPOD	Nos	% of CEPOD	Nos	% of CEPOD
North	1469	1359	92.5	124	9.1	1073	78.9	1081	79.5
North East Thames	2485	1368	55.1	213	15.5	800	58.5	863	63.2
South West	1853	1307	70.5	183	14.0	911	69.7	984	75.1
All 3 Regions	5807	4034	69.5	520	12.9	2784	69.0	2928	72.6

NB In the district breakdowns (tables 4.1SW, N and NET), following the wishes of the Joint Working Party, districts/hospitals are indicated by random number only and are not named.
*For definitions see following profiles.
**30-day deaths.

TABLE 4.1SW
South Western Region profile

District/ Hospital number	Cases reported to CEPOD		CEPOD cases consultant(s) withdrawn	CEPOD surgical forms returned		CEPOD anaesthetic forms returned	
	Nos	% of HAA*	Nos	Nos	% of CEPOD	Nos	% of CEPOD
1	46	60.5	0	46	100.0	45	98.0
2	100	81.3	0	76	76.0	91	91.0
3	108	41.1	4	85	78.7	93	86.1
4	138	120.0	11	75	54.4	69	50.0
5	14	13.5	0	14	100.0	14	100.0
6	161	120.1	3	138	85.7	140	86.9
7	180	81.4	0	170	94.5	159	88.4
8	101	54.0	30	45	44.6	64	63.3
9	105	60.7	0	74	70.4	94	89.5
10	141	128.2	24	100	70.9	115	81.6
11	67	134.0	46	18	26.9	29	43.3
12	146	49.1	65	70	47.9	71	48.6

*30-day deaths; includes all operations.
NB See table 4.1 footnote.

TABLE 4.1N
Northern Region profile

District/ Hospital number	Cases reported to CEPOD		CEPOD cases consultant(s) withdrawn	CEPOD surgical forms returned		CEPOD anaesthetic forms returned	
	Nos	% of HAA*	Nos	Nos	% of CEPOD	Nos	% of CEPOD
1	9	12.3	0	4	44.4	9	100.0
2	192	228.0	10	153	79.7	127	66.1
3	57	11.7	0	56	98.2	45	78.9
4	52·	179.3	0	45	86.5	42	80.8
5	57	162.9	17	40	70.2	39	68.4
6	122	190.5	0	107	87.7	108	88.5
7	37	92.5	0	28	75.7	35	94.6
8	79	175.6	0	74	93.7	72	91.1
9	97	101.0	1	93	95.8	95	97.9
10	38	55.9	4	24	63.1	37	97.3
11	69	95.8	42	23	33.3	20	28.9
12	91	112.3	2	81	89.0	84	92.3
13	120	60.0	0	95	79.2	111	92.5
14	96	60.0	4	81	84.4	84	87.5
15	15	214.3	0	15	100.0	14	93.3
16	60	58.3	0	47	78.3	37	61.7
17	47	146.9	1	41	87.2	39	82.9
18	60	34.9	34	18	30.0	25	41.7
19	61	107.0	9	48	78.7	58	95.1

*30-day deaths; includes all operations; if multiple operations carried out, first date
used to calculate 30 day period.
NB See table 4.1 footnote.

TABLE 4.1NET
North East Thames profile

District/ Hospital number	Cases reported to CEPOD		CEPOD cases consultant(s) withdrawn	CEPOD surgical forms returned		CEPOD anaesthetic forms returned	
	Nos	% of HAA*	Nos	Nos	% of CEPOD	Nos	% of CEPOD
1	37	48.1	4	12	32.4	23	62.2
2	14	8.0	2	8	57.1	10	71.4
3	73	73.7	35	45	61.6	27	36.9
4	66	35.5	3	43	65.2	42	63.6
5	38.	40.4	5	30	78.9	30	78.9
6	82	50.0	0	35	42.7	63	76.8
7	40	100.0	5	22	55.0	26	65.0
8	4	30.8	0	4	100.0	4	100.0
9	5	**	0	5	100.0	5	100.0
10	47	77.0	0	29	61.7	40	85.1
11	15	13.6	3	6	40.0	13	86.7
12	109	81.3	0	81	74.3	85	77.9
13	167	42.1	98	51	30.5	48	28.8
14	57	50.0	0	49	85.9	51	89.5
15	54	43.9	0	46	85.2	51	94.4
16	154	130.0	10	122	79.2	127	82.5
17	133	74.3	33	52	39.1	81	60.9
18	83	71.6	0	76	91.6	53	63.8
19	109	129.8	15	20	18.4	35	32.1
20	76	38.2	0	61	80.3	44	57.9
21	5	166.6	0	3	60.0	5	100.0
22	0	**	0	0	-	0	-

* 30-day deaths; includes all operations; including patients who were admitted by a surgeon and visited the operating theatre but may not have had an operation.
**No HAA 30-day deaths recorded under this hospital.
NB See table 4.1 footnote.

TABLE 4.2
Sex of patients

Sex	Anaesthetic form	% Surgical form
Male	52.8	53.8
Female	47.2	46.2

No regional differences.

TABLE 4.3
Sex ratios

Age group	CEPOD sex ratio Female : Male	England & Wales 1985 population sex ratio Female: Male*
0 -9	1:1.44	1:1.05
10 -19	1:2.00	1:1.05
20 -29	1:2.12	1:1.03
30 -39	1:1.76	1:1.01
40 -49	1:1.22	1:1.01
50 -59	1:1.49	1.03:1
60 -69	1:1.56	1.16:1
70-79	1:1.37	1.49:1
80 -89	1.38:1	2.59:1
90 +	2.67:1	2.59:1
All ages	1:1.11	1.05:1

*From O.P.C.S. *Population Trends* **46,** Winter 1986.

TABLE 4.4
Was the patient weighed?

Patient weighed	Total %
Yes	36.1
No	62.1
Not answered	1.8

TABLE 4.5
Operation specific death rates using CEPOD deaths and HAA data

Operation	SW	% by region N	NET	Total
Aortic aneurysm repair	12.2	40.0	16.7	20.0
HAA = 645				
CEPOD = 129				
Appendicectomy	0.04	0.0	0.04	0.04
HAA = 12212				
CEPOD = 5				
Fracture of femur	8.2	5.4	2.4	4.3
HAA = 4991				
CEPOD = 217				
Cholecystectomy	0.6	0.5	0.7	0.6
HAA = 7660				
CEPOD = 44				
Strangulated hernia repair	7.8	6.7	6.6	7.0
HAA = 767				
CEPOD = 54				
All operations	0.71	0.62	0.91	0.73
CEPOD = 4034				
HAA = 0.5 M				

HAA data from statistics departments in each region.

TABLE 4.6
Autopsies carried out on CEPOD patients who died within two days of their operation

Autopsies	SW	% by region N	NET	Total
Percentage where Autopsy carried out	53.6	38.4	39.5	44.2

TABLE 4.7
Grade of surgeon undertaking the operation

Grade of surgeon	SW	% by region N	NET	Total
Senior House Officer	7.2	3.0	3.2	4.5
Registrar	30.6	26.5	40.2	31.8
Senior Registrar	8.8	11.6	15.5	11.8
Consultant	46.3	54.3	38.4	47.1
Associate Specialist	5.3	2.5	0.7	2.9
Student	-	-	-	-
House Surgeon	-	0.1	-	1 case
Other	0.8	0.7	0.5	0.7
Not answered	1.0	1.4	1.5	1.2
Number of cases	911	1073	800	2784

TABLE 4.8
Hour of operation (grades of surgeon)

Hours	SW	% of operations N	NET	Total
Office hours (0900 - 1759)				
Consultant	54.8	60.4	45.7	54.9
Others	45.2	39.6	54.3	45.1
Out of hours (1800 - 0859)				
Consultant	31.8	42.4	27.6	33.9
Others	68.2	57.6	72.4	66.1

TABLE 4.9
Grade of surgeon by hour/day of operation

Grade of surgeon	Weekends	% of cases Weekdays	Day (0900 -1900)	Night
Senior House Officer	5.9	4.1	3.2	5.5
Registrar	46.3	29.2	24.8	44.6
Senior Registrar	13.2	11.6	11.2	12.4
Consultant	29.7	50.1	54.9	33.9
Associate Specialist	2.7	2.9	3.8	1.9
Student	-	-	-	-
House Surgeon	-	1 case	-	-
Other	0.2	0.8	0.6	0.5
Not answered	2.0	1.2	1.5	1.2
Total*	11.2	88.8	45.0	39.8

*15.2% CEPOD operations where times unknown.

TABLE 4.10
Grade of surgeon who started the operation

Grade of surgeon	SW	% by region N	NET	Total
Senior House Officer	9.5	3.4	4.0	5.6
Registrar	32.1	30.0	43.4	34.5
Senior Registrar	9.1	10.7	15.5	11.6
Consultant	42.6	51.3	35.2	43.8
Associate Specialist	5.2	2.4	0.7	2.8
Student	0.0	0.0	0.0	0.0
House Surgeon	0.2	0.3	0.0	0.2
Other	0.8	1.6	0.5	1.0
Not answered	0.5	0.4	0.7	0.5

TABLE 4.11
Most senior grade of assisting surgeon

Grade of surgeon	SW	% by region N	NET	Total
Senior House Officer	44.3	30.1	22.0	32.4
Registrar	17.1	28.8	24.0	23.6
Senior Registrar	4.1	5.0	6.6	5.2
Consultant	9.0	8.9	5.2	7.9
Associate Specialist	1.5	1.1	0.1	1.0
Student	0.3	0.6	1.0	0.6
House Surgeon	9.3	8.9	24.9	13.6
Other	1.3	2.5	2.0	2.0
Not answered	13.1	14.1	14.2	13.7

TABLE 4.12
Grade of surgeon by operation type

Grade of surgeon	Emergency	% of operation type Urgent	Scheduled	Elective	*Unable to Calculate
Senior House Officer	0.0	7.0	2.7	2.6	6.7
Registrar	33.3	40.4	26.3	28.2	35.6
Senior Registrar	11.1	12.7	11.6	8.5	12.7
Consultant	52.8	35.4	53.8	56.8	41.1
Associate Specialist	2.8	2.7	3.8	1.3	1.2
Student	0.0	0.0	0.0	0.0	0.0
House surgeon	0.0	0.0	0.0	0.0	1 case
Other	0.0	0.8	1.2	0.8	0.9
All cases	1.2	27.6	48.3	8.4	14.4

* Times unknown.
For definitions of operation types see table 1.9.
NB Columns do not total 100% where grades were not known.

TABLE 4.13
Grade of surgeon by hour of operation

Grade of surgeon	SW In	SW Out	N In	N Out	NET In	NET Out	Total In	Total Out
Senior House Officer	4.1	8.5	1.8	2.3	1.9	2.0	2.6	4.4
Registrar	18.7	36.4	20.2	29.4	21.3	40.8	20.0	35.6
Senior Registrar	8.0	5.9	7.2	16.7	12.9	8.1	9.0	9.9
Consultant	45.1	25.9	51.5	36.7	32.9	19.8	44.3	27.0
Associate Specialist	5.0	3.5	2.8	1.2	1.3	0.0	3.1	1.5
Student	0.0	0.0	0.0	0.0	0.0	0.0	0.0	0.0
House Surgeon	0.0	0.0	0.0	0.0	0.0	0.0	0.0	0.0
Other	0.5	0.7	0.6	0.0	0.2	0.5	0.5	0.4
Not answered	0.9	0.5	1.0	1.2	1.3	0.8	1.0	0.8

NB Columns do not total 100% because of grades not known.
In = in hours. Out = out of hours.
For definitions of "in hours" and "out of hours" see table 4.77.

TABLE 4.14
Ages of patients and grades of surgeons

| Age Group | % of age group per grade | | | |
	S.H.O	Reg.	S.Reg.	Cons.
0-9	0.0	23.7	3.8	73.5
10-19	5.5	38.9	5.5	50.9
20-29	0.0	37.3	11.1	44.6
30-39	2.6	31.5	7.9	57.9
40-49	2.4	28.9	7.2	57.8
50-59	2.0	27.1	10.7	57.6
60-69	2.2	26.4	13.1	55.4
70-79	3.6	28.6	13.4	50.9
80-89	7.7	42.6	12.2	37.2
90+	11.4	41.4	5.7	25.7

NB Rows may not total 100% because of other and unknown grades.

TABLE 4.15
Most senior surgeon who took history before the operation

| Grade of surgeon | % by region | | | |
	SW	N	NET	Total
Senior House Officer	7.0	4.8	3.0	5.0
Registrar	21.7	12.5	31.7	21.0
Senior Registrar	5.6	6.4	9.0	6.9
Consultant	59.4	72.4	53.6	62.8
Associate Specialist	2.3	1.5	0.9	1.6
Student	0.0	0.0	0.0	0.0
House Surgeon	2.1	1.5	1.1	1.6
Other	0.0	0.0	0.0	0.0
Not answered	1.9	0.9	0.7	1.1

TABLE 4.16
Most senior surgeon to examine patient before the operation

| Grade of surgeon | % by region | | | |
	SW	N	NET	Total
Senior House Officer	3.3	2.0	1.1	2.2
Registrar	20.4	9.9	28.0	18.5
Senior Registrar	5.9	6.2	10.5	7.4
Consultant	65.5	79.0	58.5	68.7
Associate Specialist	3.2	1.8	0.9	2.0
Student	0.0	0.0	0.0	0.0
House Surgeon	0.7	0.5	0.0	0.4
Other	0.1	0.0	0.0	0.0
Not Answered	0.9	0.6	1.0	0.8

TABLE 4.17
Specialty surgical interest of consultant surgeon

| Surgical specialty | % by region | | | |
	SW	N	NET	Total
General	24.8	25.6	17.5	23.
General (& Paediatric)	0.2	0.5	0.0	0.
General (& Urology)	10.5	5.6	2.9	6.
General (& Vascular)	13.8	23.1	24.7	20.
General (Other)	13.7	13.2	22.9	16.
A & E	0.3	0.9	0.1	0.
Cardiothoracic	7.2	1.4	0.5	3.
Dent/Oral	0.2	0.2	0.0	0.
Gynaecology	1.5	1.9	2.3	1.
Neurosurgery	4.8	1.9	5.9	4.
Ophthalmology	0.2	0.2	0.2	0.
Orthopaedic	15.1	15.6	14.5	15.
Otorhinolaryngology	1.6	1.6	1.2	1.
Paediatric	0.0	1.4	0.0	0.
Plastic	0.7	0.3	0.1	0.
Transplantation	0.0	0.2	0.3	0.
Urology	2.9	5.0	4.9	4.
Other	0.2	0.2	0.1	0.
Not answered	2.3	1.2	1.9	1.

TABLE 4.18
Autopsies carried out

| Surgical Specialty Interest | % by specialty | | | |
	SW	N	NET	To
General	37.0	25.0	35.0	31
General (& Paediatric)	0.0	20.0	0.0	14
General (& Urology)	35.0	27.9	39.1	33
General (&Vascular)	39.7	21.7	32.5	29
General (Other)	38.4	35.2	36.6	36
A & E	66.7	50.0	0.0	50
Cardiothoracic	37.9	40.0	50.0	38
Dent/Oral	50.0	50.0	0.0	50
Gynaecology	21.4	33.3	42.1	33
Neurosurgery	61.3	42.9	40.4	49
Ophthalmology	0.0	50.0	100.0	50
Orthopaedic	56.9	44.9	25.0	54
Otorhinolaryngology	40.0	11.0	10.0	20
Paediatric	0.0	40.0	0.0	40
Plastic	50.0	66.6	100.0	60
Transplantation	0.0	50.0	0.0	25
Urology	37.0	27.7	28.2	3C
Other	50.8	50.0	100.0	6C
Not answered	44.4	20.0	28.6	33

NB Each cell has its own denominator.

TABLE 4.19
Regular local mortality/morbidity meetings

Surgical Specialty Interest	% cases by specialty			
	SW	N	NET	Total
General	48.2	55.6	50.0	51.8
General (& Paediatric)	50.0	100.0	0.0	85.7
General (& Urology)	36.5	27.9	26.1	32.2
General (& Vascular)	57.1	61.7	62.9	61.1
General (Other)	56.0	65.5	81.9	69.9
A & E	33.3	30.0	0.0	28.6
Cardiothoracic	50.0	46.7	50.0	49.4
Dent/Oral	0.0	50.0	0.0	25.0
Gynaecology	35.7	28.6	31.5	31.5
Neurosurgery	25.0	23.8	10.6	18.8
Ophthalmology	0.0	0.0	0.0	0.0
Orthopaedic	8.7	7.1	18.9	10.9
Otorhinolaryngology	13.3	16.7	0.0	11.6
Paediatric	0.0	0.0	0.0	0.0
Plastic	0.0	33.3	0.0	10.0
Transplantation	0.0	100.0	50.0	75.0
Urology	55.5	79.6	30.8	58.3
Other	50.0	50.0	100.0	60.0
Not answered	22.2	80.0	64.3	50.0

NB Each cell has its own denominator.

TABLE 4.20
Attendance at local mortality/morbidity meetings

Surgical Specialty Interest				% of CEPOD deaths discussed
	SW	N	NET	Total
General	23.0	30.5	28.6	27.5
General (& Paediatric)	0.0	20.0	0.0	14.2
General (& Urology)	20.8	8.2	17.4	16.1
General (& Vascular)	30.9	41.1	46.2	40.6
General (Other)	34.4	45.7	52.4	45.3
A & E	33.3	10.0	0.0	14.2
Cardiothoracic	19.6	20.0	0.0	18.8
Dent/Oral	0.0	50.0	0.0	25.0
Gynaecology	14.3	9.5	15.8	12.9
Neurosurgery	6.8	4.8	2.1	4.5
Ophthalmology	0.0	0.0	0.0	0.0
Orthopaedic	0.7	1.2	9.4	3.3
Orthorhinolaryngology	0.0	5.5	0.0	2.3
Paediatric	0.0	0.0	0.0	0.0
Plastic	0.0	33.3	0.0	10.0
Transplantation	0.0	50.0	50.1	50.0
Urology	29.6	40.7	25.6	33.3
Other	0.0	40.0	0.0	20.0
Not answered	0.0	0.0	14.3	14.2

NB Each cell has its own denominator.

TABLE 4.21
Patient transferred from another hospital

Transfer from	% by region			
	SW	N	NET	Total
Non NHS	1.2	0.5	0.5	0.7
Same District	11.2	6.2	5.7	7.7
Same Region	5.4	3.1	5.7	4.6

TABLE 4.22
Transferred patients by specialty

Surgical Specialty interest	From non NHS	% of cases transferred From same district	From same region
General	0.5	7.2	0.8
General (& Paediatric)	-	28.6	-
General (& Urology)	-	8.3	0.6
General (& Vascular)	0.7	6.7	2.1
General (Other)	0.7	8.9	3.6
A & E	-	7.1	21.4
Cardiothoracic	2.3	7.0	12.9
Dent/Oral	-	-	25.0
Gynaecology	1.8	7.4	1.8
Neurosurgery	1.8	8.9	53.6
Ophthalmology	-	-	-
Orthopaedic	0.9	7.4	0.9
Otorhinolaryngolgy	-	11.6	4.7
Paediatric	-	53.3	20.0
Plastic	-	-	30.0
Transplantation	-	-	-
Urology	-	6.7	3.3
Other	20.0	0.0	20.0
Not answered	-	2.4	2.4

NB Each cell has its own denominator.
(- = No cases)

TABLE 4.23
Specialty of surgeon by type of operation

Surgical specialty interest	Emergency	% of specialty Urgent	Scheduled	Elective
General	0.9	28.7	45.8	8.3
General (& Paediatric)	0.0	14.3	57.1	14.2
General (& Urology)	3.3	34.4	46.1	4.4
General (& Vascular)	1.0	28.5	45.9	11.9
General (Other)	1.1	23.1	50.4	10.2
A & E	0.0	35.7	35.7	14.2
Cardiothoracic	1.2	14.1	65.9	1.2
Dental/Oral	0.0	25.0	50.0	0.0
Gynaecology	0.0	22.2	55.5	3.7
Neurosurgery	2.6	33.0	41.1	5.3
Ophthalmology	0.0	33.3	50.0	0.0
Orthopaedic	0.5	29.3	51.7	5.5
Otorhinolaryngology	0.0	27.9	44.2	13.9
Paediatric	33.3	33.3	20.0	6.7
Plastic	0.0	20.0	40.0	30.0
Transplantation	0.0	25.0	25.0	25.0
Urology	1.7	23.3	56.7	8.3
Other	0.0	0.0	60.0	0.0
Not answered	0.0	30.9	40.5	7.1

NB Rows may not total 100% because some operation types were unknown and impossible to calculate.
For definitions of operation types see table 1.9.

TABLE 4.24
Where the surgeon was not a consultant was the consultant consulted by specialty?

Surgical specialty interest	Number of cases	% where consultant consulted
General	344	67.4
General (& Paediatric)	3	66.7
General (& Urology)	84	67.9
General (& Vascular)	274	65.3
General (Other)	212	58.0
A & E	8	75.0
Cardiothoracic	31	83.9
Dental/Oral	1	100.0
Gynaecology	19	73.6
Neurosurgery	72	95.8
Ophthalmology	2	0.0
Orthopaedic	319	66.4
Otorhinolaryngology	13	53.8
Paediatric	3	100.0
Plastic	5	80.0
Transplantation	5	66.7
Urology	52	78.8
Other	3	66.7
Not answered	24	66.7

TABLE 4.25
Where the surgeon was not a consultant was there consultation with the consultant by hour of operation?

| | % by region | | | | | | | |
| | SW | | N | | NET | | Total | |
Consultant consulted	In hrs	Out of hrs	In hrs	Out of hrs	In hrs	Out of hrs	In hrs	Out of hrs
Yes	76.0	54.7	86.8	57.7	72.5	44.4	78.9	54.9
No	19.5	41.2	10.0	22.2	25.3	59.9	17.7	42.4

NB Columns do not total 100% because of cases where question not answered.
For definitions of "in hours" and "out of hours" see table 4.78.

TABLE 4.26
Consultation with consultant surgeon by grade of surgeon

| Grade of surgeon | % by region | | | |
	SW	N	NET	Total
Senior House Officer	46.9	78.1	42.3	54.0
Registrar	73.1	82.4	53.1	68.8
Senior Registrar	62.5	73.6	63.7	67.1
Consultant	-	-	-	-
Associate Specialist	66.7	81.5	66.7	71.6
Student	-	-	-	-
House Surgeon	-	1 case	-	1 case
Other	42.8	100.0	100.0	78.9
Not answered	66.7	100.0	54.5	75.8

NB Each cell has its own denominator.

TABLE 4.27
Consultation with consultant surgeon and operation type

| Operation type* | % by region | | | |
	SW	N	NET	Total
Elective	63.6	100.0	100.0	76.4
Scheduled	55.0	77.8	35.9	57.7
Urgent	73.3	84.5	71.6	76.6
Emergency	77.7	83.7	58.7	71.1
Unknown	80.7	72.0	49.1	62.8

NB Each cell has its own denominator
*For definition of operation types see table 1.9.

TABLE 4.28
Multiple operations within 30 days of the major operation

More than 1 operation	% Total
Yes	26.7
No	69.8
Not answered	3.5

No regional differences.

TABLE 4.29
Day-case patients

Day-cases	% Total
Yes	0.7
No	96.7
Not answered	2.6

No regional differences.

TABLE 4.30
Pre-operative investigations carried out by surgical
team
No regional differences

Investigation	% Total
Haemoglobin	94.1
Blood urea	92.2
Plasma sodium	91.5
Plasma bilirubin	51.6
Plasma albumin	51.2
Coagulation test	18.7
Chest X-Ray	87.0
Respiratory function tests	8.2
Urine analysis (Ward or Lab)	76.6
Ultrasound	16.8
Biopsy	11.8
Other	11.7

With regional differences

Investigation	% by region SW	N	NET	Total
Fever greater than 37°C	57.5	58.2	49.6	55.5
Serum amylase	21.5	18.5	14.4	18.3
Blood glucose	44.1	50.3	53.6	49.2
Cross matching	72.8	77.4	80.6	76.8
Sickle cell test	1.5	2.4	3.0	2.3
Electrocardiograph	86.4	77.6	86.5	83.0
Blood gases	9.8	16.2	17.4	14.4
Radiological	33.8	28.0	36.4	32.3

TABLE 4.31
Precautions or therapy undertaken immediately
pre-operatively to ensure adequate physiological
function by surgical team
No regional differences

Precaution	% Total
Pulse rate recording	97.7
Blood pressure recording	97.1
Central venous pressure measurement	18.6
Cardiac support drugs or anti-dysrythmic agents	15.2
Vasopressors	2.7
Gastric aspiration	37.3
Maintain adequate urine output	68.2
Intravenous fluid	73.5
Blood transfusion	27.5
Optimal preoperative rehydration	61.7
Anticoagulants	10.6
Antibiotics	52.7
Mucolytics	3.3
Airway protection	4.7
Tracheal intubation	18.5
Mechanical ventilation	15.9
Stabilization of spinal fractures	0.9
Stabilization of limb fractures	8.5
Parenteral feeding	4.1
Other	5.5

With regional differences

Precaution	% by region SW	N	NET	Total
Urinary catheter	55.7	58.5	61.4	58.4
Diuretics	18.6	22.5	22.4	21.2
Chest physiotherapy	38.7	42.5	39.2	40.3
Oxygen therapy	27.4	23.9	27.6	26.1

TABLE 4.32
Did the operating surgeon immediately before operation
identify the patient and notes?

Answer	% by region SW	N	NET	Total
Yes	97.4	97.9	96.5	97.3
No	1.3	0.9	1.4	1.2
Not answered	1.3	1.2	2.1	1.5

TABLE 4.33
Did the operating surgeon immediately before operation
review the notes and working diagnosis?

Answer	% by region SW	N	NET	Total
Yes	93.0	93.0	90.0	92.1
No	5.4	5.6	7.2	6.0
Not answered	1.6	1.4	2.8	1.9

TABLE 4.34
Surgeons' reply to: Was the duration of the operation too long?

Answer	SW	% by region N	NET	Total
Yes	3.4	1.3	6.7	3.6
No	93.2	95.6	87.7	92.6
Not answered	3.4	3.1	5.6	3.8

TABLE 4.35
Surgeons' reply to: Was there any intra-operative disaster?

Answer	SW	% by region N	NET	Total
Yes	9.2	5.5	8.5	7.6
No	89.0	93.2	88.5	90.5
Not answered	1.8	1.3	3.0	1.9

TABLE 4.36
Local or regional anaesthesia administered by surgeon

Answer	SW	% by region N	NET	Total
Yes	4.6	7.0	8.0	6.5
No	70.5	65.8	68.9	68.2
Not answered	24.9	27.2	23.1	25.3

TABLE 4.37
Antibiotics given post-operatively by surgical team

Answer	SW	% by region N	NET	Total
Yes	61.9	61.5	66.5	63.1
No	31.6	32.0	25.1	29.9
Not answered	6.5	6.5	8.4	7.0

TABLE 4.38
Post-operative parenteral feeding

Answer	SW	% by region N	NET	Total
Yes	10.8	9.9	10.4	10.3
No	81.9	83.2	80.1	81.9
Not answered	7.3	6.9	9.5	7.8

TABLE 4.39
Post-operative non oral (other than parenteral) method of feeding

Answer	SW	% by region N	NET	Total
Yes	6.3	4.8	4.6	5.2
No	83.7	85.6	82.6	84.2
Not answered	10.0	9.6	12.8	10.6

TABLE 4.40
CEPOD death considered at a local surgical mortality/morbidity review meeting

Answer	SW	% by region N	NET	Total
Yes	20.0	27.7	32.4	26.5
No	31.6	28.1	27.2	29.0
Not answered	48.4	44.2	40.4	44.5

TABLE 4.41
Shortage of trained personnel in the theatre according to surgeon

Answer	SW	% by region N	NET	Total
Yes	1.6	0.7	1.5	1.2
No	97.5	97.6	97.5	97.5
Not answered	0.9	1.7	1.0	1.3

TABLE 4.42
Deficiency in pre-operative management according to surgeon

Answer	SW	% by region N	NET	Total
Yes	7.2	6.9	9.7	7.8
No	91.7	92.3	89.4	91.2
Not answered	1.1	0.8	0.9	1.0

TABLE 4.43
Lack or deficiency of surgical equipment according to the surgeon

Answer	SW	% by region N	NET	Total
Yes	1.3	0.6	0.9	0.9
No	97.8	98.4	98.2	98.2
Not answered	0.9	1.0	0.9	0.9

TABLE 4.44
Technical difficulties or surgical misadventure according to the surgeon

Answer	SW	% by region N	NET	Total
Yes	12.2	8.6	15.1	11.6
No	87.0	90.1	84.0	87.4
Not answered	0.8	1.3	0.9	1.0

TABLE 4.45
Any measures which could have improved the outcome according to the surgeon

Answer	SW	% by region N	NET	Total
Yes	14.7	12.0	17.6	14.5
No	82.9	85.2	78.9	82.6
Not answered	2.4	2.8	3.5	2.9

TABLE 4.46
Organizational aspects, lack of resources or other non-clinical factors contributed to the fatal outcome according to surgeon

Answer	SW	% by region N	NET	Total
Yes	2.4	2.1	5.5	3.2
No	95.4	95.5	91.4	94.3
Not answered	2.2	2.4	3.1	2.5

TABLE 4.47
Completion of surgical forms

Completed by	SW	% by region N	NET	Total
Operating surgeon	67.2	67.7	62.5	66.0
Trainee other than operating surgeon	18.3	15.9	21.6	18.4
* Other	12.6	14.9	14.5	14.0
Not answered	1.9	1.5	1.4	1.6

* Usually consultant where trainee operator had moved on.

TABLE 4.48
Patients' notes adequate to complete the surgical form according to surgeon

Answer	SW	% by region N	NET	Total
Yes	83.1	86.6	81.4	83.9
No	15.8	11.8	17.4	14.7
Not answered	1.1	1.6	1.2	1.4

TABLE 4.49
Copies of operation notes sent with the surgical form

Copies received	SW	% by region N	NET	Total
Yes	65.0	73.4	63.4	67.8
No	35.0	26.6	36.6	32.2

TABLE 4.50
Surgeons claiming feedback required

Grade of surgeon	SW	% by region N	NET	Total
Senior House Officer	50.0	50.0	50.0	50.0
Registrar	47.7	40.0	54.0	47.6
Senior Registrar	41.2	44.8	55.6	48.0
Consultant	52.4	46.1	61.5	51.7
Associate Specialist	22.9	40.7	66.6	32.0
Student	-	-	-	-
House Surgeon	-	-	-	-
Other	42.8	37.5	100.0	52.6
Not answered	22.2	61.5	36.4	42.4

NB Each cell has its own denominator.

TABLE 4.51
Surgeons requesting feedback by telephone

Grade of operating surgeon	SW	% by region N	NET	Total
Senior House Officer	1.5	3.1	0.0	0.8
Registrar	4.6	3.5	4.9	4.4
Senior Registrar	0.0	4.0	12.1	6.1
Consultant	8.5	5.5	10.4	7.6
Associate Specialist	0.0	0.0	16.6	1.2
Student	-	-	-	-
House Surgeon	-	-	-	-
Other	-	-	-	-
Not answered	-	-	-	-

NB Each cell has its own denominator.

TABLE 4.52
Feedback requested by telephone

Surgical Specialty Interest	% of specialty
General	12.2
General (& Paediatric)	0.0
General (& Urology)	5.5
General (& Vascular)	5.4
General (Other)	5.9
A & E	0.0
Cardiothoracic	2.4
Dent/Oral	0.0
Gynaecology	3.8
Neurosurgery	1.8
Ophthalmology	33.3
Orthopaedic	0.0
Otorhinolaryngology	2.4
Paediatric	0.0
Plastic	0.0
Transplantation	0.0
Urology	0.8
Other	0.0
Not answered	2.4

NB Each cell has its own denominator.

TABLE 4.53
Surgeon assessors' opinions
Was the information adequate to make an assessment?

Answer	SW	% by region N	NET	Total
Yes	97.5	97.2	95.5	96.8
No	2.5	2.8	4.5	3.2

TABLE 4.54
Surgeon assessors' opinions
Were there avoidable elements in the entire management of the patient which if corrected, would have altered the outcome, or might at least have reduced the chance of death at that time? *ie.* Was the death avoidable?

Answer	SW	% by region N	NET	Total
Yes	22.2	19.3	26.1	22.2
No	69.7	73.7	63.4	69.4
Not answered	8.1	7.0	10.5	8.4

TABLE 4.55
Surgeon assessors' opinions
Were there departures from ideal practice?

| Answer | | % by region | | |
	SW	N	NET	Total
Yes	14.2	13.0	16.4	14.3
No	82.2	82.9	77.6	81.1
Not answered	3.6	4.1	6.0	4.6

TABLE 4.56
Surgeon assessors' opinions
Would you have decided to operate ?

| Answer | | % by region | | |
	SW	N	NET	Tot
Yes	85.2	86.7	82.4	84.9
No	5.9	4.8	6.3	5.6
Not answered	8.9	8.5	11.3	9.5

TABLE 4.57
Surgeon assessors' opinions
Do you think there should have been any surgical operation in any centre?

| Answer | | % by region | | |
	SW	N	NET	Total
Yes	89.1	91.5	86.2	89.2
No	7.2	5.0	7.5	6.5
Not answered	3.7	3.5	6.3	4.3

TABLE 4.58
Surgeon assessors' opinions
Do you consider that the death was totally or partly associated with surgery?

| Answer | | % by region | | |
	SW	N	NET	To
Yes	30.6	26.4	34.6	30
No	66.1	70.1	61.9	66
Not answered	3.3	3.5	3.5	3

TABLE 4.59
Surgeon assessors' opinions
When death was associated with surgery which factors were involved?

Factors	SW	N	% of cases NET	Total n = 2784	associated with surgery n = 839
Inappropriate operation	10.2	9.0	11.1	10.0	33.3
Inappropriate pre-op management	11.2	8.9	12.9	10.8	35.9
Inappropriate grade surgeon	8.0	3.4	9.1	6.5	21.7
Failure of organisation	4.3	3.3	4.7	4.0	13.3
Inadequate knowledge	2.5	1.5	3.4	2.4	7.9
Failure to apply knowledge	6.5	3.7	5.5	5.1	17.0
Lack of care	2.5	1.6	4.4	2.7	8.9
Lack of experience	5.0	3.4	6.1	4.7	15.7
Inadequate supervision	3.4	1.5	5.0	3.1	10.4
Fatigue	0.9	0.9	1.0	0.9	3.1
Physical impairment	1 case	0.0	0.0	1 case	1 case
Mental impairment	0.0	0.0	0.0	0.0	0.0
Other	2.9	4.0	4.1	3.7	12.2

NB Multiple answers possible.

TABLE 4.60
Surgeon assessors' opinions
Do you consider that the death was totally or partly associated with anaesthesia?

		% by region		
Answer	SW	N	NET	Total
Yes	1.6	1.4	2.5	1.8
No	65.0	63.7	55.6	61.8
Not answered	33.4	34.9	41.9	36.4

TABLE 4.61
Surgeon assessors' opinions
Do you consider that the death was totally or partly associated with the progress of the presenting surgical disease?

		% by region		
Answer	SW	N	NET	Total
Yes	66.4	69.8	65.6	67.5
No	8.5	6.8	7.1	7.4
Not answered	25.1	23.4	27.3	25.1

TABLE 4.62
Surgeon assessors' opinions
Do you consider that the death was totally or partly associated with the progress of intercurrent disease?

		% by region		
Answer	SW	N	NET	Total
Yes	43.9	44.6	44.1	44.3
No	4.6	3.0	1.6	3.1
Not answered	51.5	52.4	54.3	52.6

TABLE 4.63
Surgeon assessors' opinions
Factors relating to the death were unknown or not assessable

		% by region		
	SW	N	NET	Total
Unknown /Not assessable	3.1	3.9	5.5	4.1

TABLE 4.64
Surgeon assessors' opinions
Opinions by grade of surgeon

Grade of surgeon	Number of cases	Assessors' opinions			
		Death had avoidable elements	Death associated with surgery	Inappropriate operation	Inappropriate pre-operative management
Senior House Officer	124	27.4	40.3	8.1	22.6
Registrar	885	25.6	34.2	12.8	14.4
Senior Registrar	329	22.8	30.3	9.7	10.9
Consultant	1312	20.2	27.1	8.6	7.7
Associate Specialist	81	9.9	22.2	3.7	3.7
Student	-	-	-	-	-
House Surgeon	1	-	-	-	-
Other	19	15.8	15.8	5.2	10.5
Not answered	33	18.2	27.3	21.2	9.0

NB Each cell's denominator is in the left hand column.

TABLE 4.65
Surgeon assessors' opinions
Opinions by grade of surgeon

Grade of surgeon	% of all cases	Assessors' opinions % of deaths that had avoidable elements	% of deaths related to surgery
Senior House Officer	4.5	5.5	5.9
Registrar	31.8	36.7	36.1
Senior Registrar	11.8	12.1	11.9
Consultant	47.1	42.9	42.4
Associate Specialist	2.9	1.3	2.1
Student	-	--	-
House Surgeon	1 case	-	-
Other	0.7	0.4	0.5
Not answered			
Number of cases	2784	618	839

NB Each cell's denominator is the column total.

TABLE 4.66
Surgeon assessors' opinions
Death totally or partly associated with surgery by grade

Grade of surgeon	% by region SW	N	NET	Total
Senior House Officer	40.9	34.0	46.0	40.3
Registrar	40.1	23.9	38.2	34.2
Senior Registrar	30.0	32.8	28.2	30.3
Consultant	24.6	25.7	33.2	27.1
Associate Specialist	18.8	25.9	33.3	22.2
Student	0.0	0.0	0.0	0.0
House Surgeon	0.0	0.0	0.0	0.0
Other	14.2	25.0	0.0	15.8
Not answered	22.2	30.8	27.3	27.3

NB Each cell has its own denominator.

TABLE 4.67
Surgeon assessors' opinions
Were there avoidable elements in the entire manageme[nt]
of the patient which, if corrected, would have altered the
outcome, or might at least have reduced the chance of
death at that time? *ie.* Was the death avoidable?

Grade of surgeon	% of avoidable deaths by region SW	N	NET	T
Senior House Officer	30.3	21.8	26.9	2
Registrar	26.5	18.3	31.4	2
Senior Registrar	22.5	28.0	17.7	2
Consultant	20.1	18.0	24.4	2
Associate Specialist	6.2	11.1	33.3	
Student	0.0	0.0	0.0	
House Surgeon	0.0	0.0	0.0	
Other	14.2	25.0	0.0	1
Not answered	11.1	23.1	18.2	1

NB Each cell has its own denominator.

TABLE 4.68
Surgeon assessors' opinions
Departures from ideal practice by grade

Grade of surgeon	% by region SW	N	NET	Total
Senior House Officer	24.2	12.5	26.9	21.8
Registrar	21.1	17.3	21.4	20.0
Senior Registrar	7.5	11.2	13.7	11.2
Consultant	10.7	11.5	11.1	11.1
Associate Specialist	4.2	11.1	33.3	8.6
Student	0.0	0.0	0.0	0.0
House Surgeon	0.0	1 case	0.0	1 case
Other	0.0	0.0	25.0	5.2
Not answered	11.1	7.6	9.0	9.1

NB Each cell has its own denominator.

TABLE 4.69
Surgeon assessors' opinions
Inappropriate operation carried out by grade

| Grade of surgeon | SW | % by region | | Total |
		N	NET	
Senior House Officer	12.1	6.2	0.0	8.1
Registrar	13.6	9.1	15.2	12.8
Senior Registrar	10.0	9.6	9.6	9.7
Consultant	8.3	8.9	8.5	8.6
Associate Specialist	4.2	3.7	0.0	3.7
Student	0.0	0.0	0.0	0.0
House Surgeon	0.0	0.0	0.0	0.0
Other	0.0	12.5	0.0	5.2
Not answered	22.2	23.1	18.2	21.2

NB Each cell has its own denominator.

TABLE 4.70
Surgeon assessors' opinions
Inappropriate pre-operative management by grade

| Grade of surgeon | SW | % by region | | Total |
		N	NET	
Senior House Officer	21.2	15.6	34.6	22.6
Registrar	15.4	8.8	18.3	14.4
Senior Registrar	8.7	12.8	10.5	10.9
Consultant	8.3	8.1	6.5	7.7
Associate Specialist	2.1	3.7	16.7	3.7
Student	0.0	0.0	0.0	0.0
House Surgeon	0.0	0.0	0.0	0.0
Other	14.2	12.5	0.0	10.5
Not answered	11.1	7.7	9.1	9.0

NB Each cell has its own denominator.

TABLE 4.71
Surgeon assessors' opinions
Inappropriate pre-operative management

| Surgical Specialty Interest | SW | % by specialty | | Total |
		N	NET	
General	10.2	7.2	13.6	9.7
General (& Paediatric)	0.0	0.0	0.0	0.0
General (& Urology)	19.8	1.6	17.4	13.3
General (& Vascular)	15.9	14.6	15.2	15.2
General (Other)	13.6	9.1	13.6	12.2
A & E	33.3	10.0	0.0	14.3
Cardiothoracic	6.0	0.0	25.0	5.9
Dent/Oral	0.0	0.0	0.0	0.0
Gynaecology	0.0	14.2	0.0	5.6
Neurosurgery	6.8	0.0	2.1	3.6
Ophthalmology	0.0	0.0	50.0	16.6
Orthopaedic	5.1	7.2	12.9	8.1
Otorhinolaryngology	13.3	11.1	0.0	9.3
Paediatric	0.0	6.7	0.0	6.6
Plastic	0.0	0.0	0.0	0.0
Transplantation	0.0	0.0	0.0	0.0
Urology	14.8	11.1	10.3	11.7
Other	0.0	0.0	0.0	0.0
Not answered	11.1	0.0	21.4	11.9

NB Each cell has its own denominator.

TABLE 4.72
Surgeon assessors' opinions
Death associated with various factors

| | % of all cases | |
Factor	Partly associated*	Associated **only** with factors indicated
Surgery	30.1	6.97
Anaesthesia	1.8	0.1
Presenting surgical disease	67.5	30.1
Intercurrent disease	44.3	12.4
Unknown	1.3	0.4
Not assessable	2.8	-
Number of cases	2784	2784

*More than one factor could be recorded by assessors.

TABLE 4.73
Surgeon assessors' opinions
Deaths associated with surgery **only** by grades of surgeon

Grade of surgeon	% of each grade
Senior House Officer	8.1
Registrar	7.2
Senior Registrar	4.9
Consultant	6.9
Associate Specialist	14.8
Student	-
House Surgeon	-
Other	5.3
Not answered	0.0

NB Each cell has its own denominator.

TABLE 4.74
Surgeon assessors' opinions
Opinions by specific operations

Operation	No of cases	% Assessors' opinions Avoidable elements	Related to surgery	Inappropriate Management	Inappropriate operation	Operation types Emergency & urgent Number of cases	Other
Hernias	59	48.1	59.3	33.3	20.4	40	19
Biliary	44	31.8	54.5	15.9	22.7	-	-
AA Repair*	129	25.6	34.1	9.3	3.8	103	26
DHS**	217	13.8	21.2	7.8	1.4	-	-
Craniotomy	55	7.2	1.8	1.8	7.2	-	-
TURP	48	25.0	27.1	8.3	4.1	12	36
Laparotomy	609	22.3	29.7	12.5	12.3	-	-
Hemiarthroplasty	135	8.1	20.7	6.7	3.7	40	95
Hemicolectomy	134	40.3	45.5	17.2	14.9	-	-
Amputation	100	14.0	22.0	4.0	10.0	-	-
Embolectomy	38	18.4	26.3	7.9	10.5	-	-
Cystectomy	67	17.9	19.4	5.9	5.9	-	-
AP Resection***	56	30.4	39.3	5.4	17.9	-	-

*Aortic aneurysm repair
**Dynamic hip screw
***Abdomino-perineal resection
Denominators for assessors' opinions are in left hand column.

TABLE 4.75
Grade of anaesthetist by operation type*

Grade of anaesthetist	Emergency	% by operation type Urgent	Scheduled	Elective
Senior House Officer	14.3	26.4	16.1	15.8
Registrar	14.3	23.1	17.5	20.5
Senior Registrar	23.8	9.5	8.3	8.9
Consultant	45.2	33.9	48.2	44.4
Associate Specialist	2.4	2.8	4.8	3.4
General Practitioner	0.0	0.3	0.5	0.4
Clinical Assistant	0.0	3.0	3.8	5.6
Other	0.0	0.1	0.4	0.4
Not Answered	0.0	0.9	0.4	0.6

* For definitions see table 1.9.

TABLE 4.76
Hour of operation (grades of anaesthetist)

Hours	SW	% of operations N	NET	Total
Office hours (0900 -1759)				
Consultant	51.4	54.1	42.4	50.0
Others	48.6	45.9	57.6	50.0
Out of hours (1800-0859)				
Consultant	18.8	37.4	20.0	24.9
Others	81.2	62.6	80.0	75.1

TABLE 4.77
Grade of anaesthetists by hour of operation

Grade of anaesthetist	SW In hrs	SW Out of hrs	N In hrs	N Out of hrs	NET In hrs	NET Out of hrs	Total In hrs	Total Out of hrs
					% by region			
Senior House Officer	15.4	34.1	12.2	20.6	17.8	31.7	14.9	29.3
Registrar	16.4	26.9	11.9	20.0	24.1	25.7	16.7	24.4
Senior Registrar	10.4	12.9	6.9	7.4	10.5	6.8	9.0	9.1
Consultant	51.3	16.9	54.1	33.7	42.4	16.1	49.9	21.6
Associate Specialist	1.8	0.2	9.5	3.2	0.8	0.7	4.6	1.3
General Practitioner	0.9	0.0	0.6	0.6	0.0	0.0	0.5	0.2
Clinical Assistant	2.6	2.5	4.3	4.8	3.2	1.0	3.5	2.6
Other	9.3	0.0	0.0	0.0	0.2	0.0	0.3	0.0
Not answered	0.0	0.2	0.3	0.3	0.6	1.0	0.3	0.5

In hours = Mon-Fri 0900 - 1859.
Our of hours = Sat & Sun & Mon-Fri 1900 - 0859.
Columns do not total 100% because of cases where dates and/or times not known.

TABLE 4.78
Grade of anaesthetist by hour of start of operation

Grade of anaesthetist	Weekends	Weekdays	Day (0900-1900)	Night
		% of cases		
Senior House Officer	33.4	19.1	22.7	32.5
Registrar	29.3	18.9	20.5	26.9
Senior Registrar	11.1	8.9	9.7	10.3
Consultant	20.8	44.2	37.1	24.9
Associate Specialist	2.3	4.0	3.9	1.5
General Practitioner	-	0.4	0.5	0.2
Clinical Assistant	2.6	3.6	3.4	2.8
Other	-	0.3	0.4	-
Not answered	0.5	0.6	1.8	0.9
Totals*	11.2	88.8	45.0	39.8

* 15.2% operations where times unknown.

TABLE 4.79
Percentage of non consultant anaesthetists' cases where a
consultant helped in the management of the anaesthetic

Region	% Emergency	% Urgent	% Scheduled	% Elective
		Operation type		
South Western	21.4	13.8	11.6	13.6
North	0.0	13.5	9.5	16.7
North East Thames	28.6	10.5	12.4	11.7
Total	21.7	12.6	11.1	13.9

NB Each cell has its own denominator.
For definitions of operation types see table 1.9.

TABLE 4.80
Where the anaesthetist was a trainee, was the consultant
informed or sought advice from?

Answer		% by region		
	SW	N	NET	Total
Yes	17.2	22.8	23.1	21.0
No	38.3	21.8	39.6	32.6
Not answered	44.5	55.4	37.3	46.4

TABLE 4.81
Consultation by anaesthetist with consultant

Consultation		% of operation type		
	Emergency	Urgent	Scheduled	Elective
Consultant informed	28.5	23.6	18.5	19.6
Consultant not informed	28.5	37.5	28.9	26.4

NB Columns do not total 100% because of unanswered questions.
For operation type definitions see table 1.9.

TABLE 4.82
Percentage of non-consultant anaesthetists who informed or
sought advice from their consultants by type of operation

Region		% of operation type		
	Emergency	Urgent	Scheduled	Elective
South West	50.0	28.1	18.1	18.2
North	0.0	39.1	36.8	39.6
North East Thames	28.6	26.0	28.4	35.0
Total	39.1	30.5	27.9	33.9

NB Each cell has its own denominator.
For operation type definitions see table 1.9.

TABLE 4.83
Where the anaesthetist was not a consultant was the consultant
informed or advice sought?

Grade of anaesthetist	Total no. of cases		% yes by region		
		SW	N	NET	Total
Senior House Officer	608	31.7	48.2	25.9	34.2
Registrar	591	21.9	46.8	29.6	31.5
Senior Registrar	267	20.3	41.1	22.2	26.6
Consultant	-	-	-	-	-
Associate Specialist	111	18.2	4.3	50.0	9.0
General Practitioner	11	0.0	0.0	0.0	0.0
Clinical Assistant	103	13.3	39.2	36.4	31.1
Other	8	0.0	0.0	50.0	12.5
Not answered	14	0.0	0.0	14.3	14.3

NB Each regional cell has its own denominator.

TABLE 4.84
Grade of second anaesthetist when more than one present

Grade of anaesthetist	SW	% by region N	NET	Total
Senior House Officer	6.5	4.6	6.7	5.9
Registrar	6.0	2.3	10.7	6.0
Senior Registrar	3.4	2.5	4.5	3.4
Consultant	0.9	1.5	1.7	1.4
Associate Specialist	0.1	1.6	0.1	0.6
General Practitioner	0.2	0.2	0.1	0.2
Clinical Assistant	0.4	1.0	0.7	0.7
Other	0.0	0.0	0.1	0.0
Not answered	82.5	86.3	75.4	81.8

TABLE 4.85
Grade of third anaesthetist when more than two present

Grade of anaesthetist	SW	% by region N	NET	Total
Senior House Officer	0.0	0.1	0.0	1 case
Registrar	0.6	0.2	0.3	0.4
Senior Registrar	0.2	0.0	0.5	0.2
Consultant	0.1	0.0	0.7	0.2
Associate Specialist	0.6	0.6	0.8	0.7
General Practitioner	0.0	0.3	0.0	0.1
Clinical Assistant	0.0	0.1	0.1	0.1
Other	0.1	0.1	0.6	0.2
Not answered	98.4	98.6	97.0	98.1

TABLE 4.86
Where the anaesthetist was a trainee, was the questionnaire agreed by the consultant?

Answer	SW	% by region N	NET	Total
Yes	47.0	37.6	51.2	44.7
No	1.6	1.7	2.3	1.8
Not answered	51.4	60.8	46.5	53.3

NB Cases do not total100% because of unanswered questions.

TABLE 4.88
Anaesthetist satisfaction with general preparation of the patient

Satisfied with preparation	% of cases Total
Yes	80.5
No	13.9
Not answered	5.6

No regional differences.

TABLE 4.87
Drugs (excluding premedication) or other therapy the patient received at the time of operation (or if relevant to anaesthesia, had received prior to surgery)
No regional differences

Drug	% used
Anticholinesterase	0.8
Anticoagulant	7.4
Anticonvulsant	2.7
Antidepressant	5.3
Antidiabetic	6.8
Antidysrhythmic	4.6
Antihypertensive	11.3
Cardiac glycoside	11.0
Contraceptive	0.1
Cytotoxic	1.1
Diuretic	28.7
Phenothiazine	5.3
Steroid	10.0

With regional differences

Drug	SW	% by region N	NET	Total
Antibiotic	29.3	33.8	35.2	32.7
Other	54.1	60.1	51.6	55.6

NB There were no important regional differences in the numbers of patients who received drug therapy before operation or in the number of drugs which they received. This is another indicator that the type of caseload was similar in all three regions.

TABLE 4.89
Prescription of premedicant drugs by anaesthetist

Drug	SW	% by region N	NET	Total
Atropine	4.2	7.2	13.1	7.9
Diazepam	5.4	10.5	3.7	6.8
Droperidol	5.6	0.2	0.1	2.0
Fentanyl	0.1	0.5	0.1	0.2
Hyoscine	6.1	4.2	8.8	6.2
Lorazepam	1.9	3.8	1.2	2.4
Morphine	0.6	1.3	0.9	1.0
Oral barbiturate	0.2	0.0	0.3	0.2
Papaveretum	13.0	6.7	11.7	10.3
Pethidine	6.2	4.9	24.8	11.2
Phenoperidine	0.1	0.1	0.5	0.2
Phenothiazine	4.6	5.1	15.2	7.9
Other	15.1	15.4	14.6	15.1

NB There are some intriguing differences between regions: these probably are quite unimportant in relation to CEPOD, but nevertheless they provide an insight into different practices. *Atropine* is given to 13% patients in North East Thames but to a mere 3% in the SouthWestern region, where *Droperidol* is given to 5.6% patients but to less than 0.2% in the other regions. Both the phenothiazine drugs and pethidine are notably more frequently used in NET than elsewhere.

TABLE 4.90
Type of anaesthetic used

Anaesthetic	SW	% by region N	NET	Total
General	85.9	89.6	92.5	89.2
Local	2.7	1.9	2.5	2.4
Regional	10.1	7.0	4.2	7.2
Combined	8.9	3.0	2.7	4.9

NB There is a difference between the North East Thames and the other two regions here which may not be a reflection of a real difference in practice: nevertheless it is worth noting. The difference is confirmed in the table which also suggests that the North East Thames is particularly reluctant to use regional anaesthesia, although table 4.98 suggests that the North is also reluctant in its use of epidural anaesthesia.

TABLE 4.91
Precautions by the anaesthetist taken at induction to reduce the risk of pulmonary aspiration

Precautions		% used
Cricoid Pressure		40.6
Posture	) Head Up	3.5
	) Head Down	2.6
	) Lateral	1.1
Other		18.1

No regional differences.

TABLE 4.92
General anaesthetic agents (inhalation)

Agents	SW	% by region N	NET	Total
Diethyl ether	0.0	0.2	0.0	0.1
Halothane	21.3	11.2	21.0	17.5
Isoflurane	22.4	20.8	13.2	19.1
Nitrous oxide	64.1	61.1	55.4	60.5
Trichloroethylene	0.3	0.7	1.3	0.8
Enflurane	22.1	38.7	43.0	34.4
Other	1.6	2.1	3.2	2.3

TABLE 4.93
Parenteral drugs

Parenteral	SW	% by region N	NET	Total
Alfentanil	3.8	9.8	4.3	6.1
Diazepam	2.7	2.4	3.6	2.9
Disoprofol	0.3	0.6	0.7	0.5
Droperidol	6.6	2.5	4.6	6.4
Etomidate	25.9	28.9	11.0	22.6
Fentanyl	63.3	50.4	46.9	53.7
Ketamine	5.6	2.4	2.2	3.4
Methohexitone	4.2	6.6	3.0	4.7
Morphine	1.6	3.1	1.7	2.2
Pethidine	3.6	1.8	7.2	4.0
Phenoperidine	3.4	2.3	6.3	3.8
Phenothiazine	0.5	0.2	0.9	0.5
Thiopentone	45.2	40.4	57.7	47.1
Other	14.0	14.7	12.2	13.7

TABLE 4.94
Reversal agents

Agents	SW	% by region N	NET	Total
Atropine	31.9	27.9	36.6	31.8
Glycopyrronium	14.7	23.7	11.7	17.1
Neostigmine	45.4	50.0	45.8	47.2
Other	1.3	0.9	1.4	1.2

TABLE 4.95
Other anaesthetic drug therapy

Drug	% used
Analeptic	0.8
Antidysrhythmic	4.0
Antiemetic	2.9
Anticoagulant	2.2
Diuretic (excl. osmotic)	5.1
Electrolyte	3.5
Hypotensive	2.3
Narcotic antagonist	2.0
Inotropic	7.4
Oxytocic	0.1
Steroid	4.7
Vagolytic	4.7
Vasopressor	3.3
Other	11.8

TABLE 4.96
Ventilation during maintenance

Ventilation type	% used
Controlled manual	3.1
Controlled machine	74.6
Spontaneous	13.9

No regional differences.

TABLE 4.97
Tracheal intubation

Intubation	% Total
Yes	82.4
No	9.5
Not answered	8.1

No regional differences.

TABLE 4.98
Regional/local anaesthesia by anaesthetist

Technique	SW	% by region N	NET	Total
Epidural	7.7	2.8	2.0	4.2
Intravenous regional	0.0	0.3	0.0	0.1
Nerve//plexus	1.4	1.3	1.0	1.3
Spinal	8.0	0.6	4.4	6.4

TABLE 4.99
Regional/local anaesthetic agents

Agents	SW	% by region N	NET	Total
Bupivacaine	13.6	9.5	6.0	9.9
Cinchocaine	1.3	0.3	1.0	0.9
Lignocaine	3.4	1.4	1.5	2.1
Prilocaine	0.1	0.2	0.0	0.1
Vasoconstrictor	0.8	1.3	0.3	0.9
Other drug	2.0	1.0	0.5	1.2

TABLE 4.100
Oxygenation

Oxygen rich mixture given	SW	% by region N	NET	Total
Before and at induction	46.1	41.7	41.9	43.3
Before tracheal intubation	42.0	39.1	36.2	39.2
Alone during operation	20.0	16.3	16.1	17.5

NB This question was imprecise and gave rise to some confusion.

TABLE 4.101
Maintenance during anaesthetic

Intravenous fluids	SW	% by region N	NET	Total
Colloid	35.3	31.2	35.2	33.7
Ringer lactate	54.7	39.8	60.5	50.9
Dextrose 5%	7.6	6.9	9.5	7.9
Dextrose-Saline	12.8	26.9	19.0	19.8
Saline	21.8	19.4	20.0	20.4
Mannitol	5.4	4.7	6.7	5.5
Other	11.2	9.4	12.3	10.9

TABLE 4.102
Crossmatched blood

Available	SW	% by region N	NET	Total
Yes	70.6	77.2	77.3	75.0
No	23.4	16.8	15.4	18.6
Not answered	6.0	6.0	7.3	6.4

TABLE 4.103
Occurrence of cardiac arrest during the administration of the anaesthetic

Cardiac arrest	% cases
Yes	4.3
No	92.8
Not answered	2.9

No regional differences.

TABLE 4.104
Availability of ITU (Intensive Therapy Unit) /HDA (High Dependancy Area) facilities

	% cases
Has an ITU	89.0
Has an HDA	27.8

No regional differences.

TABLE 4.105
Patients admitted to the ITU/HDA

| Admitted | SW | % admitted by region | | Total |
		N	NET	
To ITU	25.0	30.2	27.2	27.6
To HDA	7.7	7.4	8.2	7.8

TABLE 4.106
Indication for admission to the ITU/HDA

Indication	% cases
Routine	13.3
Respiratory failure	10.4
Cardiovascular instability	14.7
Renal failure	4.6
Other	10.0

No regional differences.

TABLE 4.107
Reasons for transfer from the ITU/HDA

Reason	% cases
Elective discharge	13.1
Pressure on beds	0.6
Death	19.3
Not answered	67.1

No regional differences.

TABLE 4.108
Anaesthetists claiming feedback required

| Grade of anaesthetist | SW | % by region | | Total |
		N	NET	
Senior House Officer	39.7	51.2	63.9	51.5
Registrar	37.1	56.4	60.4	51.3
Senior Registrar	36.3	46.6	51.8	43.8
Consultant	40.8	37.9	51.3	42.1
Associate Specialist	9.0	44.5	37.5	40.5
General Practitioner	100.0	100.0	0.0	100.0
Clinical Assistant	16.7	54.9	68.2	46.6
Other	16.7	0.0	0.0	12.5
Not answered	0.0	33.3	75.0	50.0

NB Each cell has its own denominator.

TABLE 4.109
Anaesthetists requesting feedback by telephone

| Grade of anaesthetist | SW | % by region | | NET |
		N	Total	
Senior House Officer	1.8	2.4	7.8	4.1
Registrar	1.5	1.9	5.2	3.0
Senior Registrar	2.7	8.2	4.9	4.9
Consultant	5.9	4.1	7.4	5.5
Associate Specialist	0.0	3.3	0.0	2.7
General Practitioner	0.0	16.7	0.0	9.0
Clinical Assistant	3.3	0.0	9.0	2.9
Other	0.0	0.0	0.0	0.0
Not answered	0.0	0.0	0.0	0.0

NB Each cell has its own denominator.

TABLE 4.110
Anaesthetist assesssors' opinions
Was the information adequate to make an assessment?

| Answer | SW | % by region | | Total |
		N	NET	
Yes	98.6	99.1	98.0	98.6
No	1.4	0.8	2.0	1.4
Not answered	0.0	0.1	0.0	1 ca

TABLE 4.111
Anaesthetist assessors' opinions
Would you have agreed to anaesthetise?

Answer	SW	% by region N	NET	Total
Yes	89.1	89.4	87.9	88.9
No	10.4	10.1	11.5	10.6
Not answered	0.5	0.5	0.6	0.5

TABLE 4.112
Anaesthetist assessors' opinions
Do you think there should have been any surgical operation in any centre?

Answer	SW	% by region N	NET	Total
Yes	94.2	94.9	94.7	94.6
No	4.7	4.3	4.4	4.5
Not answered	1.1	0.8	0.9	0.9

TABLE 4.113
Anaesthetist assessors' opinions
Do you consider that the death was totally or partly associated with surgery?

Answer	SW	% by region N	NET	Total
Yes	16.2	11.9	14.5	14.1
No	82.7	87.0	83.7	84.6
Not answered	1.1	1.1	1.8	1.3

TABLE 4.114
Anaesthetist assessors' opinions
Do you consider that the death was totally or partly associated with the progress of the presenting surgical disease?

Answer	SW	% by region N	NET	Total
Yes	65.1	65.3	64.1	65.1
No	1.2	3.0	1.9	2.0
Not answered	33.7	31.7	34.0	32.9

TABLE 4.115
Anaesthetist assessors' opinions
Do you consider that the death was totally or partly associated with the progress of the intercurrent disease?

Answer	SW	% by region N	NET	Total
Yes	51.3	51.5	52.0	51.6
No	0.4	0.5	0.3	0.4
Not answered	48.3	48.0	47.7	48.0

TABLE 4.116
Anaesthetist assessors' opinions
Factors relating to the death were unknown or not assessable

	SW	% by region N	NET	Total
Unknown & not assessable	2.1	1.9	2.0	2.1

TABLE 4.117
Anaesthetist assessors' opinions
Do you consider that the death was totally or partly associated with anaesthesia?

Answer	SW	% by region N	NET	Total
Yes	14.7	13.7	13.6	14.0
No	84.2	85.6	84.7	84.9
Not answered	1.1	0.7	1.7	1.1

TABLE 4.118
Anaesthetist assessors' opinions
Failure to apply knowledge by grade

Grade of anaesthetist	SW	% by region N	NET	Total
Senior House Officer	10.7	13.1	9.7	11.0
Registrar	13.7	16.0	10.4	13.0
Senior Registrar	7.1	9.6	6.2	7.5
Consultant	12.4	8.6	8.4	9.8
Associate Specialist	9.1	8.7	12.5	9.0
General Practitioner	0.0	16.7	0.0	9.1
Clinical Assistant	13.3	9.8	18.2	12.6
Other	16.7	0.0	0.0	12.5
Not answered	0.0	0.0	0.0	0.0

NB Each cell has its own denominator.

TABLE 4.119
Anaesthetist assessors' opinions
Lack of knowledge by grade

Grade of anaesthetist	SW	% by region		Total
		N	NET	
Senior House Officer	4.4	0.6	6.5	4.1
Registrar	1.9	0.6	3.4	3.6
Senior Registrar	0.9	1.3	0.0	0.7
Consultant	0.3	0.9	1.4	0.8
Associate Specialist	0.0	0.0	12.5	0.9
General Practitioner	0.0	16.7	0.0	9.0
Clinical Assistant	0.0	0.0	9.1	1.9
Other	0.0	0.0	0.0	0.0
Not answered	0.0	0.0	0.0	0.0

NB Each cell has its own denominator.

TABLE 4.120
Anaesthetist assessors' opinions
Departures from ideal practice by grade

Grade of anaesthetist	SW	% by region		To
		N	NET	
Senior House Officer	45.5	47.6	51.4	48.
Registrar	44.3	42.9	41.3	42.
Senior Registrar	30.9	24.7	32.1	29.
Consultant	34.6	34.2	42.1	36.
Associate Specialist	72.7	50.0	62.5	53.
General Practitioner	40.0	33.3	0.0	36
Clinical Assistant	53.0	41.2	50.0	46
Other	83.3	0.0	100.0	87
Not answered	0.0	33.3	25.0	21

NB Each cell has its own denominator.
Senior registrars (see also table 4.119) appear to be maintainin
the highest standards of practice as assessed by these two
criteria. The immediate future of the specialty is in good hands

TABLE 4.121
Anaesthetist assessors' opinions
Opinions by grade of anaesthetist

Grade of anaesthetist	All cases	% of cases		
		Death had avoidable elements	Departures from ideal practice	Death related to anaesthesia
Senior House Officer	20.8	28.6	24.6	27.6
Registrar	20.2	21.7	21.2	23.7
Senior Registrar	9.1	6.9	6.6	5.9
Consultant	41.5	34.3	37.4	35.1
Associate Specialist	3.8	2.9	4.9	2.7
General Pra ctitioner	0.4	0.6	0.3	0.5
Clinical Assistant	3.5	4.4	4.0	4.1
Other	0.3	0.4	0.6	0.4
Not answered	0.4	0.2	0.4	0.0
Number of cases	2928	524	1192	410

NB Each cell's denominator is the bottom row.

TABLE 4.122
Anaesthetist assessors' opinions
Opinions by grade of anaesthetist

Grade of anaesthetist	Number of cases	% related to anaesthesia	% departures from ideal practice
Senior House Officer	608	18.6	48.2
Registrar	591	16.4	42.8
Senior Registrar	267	8.9	29.6
Consultant	1215	11.8	36.7
Associate Specialist	111	9.9	53.1
General Practitioner	11	1.8	36.3
Clinical Assistant	103	16.5	46.6
Other	8	25.0	87.5
Not answered	14	0.0	21.4

NB Each cell's denominator is the left hand column.

TABLE 4.123
Anaesthesia associated deaths
Where a consultant did **not** help in the anaesthetic management

Grade of Anaesthetist	SW	% of grades N	NET	Total
Senior House Officer	18.5	18.2	19.7	18.9
Registrar	19.1	16.4	16.2	17.4
Senior Registrar	12.1	7.7	5.8	9.0
Consultant	-	-	-	-
Associate Specialist	0.0	5.0	0.0	4.5
General Practitioner	0.0	0.0	0.0	0.0
Clinical Assistant	9.0	17.5	23.1	17.2
Other	0.0	0.0	0.0	0.0
Not answered	0.0	0.0	0.0	0.0

NB Each cell has its own denominator.

TABLE 4.124
Anaesthesia associated deaths
Where the anaesthetist did not have adequate help (according to anaesthetist)

Grade of Anaesthetist	SW	% of grades N	NET	Total
Senior House Officer	2.6	3.1	6.9	4.4
Registrar	2.7	0.0	0.0	1.0
Senior Registrar	0.0	0.0	0.0	0.0
Consultant	0.0	4.6	3.3	2.8
Associate Specialist	0.0	0.0	0.0	0.0
General Practitioner	0.0	0.0	0.0	0.0
Clinical Assistant	0.0	25.0	0.0	11.7
Other	0.0	0.0	0.0	0.0
Not answered	0.0	0.0	0.0	0.0

NB Each cell has its own denominator.

TABLE 4.125
Anaesthesia associated deaths
Dissatisfaction with the general preparation of the patient by the anaesthetist

Operation type	SW	% by region N	NET	Total
Elective	28.5	13.3	40.0	22.2
Scheduled	28.3	23.9	26.7	26.2
Urgent	22.7	19.7	23.8	22.1
Emergency	0.0	0.0	1 Case	1 Case
Unknown	1 Case	0.0	2 Cases	3 Cases

NB Each cell has its own denominator.
For operation type definitions see table 1.9.

TABLE 4.126
Anaesthesia associated deaths
Pre-operative precautions taken to minimise risk of pulmonary aspiration

Metoclopramide used	SW	% of deaths N	NET	Total
Yes	4.1	12.1	3.4	6.8
No	85.5	79.1	86.3	83.4
Not answered	10.4	8.8	10.3	9.8

TABLE 4.127
Anaesthesia associated deaths
Pre-operative precautions taken to minimise risk of pulmonary aspiration

H2 antagonists used	SW	% of deaths N	NET	Total
Yes	6.2	8.8	6.8	7.3
No	83.4	81.1	82.1	82.2
Not answered	10.4	10.1	11.1	10.5

TABLE 4.128
Anaesthesia associated deaths
Pre-operative precautions taken to minimise risk of pulmonary aspiration

Stomach tube used	SW	% of deaths N	NET	Total
Yes	14.5	20.2	17.1	17.3
No	77.2	69.6	75.2	73.9
Not answered	8.3	10.2	7.7	8.8

TABLE 4.129
Anaesthesia associated deaths
Pre-operative precautions taken to minimise risk of pulmonary aspiration

Antacids used	SW	% of deaths N	NET	Total
Yes	1.4	0.7	0.9	0.9
No	89.7	87.8	87.2	88.3
Not answered	8.9	11.5	11.9	10.8

TABLE 4.130
Anaesthesia associated deaths
Types of anaesthetic

Anaesthetic	SW	% used N	NET	Total
General	86.9	87.8	94.0	89.2
Local	2.8	2.0	0.8	1.9
Regional	9.7	7.4	5.1	7.6
Combined	9.6	4.7	2.6	5.9

NB The answers about the use of general, spinal, epidural, or combined anaesthetic techniques were somewhat confused by the occasional failed epidural which resulted in either a spinal anaesthetic or a combination technique. Thus the reader is cautioned about the interpretation of this data. However, the table below gives some indication of the distribution of techniques.

TABLE 4.131
Anaesthesia associated deaths
Techniques used

Anaesthetic technique	Alone	n*	With general	% anaesthesia associated
General	2612	2612	-	14.0
Spinal	154	188	34	14.9
Epidural	107	123	16	20.0

* The deficiency is made up of incomplete answers.

TABLE 4.132
Anaesthesia associated deaths
Precautions taken at induction to reduce risk of pulmonary aspiration

Postural changes: Not lateral Not head up Not head down	SW	% by region N	NET	Tot.
Yes	16.6	15.5	20.5	17.
No	1.4	2.0	0.9	1.
Not answered	82.0	82.5	78.6	81.

TABLE 4.133
Anaesthesia associated deaths
Precautions taken at induction to reduce risk of pulmonary aspiration

Postural changes Lateral	SW	% by region N	NET	Total
Yes	1.4	0.7	0.0	0.7
No	77.9	76.3	68.4	74.6
Not answered	20.7	23.0	31.6	24.7

TABLE 4.134
Anaesthesia associated deaths
Precautions taken at induction to reduce risk of pulmonary aspiration

Postural changes Head down	SW	% by region N	NET	Tot
Yes	1.4	2.7	2.6	2.
No	77.9	74.3	67.5	73.
Not answered	20.7	22.9	29.9	23.

TABLE 4.135
Anaesthesia associated deaths
Precautions taken at induction to reduce risk of pulmonary aspiration

Cricoid pressure	SW	% by region N	NET	Total
Yes	51.0	37.8	47.0	45.1
No	45.5	54.7	40.2	47.3
Not answered	3.5	7.5	12.8	7.6

TABLE 4.136
Anaesthesia associated deaths
Precautions taken at induction to reduce risk of pulmonary aspiration

Postural changes Head up	SW	% by region N	NET	Total
Yes	2.1	3.4	7.7	4.1
No	78.6	75.0	67.5	74.1
Not answered	19.3	21.6	24.8	21.8

TABLE 4.137
Anaesthesia associated deaths
Oxygenation

Before and at Induction	SW	% by region N	NET	Total
Yes	53.1	47.3	47.0	49.2
No	11.2	12.2	5.1	10.0
Not answered	35.7	40.5	47.9	40.8

TABLE 4.138
Cases with lack or defect of anaesthetic equipment (according to anaesthetist)

Anaesthetist assessors' opinion; anaesthesia associated death	SW	% by region N	NET	Total
Yes	20.0	53.3	20.8	29.6
No	73.3	46.7	75.0	66.7
Not answered	6.7	0.0	4.2	3.7

TABLE 4.139
Cases with fatigue related to outcome (according to anaesthetist)

Anaesthetist assessors' opinion; anaesthesia associated death	Total
Yes	2 cases
No	2 cases
Not answered	Nil

TABLE 4.140
Cases with misadventure during anaesthetic (according to anaesthetist)

Anaesthetist assessors' opinion; anaesthesia associated death	SW	% by region N	NET	Total
Yes	25.0	28.6	40.6	30.3
No	75.0	69.6	56.3	68.2
Not answered	0.0	1.8	3.1	1.5

TABLE 4.141
Cases with cardiac arrest during administration of anaesthetic

Anaesthetist assessors' opinion; anaesthesia associated death	SW	% by region N	NET	Total
Yes	26.9	29.3	33.3	29.6
No	73.1	67.7	64.1	68.8
Not answered	0.0	3.0	2.6	1.6

TABLE 4.142
Anaesthesia associated deaths
Cases where consultant informed or sought advice from

*ASA grade	SW	% of ASA grade N	NET	Total
1	0.0	0.0	33.3	9.1
2	15.2	18.2	4.8	13.8
3	12.2	26.8	35.5	23.9
4	21.3	22.4	31.8	24.8
5	36.8	25.0	11.7	25.0
Not answered	0.0	1 case	0.0	1 case

* For definitions see table 3.8.
NB Each cell has its own denominator.

TABLE 4.143
Consultant anaesthetist came in to help trainee anaesthetist

	SW	% by region N	NET	Total
Consultant came in	13.1	11.8	11.5	12.1

TABLE 4.144
Delay in getting the patient to the theatre

Delay due to	% of all cases According to anaesthetist	According to surgeon
Availability of surgeon	5.5	0.8
Availability of anaesthetist	0.8	0.6
Availability of portering	0.8	0.2
Availability of nurses	0.5	0.1
Availability of theatre	0.5	1.7
Other	2.3	3.3

TABLE 4.145
Percentage claiming they would like to know the assessors' scores ie. feedback

Answer	SW A	SW S	% by region N A	N S	NET A	NET S	Total A	Total S
Yes	38.2	47.9	45.0	44.5	57.4	57.1	46.3	49.2
No	52.2	40.3	42.9	43.4	33.7	26.7	43.3	37.6
Not answered	9.6	11.8	12.1	12.1	8.9	16.2	10.4	13.2

A = Anaesthetists' answer. S = Surgeons' answer.

TABLE 4.146
Feedback requested by telephone

Answer	SW A	SW S	% by region N A	N S	NET A	NET S	Total A	Total S
Yes	3.5	5.6	3.6	4.5	6.6	8.0	4.4	5.8
No	96.5	94.4	96.3	95.5	93.4	92.0	95.6	94.2

A = Anaesthetist, S = Surgeon.

TABLE 4.147
Grade of surgeon and grade of anaesthetist
(percentage of surgeons grade)

Grade of surgeon	Grade of anaesthetist S.H.O	R.	S.R.	con.	A.S.	G.P.	Cl .A.	Other
Senior House Officer	41.2	32.9	4.1	5.1	1.0	0.0	5.1	0.0
Registrar	32.1	24.1	9.2	23.6	3.6	5.3	6.3	0.0
Senior Registrar	24.4	26.5	14.3	28.3	3.2	0.0	2.1	0.4
Consultant	8.9	13.8	7.5	62.7	4.3	1.7	2.4	0.0
Associate Specialist	22.1	20.8	11.7	24.7	5.2	5.2	3.9	6.5
Student	-	-	-	-	-	-	-	-
House Surgeon	-	-	-	-	-	-	-	-
Other	33.3	20.0	0.0	13.3	26.7	0.0	6.7	0.0

NB The rows may not total 100% because some grades not known.

TABLE 4.148
Grade of surgeon and grade of anaesthetist
(percentage of anaesthetists grade)

Grade of surgeon	S.H.O.	R.	Grade of anaesthetist S.R.	con.	A.S.	G.P.	Cl.A.	Other
Senior House Officer	8.4	6.8	1.9	1.5	1.0	0.0	5.6	0.0
Registrar	50.5	38.3	32.7	17.1	28.4	40.0	52.2	0.0
Senior Registrar	14.3	15.7	18.9	7.7	9.5	0.0	6.7	16.6
Consultant	21.7	33.8	40.7	70.1	52.6	20.0	31.1	0.0
Associate Specialist	3.6	3.4	4.3	1.8	4.2	40.0	3.3	83.4
Student	0.0	0.0	0.0	0.0	0.0	0.0	0.0	0.0
House Surgeon	0.0	0.0	0.0	0.0	0.0	0.0	0.0	0.0
Other	1.1	0.6	0.0	1.9	4.2	0.0	1.1	0.0

NB The columns may not total 100% because some grades not known.
This and the previous table (4.147) do not match because cases were not completed on the same patients.

TABLE 4.149
Type of admission*

Admission	% Anaesthetic form	Surgical form
Elective	18.4	23.1
Urgent	27.5	19.6
Emergency	44.5	56.7
Not answered	9.6	0.6

*Admission
Elective - at time consented between patient and surgical service.
Urgent - within 48 hours of consultation.
Emergency - immediately following consultation.

TABLE 4.150
Complications in the operative period

Complication	According to anaesthetist % Cases	According to surgeon % Cases
Bleeding requiring transfusion or re-operation	15.1	12.5
Needing mechanical ventilation	22.1	24.0
Sepsis	32.4	39.4
Myocardial disorder	31.3	28.5
Hepatic failure	5.8	5.3
Renal failure	7.7	8.0
Endocrine system failure	2.9	1.9
Persistent coma	6.7	9.9
Other organ failure	6.0	6.5
Postoperative analgesia	3.6	2.1
Other	22.0	15.7

No regional differences.

TABLE 4.151
Do you think the assessors should pay particular attention to the other discipline's form?

Answer	Anaesthetist's form	Surgeon's form
Yes	19.4	7.8
No	76.3	87.4
Not answered	4.3	4.8

No regional differences.

TABLE 4.152
Regular local mortality/morbidity review meetings

Meetings held	% by region SW A	S	N A	S	NET A	S	Total A	S
Yes	66.7	40.7	40.1	47.8	63.4	51.0	55.9	46.4
No	32.0	57.4	57.9	50.1	33.8	46.6	42.1	51.5
Not answered	1.3	1.9	2.0	2.1	2.8	2.4	2.0	2.1

A = Anaesthetists answer. S = Surgeons answer.

TABLE 4.153
Assessors' opinions of factors associated with death

Factor				Percentage of cases	
Surgery	Anaesthesia	Presenting surgical disease	Intercurrent disease	Surgeon assessors' opinions	Anaesthetist assessors' opinions
Y	Y	Y	Y	0.4	1.1
Y	Y	Y	N	0.6	2.9
Y	Y	N	Y	0.2	2.6
Y	Y	N	N	0.4	1.6
Y	N	Y	Y	5.7	1.5
Y	N	Y	N	10.6	2.8
Y	N	N	Y	5.3	1.2
Y	N	N	N	6.9	0.5
N	Y	Y	Y	0.07	0.9
N	Y	Y	N	0.03	1.9
N	Y	N	Y	0.03	2.9
N	Y	N	N	0.1	0.1
N	N	Y	Y	20.1	19.5
N	N	Y	N	30.1	34.5
N	N	N	Y	12.4	21.8

Key: Y = Yes, N = No.
NB Columns do not total 100% because of unknown and not assessable cases.
This table indicates the incidence of each factor on its own and in conjunction with any other factor in relation to the death.

TABLE 4.154
Comparison of hospitals with equivalent catchment populations
(excluding tertiary referral centres)

Assessors' opinions	Random hospital letter	SW	% by region N	NET
Departures from	A	12.5	28.6	10.0
ideal practice (S)	B	9.4	33.3	36.1
Departures from	C	29.7	42.8	45.7
ideal practice (A)	D	51.4	39.1	60.0
Inadequate	E	29.7	14.3	14.3
monitoring (A)	F	19.4	33.0	35.3
Would not	G	16.2	7.1	11.4
anaesthetise (A)	H	11.1	6.9	4.7
Would not	I	0.0	0.0	0.0
operate (S)	J	2.8	5.2	0.0

Key: (S) = Surgeon assessors, (A) = Anaesthetist assessors.
NB These figures are the extreems of the ranges.

TABLE 4.155
Cases containing complete data
Was the information in the form adequate for an assessment?

Surgeon assessors' opinons	% by region			
	SW	N	NET	Total
Yes	97.6	97.1	95.9	96.9
No	2.4	2.8	4.1	3.0
Not answered	0.0	0.1	0.0	0.1

TABLE 4.156
Cases containing complete data
Were there avoidable elements in the entire management of the patient which, if corrected, would have altered the outcome, or might at least have reduced the chance of death? *ie.* Was the death avoidable?

Surgeon assessors' opinions	% by region			
	SW	N	NET	Total
Yes	23.4	19.9	28.2	23.3
No	68.4	72.9	62.3	68.6
Not answered	8.2	7.2	9.5	8.1

TABLE 4.157
Cases containing complete data
Were there departures from ideal practice?

Surgeon assessors' opinions	% by region			
	SW	N	NET	Total
	14.7	12.8	16.1	14.3
	81.6	82.7	78.6	81.3
answered	3.7	4.5	5.3	4.4

TABLE 4.158
Cases containing complete data
Would you have decided to operate?

Surgeon assessors' opinions	% by region			
	SW	N	NET	Total
	85.1	87.2	83.7	85.5
	6.5	4.8	5.7	5.6
answered	8.4	8.0	10.6	8.9

TABLE 4.159
Cases containing complete data
Do you think there should have been any surgical operation in any centre?

Surgeon assessors' opinions	% by region			
	SW	N	NET	Total
Yes	88.7	91.4	87.0	89.3
No	7.7	5.0	7.0	6.4
Not answered	3.6	3.6	6.0	4.3

TABLE 4.160
Cases containing complete data
Do you consider that the death was totally or partly associated with surgery?

Surgeon assessors' opinions	% by region			
	SW	N	NET	Total
Yes	32.2	27.3	36.6	31.4
No	64.5	69.1	60.1	65.2
Not answered	3.3	3.6	3.3	3.4

TABLE 4.161
Cases containing complete data
When death was associated with surgery, which factors were involved. (Surgeon assessors' opinions)

Factor	% by region			
	SW	N	NET	Total
Inappropriate operation	11.0	9.3	10.6	10.2
Inappropriate pre-operative management	12.1	9.2	13.1	11.3
Inappropriate grade operating surgeon	8.3	3.6	9.8	7.0
Failure of organisation (system)	4.4	3.5	5.1	4.2
Technical failure by surgical team due to:-				
Inadequate knowledge	2.7	1.4	3.8	2.5
Failure to apply knowledge	6.6	3.8	6.8	5.6
Lack of care	2.8	1.7	5.2	3.0
Lack of experience	5.5	3.5	6.6	5.0
Inadequate supervision	3.8	1.3	5.2	3.2
Fatigue	1.0	1.0	0.8	0.9
Physical impairment	1 case	0.0	0.0	1 case
Mental impairment	0.0	0.0	0.0	0.0
Other	2.7	3.7	4.3	3.5

NB Multiple answers possible to the above factors.

TABLE 4.162

Cases containing complete data

Do you consider that the death was totally or partly associated with anaesthesia?

Surgeon assessors' opinions	SW	% by region N	NET	Total
Yes	1.6	1.6	2.5	1.8
No	65.6	63.4	56.8	62.4
Not answered	32.8	35.0	40.7	35.8

TABLE 4.163

Cases containing complete data

Do you consider that the death was totally or partly associated with disease?

Surgeon assessors' opinions	SW	% by region N	NET	To
Progress of presenting surgical disease.	65.9	69.3	64.9	6
Progress of inter-current disease.	44.4	46.1	44.3	4

NB Multiple answers possible.

TABLE 4.164

Cases containing complete data

Assessment could not be made by surgeon assessors

Surgeon assessors' opinions	SW	% by region N	NET	Total
Unknown	1.0	1.3	2.1	1.4
Not assessable	2.2	2.9	3.5	2.8

TABLE 4.165

Cases containing complete data

Was the information in the form adequate for an assessment?

Anaesthetist assessors' opinion	SW	% cases by region N	NET	To
Yes	99.0	98.9	98.3	98
No	1.0	1.1	1.7	1

TABLE 4.166

Cases containing complete data

Were there avoidable elements in the entire management of the patient which, if corrected, would have altered the outcome, or might at least have reduced the chance of death at that time? *ie.* Was the death avoidable?

Anaesthetist assessors' opinion	SW	% cases by region N	NET	Total
Yes	19.3	16.2	17.2	17.6
No	79.8	82.3	81.5	81.2
Not answered	0.9	1.5	1.3	1.2

TABLE 4.167

Cases containing complete data

Were there departures from ideal practice?

Anaesthetist assessors' opinions	SW	% by region N	NET	To
Yes	39.9	38.2	44.0	4
No	59.5	61.0	55.2	5
Not answered	0.6	0.8	0.8	

TABLE 4.168

Cases containing complete data

Would you have agreed to anaesthetise?

Anaesthetist assessors' opinions	SW	% by region N	NET	Total
Yes	89.1	90.1	88.4	89.3
No	10.4	9.2	11.1	10.1
Not answered	0.5	0.7	0.5	0.6

TABLE 4.169

Cases containing complete data

Was the monitoring used adequate?

Anaesthetist assessors' opinions	SW	% by region N	NET	To
Yes	77.8	80.3	76.9	7
No	21.8	19.1	22.5	2
Not answered	0.4	0.6	0.6	

TABLE 4.170
Cases containing complete data
Do you think there should have been any surgical operation in any centre?

Anaesthetist assessors' opinions	SW	% by region N	NET	Total
Yes	94.0	95.6	94.8	94.9
No	4.8	3.6	4.4	4.2
Not answered	1.2	0.8	0.8	0.9

TABLE 4.171
Cases containing complete data
Do you consider that the death was totally or partly associated with surgery?

Anaesthetist assessors' opinions	SW	% by region N	NET	Total
Yes	15.8	11.5	13.3	13.4
No	83.8	87.6	85.8	85.8
Not answered	0.4	0.9	0.9	0.8

TABLE 4.172
Cases containing complete data
Do you consider that the death was totally or partly associated with anaesthesia?

Anaesthetist assessors' opinions	SW	% by region N	NET	Total
Yes	14.7	13.7	13.6	14.0
No	84.9	85.6	85.4	85.3
Not answered	0.4	0.7	1.0	0.7

TABLE 4.173
Cases containing complete data
When death was associated with anaesthesia which factors were involved. (Anaesthetist assessors' opinions)

Factor	SW	% yes answers N	NET	Total
Failure of organisation	3.9	3.5	3.2	3.6
Failure of equipment	0.0	0.3	0.5	0.3
Drug effect	1.5	1.3	1.1	1.3
Lack of knowledge	1.5	1.5	2.8	1.8
Failure to apply knowledge	12.0	10.4	9.5	10.7
Lack of care	4.5	3.6	4.1	4.1
Lack of experience	3.2	2.4	4.3	3.2
Fatigue	0.0	0.0	0.0	0.0
Impairment	0.0	0.0	0.0	0.0
Other	0.6	0.3	0.2	0.4

TABLE 4.174
Cases containing complete data
Do you consider that the death was totally or partly associated with disease?

Anaesthetist assessors' opinions	SW	% yes N	NET	Total
Progress of presenting surgical disease.	66.5	67.2	66.5	66.8
Progress of intercurrent disease.	51.9	50.1	51.3	51.0

NB These questions could be answered in multiples.

TABLE 4.175
Cases containing complete data
Assessment could not be made by anaesthetist assessors

Anaesthetist assessors' opinions	SW	% by region N	NET	Total
Unknown	1.0	0.6	0.6	0.8
Not assessable	0.5	1.3	0.6	0.8

TABLE 4.176
Cases containing complete data
Consultant anaesthetist/surgeon consulted
pre-operatively

Consultant of either discipline consulted	SW	% by region N	NET	Total
Yes	82.9	91.7	79.7	85.6
No	10.2	1.4	14.6	7.8
Not answered	6.9	6.9	5.7	6.6

TABLE 4.177
Cases containing complete data
Assessors' opinions

Factor	Assessors' opinions % Anaesthetist	Surgeon
Avoidable elements	17.6	23.3
Departures from ideal practice	40.3	14.3
Would not operate/anaesthetise in circumstances?	10.1	5.6
Monitoring inadequate	20.0	-
No operation should have been performed	4.2	6.4
Death associated with:		
Surgery and (or)	13.4	31.4
Anaesthesia and (or)	14.0	1.8
Surgical disease and (or)	66.8	67.0
Intercurrent disease	51.0	45.0
Unknown	0.8	1.4
Not assessable	0.8	2.8

NB For details of each item in the above table including
details by region, see Part 4, tables 4.155-4.176 inclusive.

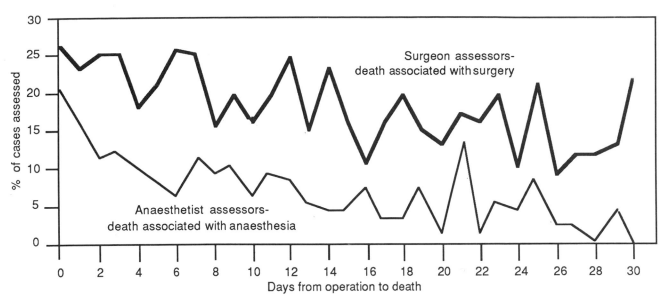

Figure 4.1 Assessors` opinions: Deaths associated with surgery or anaesthesia

NB The peak at 21 days can not be explained by us except that at this end
of the graph the numbers involved are small.

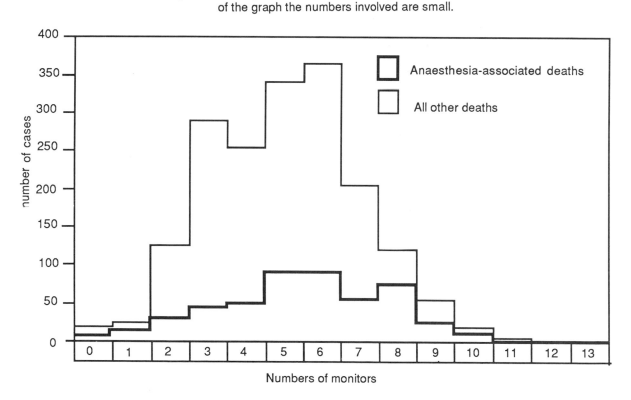

Figure 4.2 Frequency of number of monitors used

NB One interpretation of this figure (4.2) is that since the frequency distribution
of the monitors looks approximately normal and is not greatly different between the
two populations it is likely that assessors did not use this as a criterion to assess
a death as anaesthesia-associated. It is possible that assessors attempted to make
qualitative rather than quantitative judgements about monitoring in individual cases
(eg. the 30-minute interval between single blood pressure and pulse recordings
during an operation).

APPENDIX 2

JOINT WORKING PARTY

(at May 1987)

Chairman	Professor M D Vickers
Vice Chairman	Dr E A Cooper
Treasurer	Dr M M Burrows
Secretary	Mr H B Devlin
Members	
	Professor P G Bevan
	Professor M Clarke (from February 1987)
	Mr J L Craven
	Mr D R Harper
	Dr M T Inman
	Professor A G Johnson (from May 1985)
	Professor J S P Lumley
	Dr J N Lunn
	Professor I McColl (resigned May 1985)
	Dr P Morris
	Professor R Owen (from February 1987)
	Mr S Simmons (from February 1987)
Coordinators	
	Mr H B Devlin (surgeon)
	Professor J S P Lumley (surgeon) (resigned as coordinator in November 1986)
	Dr J N Lunn (anaesthetist)

Administrator	Mr N Buck
Coordinator's assistant	Dr R D Jack (anaesthetist)
Administrator's assistant	Ms G Sims

ASSESSORS

SURGEON ASSESSORS

General surgeons

MR N V ADDISON*	Bradford
MR J ALEXANDER-WILLIAMS	Birmingham
MR A H AMERY	Frimley
MR A D BARNES	Birmingham
MR T BATES	Ashford, Kent
MR R J BENTLEY	Hexham
PROF P G BEVAN	Birmingham
PROF L H BLUMGART	London
PROF M P BRADY	Cork
PROF D C CARTER	Glasgow
MR T P COLE	Carlisle
MR J L CRAVEN	York
MR M K H CRUMPLIN	Wrexham
MR J L DAWSON*	London
MR A C B DEAN	Edinburgh
MR H B DEVLIN	Stockton on Tees
MR B L DOWLING	Northampton
PROF H A F DUDLEY	London
PROF SIR Herbert L DUTHIE	Cardiff
MR R J EARLAM	London
MR D S EVANS*	Shrewsbury
MR J R FARNDON	Newcastle
MR L B FLEMING	Newcastle

* Indicates those assessors outside of the regions studied who attended seminars to discuss CEPOD results with the coordinators.

MR R J E FOLEY*	Bedford
MR H FORREST	Glasgow
PROF G R GILES	Leeds
PROF I E GILLESPIE	Manchester
MR A GUNN	Ashington
MR A A GUNN	Broxburn
MR B D HANCOCK	Manchester
MR A W HARGREAVES	Salford
LT COL I R HAYWOOD	London
PROF M HOBSLEY	London
MR R W HOILE	Rochester
MR E R HOWARD*	London
PROF L E HUGHES	Cardiff
MR B T JACKSON	London
PROF A G JOHNSON*	Sheffield
PROF I D A JOHNSTON	Newcastle
MR N C KEDDIE	Whitehaven
MR T L KENNEDY	Belfast
MR R M KIRK	London
MR D J LEAPER	Bristol
MR C J H LOGAN	Belfast
MR P H LORD	Beaconsfield
MR J B MCFARLAND	Liverpool
MR I A MILLER	Gateshead
PROF P J MORRIS	Oxford
PROF N O'HIGGINS	Dublin
MR A V POLLOCK	Scarborough
MR M C T REILLY	Yelverton
MR R C G RUSSELL	London
MR G R SAGOR	St Albans
PROF R SCOTT	London
PROF R SHIELDS	Liverpool
MR R M R TAYLOR	Newcastle
MR J TEMPLE*	Birmingham
MR K VOWLES	Exeter
MR J S H WADE	Cardiff
MR H WHITE	London
MR M G WHITTAKER	Darlington
CAPT F R WILKES	Plymouth
PROF R C N WILLIAMSON	Bristol
MR P D WRIGHT	Newcastle
MR A E YOUNG	London

Vascular surgeons

MR R BAIRD	Bristol
PROF P R F BELL	Leicester
PROF N L BROWSE	London
MR S G DARKE*	Poole
MR W T DAVIES	Cardiff
MR D R HARPER	Falkirk
MR C W JAMIESON	London
PROF J S P LUMLEY	London
MRS A O MANSFIELD	London
MR J A P MARSTON	London
MR M C PIETRONI	London
MR C V RUCKLEY	Edinburgh
MR W F WALKER*	Dundee

Ophthalmic surgeons

PROF A L CROMBIE	Newcastle
MR B MARTIN	Leeds

Neurological surgeons

MR M BRIGGS*	Oxford
MR H COAKHAM	Bristol
PROF J HANKINSON	Newcastle
PROF B JENNETT*	London
MR R M KALBAG	Newcastle
MR R S MAURICE WILLIAMS	London
PROF G TEASDALE	Glasgow

Otorhinolaryngological surgeons

MR T L BRADBEER	Exeter
MR J N G EVANS	London
MR D W HAND	Carlisle
MR I HOPPER	Sunderland

Plastic surgeons

MR I W BROOMHEAD	London
AIR CDR R F BROWN	Aylesbury
MR T M MILWARD	Leicester
MR R W PIGOTT	Bristol

Cardiothoracic surgeons

MR A H BROWN	Newcastle
MR P B DEVERALL	London
MR C J HILTON	Newcastle
MR K JEYASINGHAM	Bristol
MR A J MEARNS*	Bradford
MR K MOGHISSI	Humberside
SIR J KEITH ROSS*	Southampton

Colorectal surgeons

PROF J D HARDCASTLE*	Nottingham
PROF M H IRVING*	Manchester
PROF M R B KEIGHLEY	Birmingham
MR A A M LEWIS	London
MR G OATES	Birmingham
MR J P S THOMSON	London
PROF N S WILLIAMS	London

Dental/oral surgeons

MR P BANKS	East Grinstead
PROF G R SEWARD	London
MISS A M SKELLY	London

Paediatric surgeons

MR J D ATWELL*	Southampton
MR W H BISSET	Edinburgh
MR J J CORKERY	Birmingham
MR J A S DICKSON	Sheffield
MISS C M DOIG*	Manchester
MR D FORREST	West Wickham
PROF E GUINEY	Dublin
MISS L KAPILA	Nottingham
PROF J LISTER	Liverpool

MR J E S SCOTT	Newcastle
PROF L SPITZ*	London
MR D G YOUNG	Glasgow

Gynaecological surgeons

MR A G AMIAS	London
MR R T BOOTH	Brentwood
SIR Rustam FEROZE*	London
PROF B M HIBBARD	Cardiff
MR T L T LEWIS	London
MR J D O LOUDON	Edinburgh
MR E D MORRIS	London
MR J F PEARSON	Cardiff
MR S C SIMMONS*	Windsor
MR D TACCHI	Newcastle
MR D W WARRELL	Manchester

Urological surgeons

MR C P BATES	Nottingham
PROF J P BLANDY	London
MR C A C CHARLTON*	Bath
MR E CHARLTON EDWARDS	Manchester
PROF G D CHISHOLM*	Edinburgh
MR R C L FENELEY	Bristol
MR R R HALL	Newcastle
MR R G NOTLEY	Guildford
MR R SCOTT*	Glasgow
MR K E D SHUTTLEWORTH	London
MR J VINNICOMBE*	Portsmouth
MR R H WHITAKER	Cambridge

Orthopaedic surgeons

MR B G ANDREWS	London
MR N J BARTON	Nottingham
MR D CAMPBELL	Chester
MR P H CORKERY	Clwyd
PROF R A DICKSON	Leeds
MR J H DIXON	Weston s/Mare
PROF T DUCKWORTH*	Sheffield
PROF R B DUTHIE	Oxford
MR D K EVANS	Sheffield
MR D L EVANS	London
MR S C GALLANNAUGH	Hastings
MR C J M GETTY	Sheffield
MR J M C GIBSON	Aberdeen
PROF P J GREGG	Leicester
MR R HORNBY	Newcastle
PROF S P F HUGHES	Edinburgh
MR J R KIRKUP	Bath
MR I J LESLIE	Bristol
PROF B McKIBBIN	Cardiff
MR P J MULLIGAN*	Birmingham
MR R L M NEWELL	Barnstaple
PROF R OWEN*	Liverpool
MR A H C RATLIFF	Bristol
PROF W J W SHARRARD	Sheffield
MR J L SHER	Ashington
MR T W D SMITH	Sheffield
PROF J STEVENS	Newcastle
MR K H STONE	Barnet

PROF W WAUGH	Peterbrough
MR P M YEOMAN*	Bath

ANAESTHETIST ASSESSORS

DR A K ADAMS	Cambridge
DR A R AITKENHEAD	Leicester
DR R S ATKINSON	Southend
DR J BALDASERA	Sunderland
DR P J F BASKETT	Bristol
DR D G M BISHOP	Darlington
DR G W BLACK	Belfast
DR C E BLOGG	Oxford
DR T B BOULTON	Reading
DR D J BOWEN	Winchester
DR M A BRANTHWAITE	London
DR D R G BROWNE	London
DR M M BURROWS	Merseyside
DR J A BUSHMAN	London
PROF D CAMPBELL	Glasgow
PROF C M CONWAY (Deceased)	London
DR E A COOPER*	Newcastle
DR H T DAVENPORT*	Harrow
PROF J W DUNDEE	Belfast
DR L J DUNKIN (Deceased)	Newcastle
DR J C EDWARDS	Southampton
DR F R ELLIS	Leeds
DR A T FISHER	Oxford
DR W FITCH	Glasgow
DR G D FLOWERDEW	Nottingham
DR C B FRANKLIN	Manchester
DR E P GIBBS	Billericay
DR A A F GILBERTSON	Liverpool
DR J E S GOODWIN	York
DR M HARMER*	Cardiff
DR G HARRIS	Stockton on Tees
DR W H K HASLETT	Belfast
DR D J HATCH	London
DR P B HEWITT	London
DR D F HOGAN	Dublin
PROF C J HULL	Newcastle
DR J McG IMRAY	Aberdeen
DR M T INMAN	Plymouth
DR R D JACK*	Slough
DR I R JENKINS	Carmarthen
DR R M JONES	London
DR L KAUFMAN	London
DR J H KERR*	Oxford
DR P G P LAWLER	Middlesbrough
DR J I M LAWSON	Dundee
DR J N LUNN	Cardiff
DR W R MACRAE	Edinburgh
DR I P McEWAN*	Norwich
DR M MARSHALL	Newcastle
DR R A MASON*	Swansea
DR P MORRIS*	Manchester
PROF W S NIMMO	Sheffield
DR W K PALLISTER	London

* Indicates those assessors outside of the regions studied who attended seminars to discuss CEPOD results with the coordinators.

PROF J P PAYNE	London	
DR D J PEARCE	Southampton	
DR B W PERRISS	Exeter	
PROF C PRYS-ROBERTS	Bristol	
DR R J PURNELL*	Norwich	
DR L R REDMAN	Bath	
DR A M REID	Glasgow	
DR G S RIDDELL	Ashington	
DR J E RIDING	Liverpool	
PROF M ROSEN	Cardiff	
DR M A RUCKLIDGE	Lancaster	
DR W RYDER	Newcastle	
DR D B SCOTT	Edinburgh	
DR P V SCOTT*	Bromsgrove	
DR J W SEAR	Oxford	
DR J F SEARLE	Exeter	
DR P J SIMPSON	Bristol	
MISS A M SKELLY	London	
PROF A A SPENCE*	Edinburgh	
DR J C STODDART	Newcastle	
PROF M K SYKES	Oxford	
DR A B M TELFER	Glasgow	
DR P W THOMPSON	Cardiff	
DR C W THOMSON	Newcastle	
PROF J E UTTING	Liverpool	
DR I R VERNER	London	
DR D C WHITE	Harrow	
DR S M WILLATTS	Bristol	
DR J S M ZORAB	Bristol	

OTHER DISCIPLINE ASSESSORS

PROF G A J AYLIFFE
  Birmingham (Medical Microbiology)
PROF D N BARON
  London (Chemical Pathology)
DR J H BARON   London (Physician)
MR D BOWDEN   Brighton (Administration)
MR F R BRAMBLE   Eastbourne (Nursing)
DR C K CONNOLLY   Darlington (Physician)
PROF B CORRIN
  London (Thoracic Pathology)
MISS J A DANIELS   Prescot (Nursing)
MRS S J DIVER   Carlisle (Nursing)
MRS M DONNE   Brighton (Nursing)
MRS P D EDWARDS   London (Nursing)
MR T E GRADY   Exeter (Nursing)
MR J D HAGUE   Newcastle (Administration)
DR P S HASLETON
  Manchester (Histopathology)
MRS K JAMES   Warrington (Nursing)
DR H KENNEDY   Norwich (Physician)
MISS C M A McLOUGHLIN
  London (Nursing)
MRS B ROBERTS   Prescot (Nursing)
DR R H SMITH   North Tees (Physician)
DR P STRICKLAND
  Middlesex (Radiotherapy)
MRS J TOMASONE   Halifax (Nursing)
DR I WICKINGS   London (Administration)
MR J YATES   Birmingham (Administration)

LOCAL REPORTERS

SOUTH WESTERN REGIONAL HEALTH AUTHORITY

DR A ADAM	Somerset	Taunton
DR R FORWARD	,,	Yeovil
DR Y SIVATHONDAN	Cornwall	Truro
DR J L DUNSCOMBE	,,	Penzance
MR W J GALL (retired)	Plymouth	General
MR A S DAVIES	,,	Derriford (Freedom Fields)
DR J CHAPMAN	,,	General
MR N SEYMOUR	,,	Mount Gould
SRG CPT N G B HERSEY	,,	Royal Naval
DR A BENNETT	Frenchay	
DR P BRIGHTEN	North Devon	
DR J A CLEMENT	Bristol	Royal Infirmary, Dental, Weston, & Children's Hospital
DR N GUBBAY	Cheltenham	
DR C HAY	Torbay	
DR A NICOL	Gloucester	
DR B W PERRISS	Exeter	
DR E WALSH	Southmead	

NORTHERN REGIONAL HEALTH AUTHORITY

DR W B SHAW (deceased)   N Tyneside
  Deputy: Dr I M S Gillie

DR J HALSHAW   Sunderland   District General
DR H WACKS   „   Royal Infirmary
MR J LENNOX   „   Ryhope General

DR J McCARTHY   S Tyneside

MR K B QUEEN   N W Durham
  Deputy: Mr J R Mason
DR D C TOWNSEND   S W Durham
DR D W WOOD   Durham
DR K H DAVIES   W Cumberland

DR E D LONG   E Cumbria
DR M A RUCKLIDGE   S Cumbria   Royal Lancaster Infirmary (for
                                                   Westmorland County)
DR L J WILLIAMS   S Cumbria   Barrow in Furness

MR R F MATHER   Northumberland   Berwick Infirmary
DR G S RIDDELL   „   Ashington & Alnwick
DR J D M JEFFERY   „   Hexham

DR C BEETON   Darlington
  Deputy: Mr E N McKenzie

DR M RICHARDSON   Gateshead
  Deputy: Dr A Brown

DR I D CONACHER   Newcastle   Freeman
DR D SCOTT   „   General
MR L RANGECROFT   „   Fleming Memorial
MR J FARNDON   „   Royal Victoria Infirmary
  Deputies: Dr E Charlton
           Dr L Thompson Hill
MR D J LOVELOCK   „   Dental

DR P CAUCHI   Hartlepool

DR E W WALTON   N Tees
MR M HOROWITZ   S Tees   North Riding
DR P G P LAWLER   „   South Cleveland
DR Z MASRI   „   Middlesbrough General

NORTH EAST THAMES REGIONAL HEALTH AUTHORITY

DR R M BOWEN-WRIGHT   Bloomsbury   Middlesex, Royal National
                                                   Orthopaedic Hospital and
                                                   Hospital for Women.

DR P PAINTER   „   Elizabeth Garrett Anderson

DR J ORMROD   „   University College Hospital &
                                                   Dental Hospital

MR G DOWD   „   Royal National Orthopaedic
  Deputy: Dr D R J Seingry   Hospital in Stanmore

DR J R SAMUEL   „   St Peter's Group and The
                                                   Shaftesbury

MR A WRIGHT   „   Royal National Throat, Nose &
                                                   Ear Hospital

MR J P S THOMSON   City & Hackney   St Mark's, Hackney &
                                                   Homerton

PROF R F M WOOD   ,,   St Bartholomew's

DR S G SUBBUSWAMY   Basildon & Thurrock
DR D ERWIN   Waltham Forest
MR B S ASHBY   Southend
DR J DYSON   Islington
DR T D McGHEE   Newham
MR K LINDSAY   Hampstead
DR W A KONARZEWSKI   North East Essex
DR K AGARWAL   West Essex
DR G DAVIES   Mid-Essex
  Deputy: Dr D Walmsley
MR R J HAM   Tower Hamlets
  Deputy: Mr D G A Eadie
DR W J HARRISON   Haringey
DR V STANHILL/DR K PATTERSON   Redbridge
  Deputy: Mr C F Noon
MR M W N WARD   Enfield
  Deputy: Dr A Sampson
DR D A THOMAS   Barking, Havering & Brentwood   Harold Wood & Brentwood

MR M SPIRO   ,,   Rush Green

DR D T LOVELL   ,,   Oldchurch

PARTICIPANTS

NORTHERN REGION

The following consultants agreed to participate in writing but did not necessarily have any deaths, nor complete any forms:

Surgeons

P J Adams	R B Berry	C A Campbell	K Fanibunda	J Hindmarsh
A K L Addison	J A Betts	J Carlin	J R Farndon	M P Holden
D Allan	A J M Birnie	B D Case	J G W Feggetter	J D Holdsworth
R Allchin	J B McK Black	J Chamberlain	T J Fernandes	J W Hooley
E D Allen	J E Black	R G Checketts	L B Fleming	I Hopper
G E Anderson	M J M Black	M B Clague	L M Flood	R Hornby
J Anderson	G S Blair	D Clarke	J C Foster	M Horowitz
P J Armon	A Blesovsky	P R R Clarke	J W Foulds	J W Howe
J Ashworth	S A Bober	S Cohen	R C Francis	I H Hubbard
A F J Atkins	R C Bosanquet	T P Cole		J M Hudson
P M Atkinson	W M Bowden	H B Contractor		R S Hutchison
R Attard	P H Brakenbury	P J Cook	R F R Gardner	D T R Hutchon
B Avery	J K Brigg	J A Cosbie Ross	R Garry	
	F T Brough	D G Cottrell	D Gatehouse	
	A H Brown	A Coxon	A D Gayner	J C Jago
R Baker	H Brown	P J Crawford	D G Ghanekar	J H James
G A Balmer	R Brown	A D Craxford	R F Gillie	F S Johnson
S C Banerjee	J M Buchanan	A L Crombie	M J Goakes	I D A Johnston
D T C Barber	C H W Bullough	A T Cross	K A Godfrey	A J Jones
H Barber	C H Bulman	R B Cubey	C R Gomersall	D H Jones
S L Barron	M Burke		T P Griffith	K Jones
A R Bearn	V W Burton	E P Davison	A Gunn	
J R Bell		J M Davison		
R J Bentley	A Calder	W G Dawson		R M Kalbag
	A S Campbell	E Dayan		S Karat
	D S Cameron	R A Dendy	J B Hall-Parker	N C Keddie
		H B Devlin	R R Hall	J F Kelly
		C Diamond	D M Hancock	D Kilby
		P H Dickinson	D W Hand	J H Kilshaw
		D C D'Netto	R Harrison	R Kirby
		W Dunlop	J E Hawkesford	
		G H Dunstone	D V Heath	
			C D Hierons	J E R Lart
		A N Edwards	M J Higgs	T A Lavin
		M H Edwards	C J Hilton	J Lawson
		F Ellis	P Hilton	R Layton
		D M Essenhigh	A Hind	T Layzell

Northern Region
Surgeons

J M Lennox
M A Leonard
D G Limb
T Lind
R Loffill
N Longrigg
J D Lorimer
D J Lovelock
L Lyness
M J Lyons

G Mackay
I W Mackee
G M Maclure
B McEvedy
J McGlone
C G A McGregor
A S McIntosh
E N McKenzie
G McLatchie
G MacNab
B J McNeela
I McNeill
A K Maitra
N Manson
H F Marshall
F W Martin
P J K Maskery
J R Mason
R F Mather
D B Mathias
I K Mathie
C Metcalfe-Gibson
I A Miller
I T Miller
D D Milne
G N Morritt
D S Muckle
S Mukherjee
J Murgatroyd
B J Murray

V S Nargolwala
F P Nath
R Neale

P J O'Rourke
R A Ord
V H Oswal

B Y Pai
C Parker
R D Peduzzi
A L G Peel
A H Petty

T A Piggot
S S Pillai
I M Pinder
R Pollard
J Pooley
I D Porteous
R Porter
J Potter
P H Powell
T G Price
G Proud

A A Qazi
K B Queen

C R G Ramachandra
P D Ramsden
L Rangecroft
R G Rangecroft
V A C Reece
C A Reid
W Reid
J R Rhind
D G Richards
J Richardson
R E W Ridley
J H Rizvi
C Roberts
A A Robertson
I R Robertson
H I Robinson
I Rogers
I L Rosenberg
R R Roy

P R Samuel
K Sarang
D Sarson
D J Scobie
J E S Scott
R P Sengupta
B P Sethi
A Seymour
C B Shah
J E G Shand
C Sharp
R J Shepherd
J L Sher
P I Silverstone
P F Sims
W Y Sinclair
M M Singh
S P Singh
D P Sinha
V Siva
S R Smith
C A Snodgrass
J Stafford
T J Stahl
G D Stainsby

J G Stephen
J Stevens
A J Strong
G B Summergill
R A Sutton

D Tacchi
J T Taylor
R M R Taylor
R W Thomson
A H Tooley
G A Turnbull
W J Twibill

C W Venables

J Wagget
T I Wagstaff
W K Walsh
S M Walton
R P Ward Booth
A J Warrington
A Watson
R T Watson
B D Weerasinghe
A R Welch
J S W Whitehead
D G Whittaker
R G Wilson
R Y Wilson
T T Win
P D Wright

Anaesthetists

J C S Ainley Walker
P R Allen
M Amanullah
I Anderson
J I Andrews
P L Archer
A Arrowsmith

D H T Bain
J Baldasera
C E Baptiste
C Beeton
M Berry
B B Bhala
M J Biggart
D G M Bishop
R J Bray
A E Brown
M R Bryson
F B Buckley
R E Bullock
M C Burn

K S Cameron
R F Carter
S J Carter
P Cauchi
J E Charlton
R J M Colback
I D Conacher
S W Coniam
H B Contractor
S Cook
P F Copeland
S C Craddock
S G H Cruickshank

D J H Daniel
I W Davidson
J R Davies
K H Davies
P A Davies
B Dennison
W R Desira
T Dowell
R S Drummond

G N Elliott

I R Fletcher
E N S Fry

R Gautam
M I Gergis
N Ghosh
R E C Gibson
D Girling
R Goodwin
J D Greaves
S K Greenwell

J Halshaw
J Hamilton
S A Hargreave
G Harris
D W Heaviside
N M Heggie
J B Hicks
J N Hodkinson
B L Holt
D G Hughes
C J Hull
J D Hunter

L A G Jayasekera
J Jeffery
G Johns
M K Johnson
D F Jones

A Kilpatrick
R A Knight
G W Kuvelker

P G P Lawler
D L Leaming
J A Little
M Lothian

D G McGregor
A McHutchon
C K McKnight
L J Mackay
D I MacNair
A R Mahroo
I M Mair
M Marshall
Z Masri
I M Mathias
M Mehta
K C Misra
S P Moffett

J M Newbery
P T P Newham
K W Nightingale

M L Paes
P K Pal
W G Park
D T Pearson
A G B Poole
S Pratt
A K Pridie

M A Quader

M S Rana
A Redpath
M E Richardson
G S Riddell
I F Riddle
P Ritchie
M A Rucklidge
D W Ryan
W Ryder

N Salari
J J H Sherriff
B C H Smith
S Srivastava
M A Stafford
J C Stoddart
J Storrs
P Stuart
B G Swales

L Thompson-Hill
C W Thomson
D C Townsend

I Ulyett

C J Vallis
N Vellore

B G Watson
D M Watson
O G W Weldon
B Welsh
R Will
L J Williams
D W Wood

1. There were **no** consultants in this region who completed forms but did not indicate their agreement to participate.

2. There were 27 consultants (5 anaesthetists and 22 surgeons) in this region who declined to take part in this study, of whom 12 (2 anaesthetists and 10 surgeons) withdrew after the study began.

3. There were **no** consultants in this region who did not reply to our invitations to participate.

4. There was one consultant surgeon who declined to participate but specifically requested that one of his cases be included because it was "relevant".

5. There were also a number of consultants who were unknown to us at the start of the CEPOD Enquiry, and did not, as far as we knew, have any cases reported to this office, but who later appeared on the staffing lists supplied by the Regional Health Authorities:

P L Bali
R K Banjeree
J G Banks
J R Cherry
M S Dang
H J B Gonsalves

J D Haslam
J E Milson
R J Pratt
L Singh
P J Taylor

NORTH EAST THAMES REGION

The following consultants agreed in writing to participate but did not necessarily have any deaths nor complete any forms:

Surgeons

K P Abel
J D Abrams
M Adieshiah
F Afshar
N Ahmad
W L Alexander
A Amen
M Amin
J Angel
H G Annan
B S Ashby
D W Atkinson

C M Bailey
R W M Baldwin
A J Ball
G S Banwell
J M Beaugie

A Beckingsale
T Beedham
G Bentley
B F Beveridge
G Bewtley
M Bhamra
R Birch
M Birnstingl
J P Blandy
R P Boggon
J P Bolton
P J Bolton
C M Booth
J B Booth
D A Boston
P B Boulos
J M Boulton
A A Boutwood
N R M Boyd
H A Brant

A P Bray
G B Brookes
M D Brough
J P Browett
D B Brown
G Buchanan
T M Bucknill
E B Burton

H Cannell
A Catterall
J H Challis
M T Challis
P A F Chalk
J Chalstrey
A D Cheesman
S C Chen
G Cherfan
B D Chopra
C G Clark
J Clarke
R V Clements
M A Clifton
G W Cochrane
J Cochrane
R A Coles
H P Cook
R F P Copland
A G A Cowie
C B Croft
R J Croft
G J Crow
J C M Currie

D G Davies
R S Dawkins
M H Devereux
G S Dowd
L N Dowie
T P Dutt

D G A Eadie
R Earlam
J W Eddy
M A Edgar
S J Edmondson
P Emery
P England
T English
L Epsztejn
R J Etheridge
D G Evans
F J H Evans
V J Everett

D V I Fairweather
M Z Farag
D G Fife

J A Fixsen
J P Flanagan
D M C Forster
J G Fraser
M A R Freeman
K Frith
N J Frootko
A P Fuller
D V Furlong

J R C Gardham
A Gardner
N Garvan
P George
M Ghilchik
M G Gillard
O J A Gilmore
R E Glass
C J Good
A W Goode
C F Goodfellow
P Gortvai
L Gracey
J M Graham
W J Grange
H Grant
J D Griffiths
J Groves
J Grudzinskas
J Guillebaud

M E J Hackett
M H Hall
R J Ham
R A Harlow
M Harris
D F N Harrison
J Hartgill
R Hartwell
P R Hawley
J W Hazell
A D Heath
M R Heath
B Helal
W F Hendry
M B Heywood-
   Waddington
J D Hill
J T Hill
K E F Hobbs
M Hobsley
A A Hooper
J P Hopewell
D Howard
A C Hume
J Hungerford
R Hurt
V M Husband

A M Jackson

S M T Jaffery
J D Jagger
O D Jahanbakach
O A Jamall
D R James
P L James
J D Jeremiah
B M Jones

N Kayali
V Kearney
M H Keene
A J Kellerman
J V H Kemble
H B S Kemp
J Kersey
I G Kidson
J B King
R M Kirk
E O'G Kirwan
P Kitchen
K M N Kunzru

G Lachelin
C E M Lamb
R J Lavelle
M G Lawlor
D Lawrence
D Learmont
A W F Lettin
I S Levy
A A M Lewis
C T Lewis
A Leyshon
C D R Lightowler
K W Lindsay
R Liversedge
R Lloyd-Jones
M R Lock
W Love
M Lowy
C Lucas
J S P Lumley
M G Lyall

D M Mackinnon
A D W MacLean
P McKelvie
D L McMillan
R McNab Jones
D Madan
T C A Madgwick
M R Madigan
P G Magee
J Magri
C V Mann
B D Markwell
J A P Marston
M R Martin
J G Mathie

North East Thames Region

R S Maurice-Williams
A R L May
M H Mehta
D M Millar
E J Milroy
A J Minchin
D A Moffat
C J Moore
B D G Morgan
H Morgan
M W E Morgan
R J Morgan
T R Morley
A W Morrison
D L Morrison
R W Motson
P D Moynagh
H Mulnier
A H G Murley
A Mushin

A Naftalin
H G Naylor
E Nicholls
R J Nicholls
C F Noon
J M A Northover

P M S O'Brien
E P N O'Donoghue
T G O'Driscol
B C O'Riordan
B C Obiekwe
D N Offen
D Oram
M H Ornstein
N Orr
D R Osborne
J L Osborne

S P Parbhoo
B J Pardy
A M I Paris
D F Paton
R A Payne
J B Pearson
B W T Pender
R M Phillips
M Pietroni
R Pilkington
P Pitt
T J Pocock
M Powell
S V L Prasad

D M C Price
J Primrose
J Pryor
M Pugh
R J Pusey

G Radcliffe
G L S Rankin
A O Ransford
P G Ransley
J L Read
G M Rees
B Ribeiro
D R Richard
P R Riddle
P H Rivas
D J Robert
P Roberts
B A Roper
A H McLean Ross
R A Roxburgh
C Rudge
C J Rudge
J A Rumble
R C G Russell
R W Rushman

W D Savage
J H Scurr
M Setchell
G R Seward
P J R Shah
O H Shaheen
N B Shaikh
W S Shand
R W Shaw
J H Shepherd
N Shotts
N Siddle
A Silverstone
A Singer
M Singh
W W Slack
B C Sommerlad
P M Spencer
M Spiro
C J Spivey
M B Stanton
M P Stearns
R D Stedeford
A E Steel
S J Steele
K H Stone
A E Stuart
M F Sturridge
A P Su
R A Sudlow
M Sullivan
D R Sweetnam
M Al Syada
E McKim Sycamore

E Taylor
L K M Therkildsen
P Thomas
T L Thomas
H H Thompson
J P S Thomson
M T Thoung
R C Tiptaft
I P Todd
R C Todd
R M Todd
T Treasure
I Treharne
R E Turner-Warwick

M R A Utidjian

D A Viniker
J S Virdi

R K Walesby
C C Walker
J E G Walker
A F Wallace
C E Wallace
J K Ward
M Ward
M W N Ward
R H T Ward
C C Ware
W C Wathen
E S Watkins
E J M Weaver
P J Webb
C C Welch
A R L Weekes
J Wellwood
B L Whitaker
A J White
R A F Whitelock
H N Whitfield
H P Williams
N S Williams
R A Williams
D W Wilson
P C Wilson
D Winstock
E H Wisely
M J Witt
R F M Wood
C R J Woodhouse
P H L Worth
A Wright
V M Wright
P S Wright
J H Wyllie

H L Young

A G Zahir

Anaesthetists

G G Abbondati
T G L Allum
R F Armstrong
B Astley
R S Atkinson
W Aveling

J Barber
P M Bashir
A Beague
P J Bennett
J Bevan
D G Beynon
D M Birley
C Birt
M Biswas
I J Blair
P O Bodley
H Boralessa
R M Bowen-Wright
R I J Brain
C Browne
D R G Browne
C Bullen
D E Burt
J A Bushman

I Calder
J Cantrell
F F Casale
H E R Chew
L Chippindale
G Clark
E Clements
P Cole
B Collett
B Collier
K M Collins
M P Colvin
H A Condon
S K Coombes
J Cotter
M Cronin
W V Cuschieri

S D Dalal
P E Daly
D N Davies
G M Davies
A M Day
S Day
A R Deacock
N H A Doctor
G W Duckworth

G M Eames
D B Ellis

R H Ellis
D H Enderby
D Erwin

M Fanning
P Flynn
J M G Foster
M Frank

L A Gergis
E P Gibbs
G B Gillett
R Greenbaum
R W Griffin
E M Grundy

J L Handy
S A I Helwa
S K Hepton
J D Hill
C J Hinds
P G Hollywood
R J Hope
T H Howells
J A Hulf

S Ingram
L N Iskander

K Jash
E B Javed
R L A Jayaweera
R E Jones
M Jordan

L Kaufman
P A Keeling
T Khanam
W H Konarzewski
J R Krapez

G L Leader
P Lee
D J Lightman
G H Lim
R M Liscombe
D T Lovell

A McAra
E J McAteer
P B McComish
T D McGhee
J J Maher
A G Marshall
J E Mason-Jordan

A K Mathur
R F J Matthews
R M Mehta
L M Mendonca
R E Molloy
P S Monks
J Mulryan

A F Naylor

P J O'Shea
B Oliver
J Ormrod

P Painter
W K Pallister
D B Pallot
M S Pegg
M J Pick
N Poobalasingam
V Pradhan
V G Punchihewa
S A Purdie

T Rajasekaran
R Rajendram
A Ramachandran
D Rees
M J S Robertson
R H Robinson
M G Rolfe
A P Rubin
G B Rushman

N Sampson
J R Samuel
T M Savege
J Secker-Walker
D R J Seingry
R C Shah
P H Simmons
P H Simmons
R S Simons
J Skinner
W K Slack

F C Smales
J R Spears
R A Spilsbury
S M Srivatsa
V Stanhill
G L Steer
C J Stephens
P M Stracey
D Swallow

D B Talwatte
T H Taylor
G C Thick
D A Thomas
D Thomas
A Thorogood
K Tusiewicz
A G Tyers

H J Utting

B Q Varley
C Verghese
I R Verner
M S Vernon
P J Verrill

D A Walmsley
E Walsh
B Walton
S Ward
C R Wijesurendra
D J Wilkinson
W M Wilkinson
D J M Williams
C M Wisely
S D Woods

P M Yate
J V I Young
P M E Youngman

D Zuck
Z Zych

NOTES

1. There were 3 consultant surgeons and 3 consultant anaesthetists in this region who completed forms but did not indicate their agreement to participate (we have considered this as a request for privacy and have not published their names).

2. There were also 29 consultants (24 surgeons and 5 anaesthetists) in this region who declined to take part in this study, 18 of whom (3 anaesthetists and 15 surgeons) withdrew after the study began.

3. There were 15 consultants (4 anaesthetists and 11 surgeons) in this region who did not reply to any of our invitations to participate nor did they return any forms.

4. There was one consultant anaesthetist on the above list who joined the study after 1.9.86 but had declined to take part before this.

5. One illegible consent form was returned in this region but alas only identifiable by a London postmark.

6. There were also probably, as in the other two regions, a number of consultants who were unknown to us at the start of the CEPOD Enquiry, and did not, as far as we knew, have any cases reported to this office. The Regional Health Authority were unable, at the time of publication, to supply us with a complete list of consultants.

SOUTH WESTERN REGION

The following consultants agreed in writing to participate but did not necessarily have any deaths or complete any forms:

Surgeons

P Abrams
C E Ackroyd
R M Adam
D A P Ainscow
G Angel

R N Baird
N J Barwell
P Beasley
J Bertram
J Bevan
P G Bicknell
B P Bliss
A H W Boyle
P Boreham
T L Bradbeer
D J Bracey
R Bradbrook
W P Bradford
M W M Bridger
A J M Brodribb
C Brown
I Buchanan
W Bunting
M A Burley

P J Callen
D G Calvert
W B Campbell
W A F Carruthers
L R Celestin
A N Chakraborty
C W Chapman
R G Choa
R J Clarke
J R Clough
C A C Clyne
H Coakham
R Coates
C D Collins
G J Conrad
J A Cooper

M J Cooper
T C Crewe
M L Crosfill
B Cummins

C M Davidson
G M Davidson
A J Davies
A S Davies
R A C Davies
J P Dhasmana
J H Dixon
J W Dixon
R Donovan

N Edwards
W K Eltringham
H J Espiner

J Fairgrieve
H D Fairman
A D Falconer
R C L Feneley
A D Fisher
T J Flew
P J Folca
C P Forrester-
Wood
R P Foster
J Foulkes
G C Fox
C E Fozzard
J D Frank
J Friend

W J Gall
M W L Gear
J C Gingell
M Golby
A Gough
H B Griffith
D A Griffiths
H E D Griffiths

M J Griffiths
M F B Grundy
D H Gudgeon

J F Hamlyn
J Hammonds
D J Hanley
M A Hannon
M Hardingham
D L Harris
J M Harrison
C T Hart
D R Harvey
S Hasan
S Haynes
R W Hiles
A Hinchliffe
J V Holland
M Horrocks
R Hughes
R B Hutcheson
P M Hutchins
J D Hutchison

G H Irvine

J S H Jacob
D K James
C D Jefferiss
I Jelen
K Jeyasingham
C K Jones
P Jones
S M Jones
D N Joyce

G Keen
R H J Kerr-Wilson
N J Knight
P Knipe

D J Leaper
P H D Lewars
I J Leslie
G N Lumb

N N S MacKay
M MacKenzie
D R McCoy
J McGarry
J A W McKelvey
F N McLeod
N J McC Mortensen
B K Madden
M J Maxted
R E May
M Midda
J Mohan
P J W Monks
B D A Morris
J M Morsman

South Western Region
Surgeons

R L M Newell
P A R Niven
H R Noblett

P J O'Boyle
L Oldham

G Pell
B D Pentlow
B N Pickering
R W Pigott
L H Poberskin
Le Roy Priaulx

H A Rainey
N I Ramus
A H C Ratliff
I D Rawlings
M W Reece
C D Reid
W Rich
J A Richardson
J W S Rickett
C R K Rickford
J B M Roberts
P H Roberts
R H C Robins
J M Robinson
R K Roddie
J W Ross
G D Rooker

P E Savage
S G Scanlan
P J Scott
D W Seargeant
N Seymour
J P Shepherd
J F L Shaw
K Sivathondan
H M Smith
L Solomon
J O Soul
P G Stableforth
P J Stannard
R V Stephenson
I P Stewart
W E Strachan
G D Sturrock
M Sutton
G R Swingler
D W Sykes

T P B Tasker
C Teasdale
M H Thompson
J Thomsitt
D S Thomson

W H F Thomson
M J Torrens
P L G Townsend
J Tricker

J Upton

S Vethanayagam
K D J Vowles

H Walters
D M Ward
A J Webb
S C Wells
H J O White
F R Wilkes
D C Wilkins
R C N Williamson
P C Windle-Taylor
J D Wisheart
P J Witherow
S M Wood

J R Young

Anaesthetists

J I Alexander
C J H Andrews

P Ballard
P G Ballance
H G R Balmer
P J Baskett
H L R Bastiaenen
J A Bennett
F J Beswick
A M S Black
R W Boaden
T A Boliston
J B Bowes
P Brighten
T M Bull
A N Burlingham
G W Burton

D R Cadle
J A Carter
T I Cash
J M Chapman
M Churcher
W B Clarkson
J A Clement
M B Coates
D Cochrane
V A Codman
J C Coghill
C H Collins
G Cooper
K J Covell
S Currie

R M Davies
R E Davis
R C Desborough
A W Diamond
I A R Dunnett
M A P Durkin

J M Eaton
R Eltringham

D Faulkner
R F M Forward
S J Forster
J G Francis
M K Freeman

N W Goodman
G G Grayling
D P G Griffiths

C R Hall
F G Hall
N F Harley
R A Harrison
C R Harvey
P B Harvey
N G B Hersey
M M Hills
A M Hipkin
R M H Hodgson
D G Hughes
P Hut
J Hyland

M T Inman

A Jackson
A S Jackson
M L James
G Jephcott
R W Johnson

F S Keddie
S W Kemp

S K Lahiri
R J Lenz
J Lytle

A P Madden
F P F Marshall
S Masey
S J Mather
S B Merrill
J S Miller
G A R Morgan
B J Muir
J T Mulvein

A E Nesling

N O'Donovan
J W O'Higgins
K L Owen

J C Pappin
J B Parsons
V W Penning-
 Rowsell
B W Perriss
B A Poley
J Powell
J Pring
J Prior
D L Pryer
C Prys-Roberts
G R G Purcell

P J Ravenscroft
G Routh

J F Searle
D H Short
L E Shutt
W J W Siddall
A D Simcock
P J Simpson
G R Sowden

G H M Stanley-
 Jones
J A C Strachan

P A Taylor
T A Thomas
J L Thorn
P G N Thornton
J K Trotter

B Le G Waldron
A K Y Walker
M A Walker
E Walsh
F J M Walters
T D Waterhouse
R Weller
P White
B R Whittard
D B Whittingham
D G Wilkins
S M Willatts
N B Williams
G Wray

P N Young

J Zorab

NOTES

1. There were 4 consultants in this region (3 surgeons and 1 anaesthetist) who completed forms but did not indicate their agreement to participate (we have considered this to be a request for privacy and have not published their names).

2. There were 21 consultants in this region (one anaesthetist and 20 surgeons) who declined to take part in this study. Eight of the surgeons withdrew after the study began.

3. There were also 2 consultants (one surgeon and one anaesthetist) in this region who did not reply to any of our invitations to participate nor did they return any forms.

4. There was one consultant surgeon who appears in the list above who wished to join the study from 1.1.86 but had not joined for the first 8 weeks.

5. There were also a number of consultants who were unknown to us at the start of the CEPOD Enquiry, and did not, as far as we knew, have any cases reported to this office, but who later appeared on the staffing lists supplied by the Regional Health Authorities:

R R Acheson
R J Andlaw
J R S Barton
N L Dallas
J C Dean Hart
R N L Doran
Prof D L Easty
R P Ellis
B E Enoch
F I K Feddo
R A Gibson
R H B Grey
D R W Hartley
R Hensher
M Houlton
C R H James

A H John
M Joyce
D E Lyons
D M Magauran
R K Mal
R H C Markham
V J Marmion
J P Martin
A Midwinter
I W Payne
S S Prime
M D Read
Prof C M A Scully
Prof G M Stirrat
G M Turner
A H Young

Association of Anaesthetists

of Great Britain and Ireland

APPENDIX 3

NOVEMBER 1984

(Reprinted June 1985)

Association of Surgeons

of Great Britain and Ireland

Confidential Enquiry into Perioperative Deaths

1.0 PREAMBLE

1.1 The medical profession has a responsibility to the public and to itself to assess its own standards and to be in a position to meet criticism, from whatever source, in an authoritative fashion. Accurate audit can establish current standards of medical organisation and care; it allows for comparisons and helps to determine the value of procedures. It also directs future developments and influences teaching and training.

1.2 Although the longer we live the more likely we are to die, the timing of this event can be markedly influenced by an intercurrent operative procedure. Mortality does not lend itself to prospective controlled trials, however a great deal of information can be obtained from individual case studies.

1.3 Since 1952, the Department of Health has collected figures on maternal mortality (Confidential Enquiries into Maternal Deaths, HMSO, Triennial Reports) and over the last 35 years the Association of Anaesthetists of Great Britain and Ireland has commissioned three reports on mortality associated with anaesthesia (Edwards et al, 1956; Dinnick, 1964; Lunn and Mushin, 1982). The surgical input to the latter studies was limited and, in view of the interdependence of the two specialities, the Association of Anaesthetists are combining with the Association of Surgeons to obtain mortality figures for surgical procedures carried out in Great Britain and Ireland.

1.4 For the Enquiry to be successful and have the confidence of the public and the profession it is important that:-

    1.4.1 the data is **confidential** throughout

    1.4.2 Assessments of the data are **independent** of the operating team

    1.4.3 the assessments are **authoritative.**

1.5 The design of the Enquiry is derived from a previous study of anaesthetic mortality (Lunn and Mushin, 1982).

1.6 To this end it is proposed to mount a pilot study involving three Districts and then extend the Enquiry in the light of lessons learned to three Regions.

1.7 It is then intended that the Enquiry be extended countrywide on a continuing basis.

2.0 CONFIDENTIALITY

2.1 Confidentiality is the nub of any audit system. Clinicians are assured that the secrecy of the enquiry is absolute; they will never be 'named', sued, or otherwise denigrated by information contained in the study. Previous multicentre studies of surgical activity have maintained confidentiality (e.g. St. Mary's Large Bowel Cancer Project) and this study will achieve the same end.

2.2 Confidentiality is a numeric concept, the fewer persons who know a secret the less likely it is to leak. Therefore only the clinical Co-ordinators and their office staff, to a maximum of five persons (three Co-ordinators and two office staff) would have **access** to personal data about consultants/doctors and names of patients.

3.0 THE DEFENCE SOCIETIES

3.1 The defence societies have been consulted and can see no grounds for concern. Previous experience with the anaesthetic studies, the Confidential Enquiries into Maternal Deaths and with the St. Mary's Large Bowel Cancer Project have not raised any medico-legal problems.

Extract from memorandum of solicitors to the Medical Protection Society

'We cannot, however, see in this instance that the Committee can do any more to preserve confidentiality than is proposed in the protocol. Unless there should be either a deliberate leak or gross carelessness on the part of one of the Co-ordinators or their office staff, the precautions seem to be very strong and the risk is minimal of information becoming public in a form in which any individual could be identified.'

4.0 INDEPENDENCE OF ASSESSMENT

4.1 Assessment must be carried out entirely independently of the operating team. To ensure adequate independence the **assessors will not know** the names of the operating team, nor its geographical location. Assessors will make the assessment purely on the basis of facts presented to them. If the assessors receive data which is inadequate to make a firm judgement the matter will be referred back to the Co-ordinators who will obtain the additional data the assessors require to complete their task. Equally, those reporting cases to the study need to remain unaware of the identity of the individual assessors.

5.0 AUTHORITY

5.1 The assessors need to be authorities on their particular topics. The assessors appointed by the Joint Working Party are persons with a broad spread of knowledge and expertise and who represent acceptable standards and opinions within the professions. This will be made clear to participating operating teams at the commencement of the enquiry.

6.0 AIMS OF THE STUDY

6.1 To determine mortality rates associated with surgical operations in hospital considering the events before, during and within thirty days after these procedures.

6.2 H.A.A. data and other routinely collected N.H.S. statistics will be used as a denominator for these rates.

6.3 To identify remediable factors in the practice of anaesthesia and surgery.

6.4 To evolve an Enquiry design capable of continuing implementation on a national scale to keep those matters under review.

6.5 The Enquiry will consider the disease process, its duration and severity and the general state and age of each patient. It will examine the decision to operate, the appropriateness of the operation and its timing, whether an elective or emergency procedure and the preliminary resuscitation and pre-operative preparation. Assessment of the technical skills and training of the anaesthetist will include management of the airway and ventilation and the manipulation of anaesthetic drugs. The surgeon's operative technique will be considered and the combined assessment will include the management of fluid balance and medication.

6.6 These technical details will be linked to the location of the procedure, the time of day, the staffing, seniority, experience and possible fatigue and the consultation that had taken place between the surgeon and anaesthetist and junior and senior members of each team. Autopsy results will be scrutinized. These do not always agree with pre-mortem diagnoses, however, and the sequence of events leading to death will be analysed, as these may be more relevant than the specific cause.

6.7 From the documented information an opinion will be made as to whether the procedure was a justifiable risk and whether death was inevitable or avoidable. Factors implicated in the death will be considered, together with the adequacy of both the local facilities and the patients records.

6.8 To ensure absolute confidentiality, all the data sheets and correspondence concerning individual patients will be shredded at the completion of the study of each individual case.

7.0 IDENTIFICATION OF DEATHS

7.1 All deaths occurring in hospital within 30 days of an anaesthetic or surgical procedure carried out in hospital are to be included in this review and studied. It is recognised that some deaths at home within this period after discharge may be overlooked.

7.2 It is proposed to exclude:-

7.2.1 deaths covered by the Triennial Enquiries into Maternal Deaths

7.2.2 death following cardiac surgery.

7.3 Deaths which fall within the study definitions will be identified locally according to a detailed protocol. Co-operation of Medical Records Officers will be needed and this co-operation will be specifically sought at the commencement of the study.

8.0 COLLECTION OF DATA

8.1 Each study district will be visited by the clinical Co-ordinators who will explain the purpose of the Enquiry and the safeguards. Local participation and consent will be obtained from the consultant anaesthetists and surgeons. The consultants in each district will themselves choose a local consultant colleague to be the local reporter of deaths. The local reporter will identify all the deaths in co-operation with the records staff in the district and with the consultants concerned. Participating consultants will receive a confirmatory letter from the Enquiry centre.

8.2 The initial case selection must ensure that all relevant cases are collected. The local reporter will report to the centre the name of the deceased, date of birth of the deceased, the date of death and the names of the surgeon and anaesthetist responsible for the deceased's care. The local reporter will not be asked to report on or pass any judgement on any clinical procedure.

8.3 When the Enquiry centre is advised of a death the clinical Co-ordinators will write to the consultant anaesthetist and consultant surgeon responsible and ask them each to complete a questionnaire and self-assessment form; these forms when completed will be returned to the Enquiry centre.

8.4 Returned forms will be checked for completeness by the clinical Co-ordinators at the Enquiry centre. The patient's, surgeon's, anaesthetist's names and hospital identification will then be removed from the record and the participating consultants self-assessment forms filed. The Co-ordinators will refer each completed questionnaire identifiable only by Enquiry centre index number, to the independent assessors.

8.5 The aim of the assessment is to:-

    8.5.1 Decide on the clinical cause of the death.

    8.5.2 Determine the extent of contributory factors of the anaesthetic.

    8.5.3 Determine the extent of contributory factors of the surgery (including surgical decisions).

    8.5.4 Determine the part played by other causes.

    8.5.5 Identify avoidable and unavoidable factors.

    8.5.6 Identify clinical deficiencies.

    8.5.7 Identify organisational deficiencies.

8.6 The assessors will complete assessment forms, similar to those completed by the participating consultants and their junior colleagues, basing their (the assessors') judgement on the responses given in the questionnaires they review. If the assessors think any further relevant questions need to be asked and answered, they will return the assessment forms to the Enquiry centre and the clinical Co-ordinators will approach the consultant concerned with the questions the assessors have raised.

8.7 The assessors will return their completed assessment forms to the Enquiry centre. The study centre will telephone to the participating surgeons/anaesthetists the assessor's opinion if the participating clinicians have asked for it and have supplied an appropriate telephone number.

8.8 Any deaths which are unresolved by the assessors will be considered again anonymously by the Joint Working Party of the Confidential Enquiry into Perioperative Deaths.

8.9 It is intended to complete the study of each death within six weeks. Once the assessment is complete the outcome data but **not** the patient's name, address, surgeon's or anaesthetist's name, or hospital name, will be filed in chronological order on a computer at the study centre. As soon as data collection is complete all the questionnaire sheets and correspondence referrable to an individual case will be shredded.

9.0 THE ENQUIRY CENTRE

9.1 To ensure the overall direction of the study three clinical Co-ordinators have been appointed. These Co-ordinators will liaise with participating clinicians. They will refer cases to the assessors and convey results back to clinicians. They will assemble the data and analyse it. The Co-ordinators will be accountable to the Joint Working Party of the Confidential Enquiry into Perioperative Deaths.

9.2 The Committee and study will be serviced by a whole time administrative officer with an interest and training in administration and information systems. There will also be a need for one or two secretarial assistants and the main office of the Enquiry centre will be located in central London.

10.0 PILOT STUDY

10.1 It is proposed to launch the pilot study in three districts to test the protocol and its feasibility. These will be:-

    10.1.1 Bloomsbury District (N.E. Thames Region)

    10.1.2 Darlington District (Northern Region)

    10.1.3 Exeter District (S.W. Region)

11.0 REGIONAL STUDY

11.1 A study using a similar protocol, will then be undertaken in three Health Regions in England. It is hoped that at least two (Northern and S. Western) will include Districts which have participated in the pilot study. The third Region will be a Thames Region.

11.2 The regional study will follow approximately six months after the completion of the pilot study, to allow time for analysis of the methodology and to recruit the local reporters in each District in the chosen Regions. Data collection will be continued for twelve months.

12.0 RESULTS

12.1 Reporting Results

It is proposed that all participating consultants be invited to a launch meeting to discuss the protocol and then to further meetings to discuss the results. These meetings will be confidential and limited only to participating consultants. Pooled data will be available for all attending the meeting. Consultants will not be able to obtain unique information other than requested telephoned assessments. The storage of unique identifiable information would compromise the overall confidentiality of the system.

12.2 The clinical Co-ordinators, the administrative officer, members of the joint working party or assessors will not enter into correspondence with participating consultants regarding details of assessments.

13.0 PERSONNEL AND HONORARIA

13.1 Local reporters and expert assessors will be paid honoraria.

14.0 CO-ORDINATORS

14.1 The Joint Working Party of the Confidential Enquiry into Perioperative Deaths have appointed as Co-ordinators:-

Mr. H. B. Devlin
Professor J. S. P. Lumley
Dr. J. N. Lunn

15.0 WORKING PARTY

15.1 The members of the Working Party consisted of:-

Chairman:-	Professor M. D. Vickers
Vice-Chairman:-	Professor J. S. P. Lumley
Treasurer:-	Dr. M. M. Burrows
Secretary:-	Mr. H. B. Devlin

Professor P. G. Bevan
Dr. E. A. Cooper
Mr. J. L. Craven
Mr. D. Harper
Dr. M. T. Inman
Dr. J. N. Lunn
Professor A. G. Johnson
Dr. P. Morris

16.0 SUPPORTING BODIES

16.1 This Protocol has been scrutinized by all, and comment received from some of, the following professional institutions:-

1. The Royal College of Surgeons of England
2. The Royal College of Surgeons of Edinburgh
3. The Royal College of Physicians and Surgeons of Glasgow
4. The Royal College of Surgeons in Ireland
5. The Royal College of Obstetricians and Gynaecologists
6. The Faculty of Dental Surgery of the Royal College of Surgeons of England
7. The Faculty of Anaesthetists of the Royal College of Surgeons of England
8. The Faculty of Anaesthetists of the Royal College of Surgeons in Ireland
9. The Faculty of Dentistry of the Royal College of Surgeons in Ireland
10. The Royal College of Physicians of Ireland
11. The Royal College of Physicians of London
12. The Royal College of Radiologists
13. The Royal College of Pathologists.
14. The Royal College of Physicians of Edinburgh
15. The Royal College of Psychiatrists
16. The Royal College of Nursing
17. The Faculty of Community Medicine of the Royal College of Physicians of the United Kingdom

17.0 OTHER BODIES CONSULTED

The Joint Consultants Committee
The Central Committee for Hospital Medical Services
The British Medical Association
The National Association of Health Authorities
The Association of Clinical Pathologists.
The Association of Nurse Administrators
Department of Health and Social Security
The General Medical Council
The Office of Population Censuses and Surveys
The Institute of Health Service Administrators
The Medical Defence Union Ltd
The Medical Protection Society Ltd
The British Thoracic Society
The American College of Surgeons
The British Association of Paediatric Surgeons
The Coroners Society of England & Wales
The British Orthopaedic Association
The Society of Thoracic and Cardiovascular Surgeons of Great Britain and Ireland
The Cremation Society of Great Britain
The British Association of Urological Surgeons
ENT Societies
Society of British Neurological Surgeons

Further information may be obtained from the Administator: Mr Nigel Buck MSc, 14 Palace Court, London W2 4HT. Tel: 01-727 4547

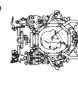

JUNE 1985

Supplementary Notes to the Protocol

Confidential Enquiry into Perioperative Deaths

1. Litigation

(Paragraphs 2.0 and 3.1 of the Protocol)

Written confirmation has now been received from the Secretary of State to the Department of Health and Social Security that the Department will support the total confidentiality of this Enquiry.

The Secretary of State is satisfied that the disclosure of documents about individual cases prepared for the Enquiry into Perioperative Deaths would be against the public interest and would undermine the whole basis of a confidential enquiry. The Secretary of State has confirmed that the same support will be provided for the Confidential Enquiry into Perioperative Deaths as is already given to the Enquiry into Maternal Deaths. The Secretary is satisfied that disclosure of documents about individual cases prepared for these Enquiries would be against the public interest. The courts have always had regard to overriding public interest as grounds for refusing requests for disclosure of documents, and Section 35 of the Supreme Court Act 1981, which provides that the Court shall not make an Order, under Sections 33 or 34 of that Act, for disclosure 'if it considers that compliance with the Order, if made, would be likely to be injurious to the public interests' has provided additional support for such opposition. The Department has been assured that if it should be necessary, the claim for public interest immunity from disclosure would be pressed vigorously by the Crown.

The Department in addition states that in its opinion a fruitful outcome to the Enquiry will be a major achievement by the medical profession in the field of medical audit.

Therefore, the data/information sent to the Confidential Enquiry into Perioperative Deaths is protected from subpoena. However, if any participant takes a photocopy of the form, that photocopy is his property and is open to subpoena by the courts and the Confidential Enquiry into Perioperative Deaths cannot protect that copy. It is therefore essential that participants or others *DO NOT PHOTOCOPY ANY OR PART OF THE COMPLETED QUESTIONNAIRE.*

1

2. Local Reporter

The local reporter will be a *consultant* chosen and respected by his/her colleagues in each District for the full duration of the study.

This person's role will be *solely* to ensure that each death is reported to the *CEPOD* office, the names of the patient, the consultant anaesthetist, the consultant surgeon, the operating surgeon and anaesthetising anaesthetist, together with the date of death will be reported. The local reporter will not be asked to comment.

3. Reporting Deaths

How does the local reporter find out about deaths? This is a matter for local arrangement but we suggest that the local reporter firstly discusses the mechanics of the enquiry with the District General Manager and the District Medical Officer who can help. Then one or more of the following methods may prove useful. The local reporter

(i) talks to the Administrator in charge of Medical Records who has access to a list of deaths.

(ii) arranges a weekly review of death certificates: NB—some hospitals have one death certificate book. From June 1st, 1985 new death certificates require the name of the consultant responsible if patients die in hospital.

(iii) has the junior medical staff, who fill in death certificates, report to him on a regular basis.

(iv) in collaboration with the mortuary technician reviews the mortuary register.

4. Case Selection

The confidential enquiry into perioperative deaths is interested in all deaths which occur in hospital within 30 days of an operative procedure carried out by a surgeon of any specialty (including

dentistry and gynaecology) and including procedures carried out in the ward or intensive care unit, etc. (eg, tracheostomy).

The Study Centre would like to assess all deaths occurring in patients being prepared for operation. An operation will normally be said to commence with the administration of the premedication or, in an emergency case, the booking of the operating theatre. If you are in any doubt as to whether a patient should be included, please report the death, since inappropriate cases can be excluded from the analysis.

The enquiry does *not* include deaths relating to:

(i) diagnostic procedures carried out by physicians or other non-surgeons.

(ii) therapeutic procedures carried out by physicians and other non-surgeons.

(iii) radiological procedures performed solely by a radiologist without a surgeon present.

(iv) maternal deaths (See 7.2 of the Protocol).

(v) cardiac surgery (See 7.2 of the Protocol).

5. The Enquiry does not include deaths in private hospitals, but we stress that all patients, including private patients in NHS hospitals, are included.

6. Deaths at Home

Deaths which occur at home within 30 days of surgery should be reported to us whenever possible. However, we are not (for logistic reasons) asking the General Practitioners to report them. We have informed all the Family Practitioner Committees that the Enquiry is proceeding and welcome information from any source (See 7.2 of the Protocol). It is estimated from linkage data that we will lose approximately 6% of deaths as a result of this exclusion.

A list of assessors is available from CEPOD on request to:

Mr Nigel Buck, MSc
14 Palace Court
LONDON W2 4HT
Tel: 01-727 4547

Assessors have been chosen because they are respected authorities within their specialty. The list of assessors includes academic, non-academic, teaching, non-teaching hospital staff, from metropolitan, provincial, regional and small town practises, both newly appointed and senior consultants; assessors will be chosen appropriately so that the study results will reflect the practice of surgery and anaesthesia as it exists in the study regions. It is not the intention to apply novel or unrealistic standards.

Assessors appropriate to the case in question will be selected from the list and will normally practise outside the region from which the questionnaire came.

8. Completion of Questionnaire

Once we have heard from the local reporters that a death has occurred, provided the consultant anaesthetist *and* the consultant surgeon have previously agreed to participate in the study, a questionnaire will be sent to the consultant surgeon and consultant anaesthetist.

It is our recommendation that consultants ask their junior staff to complete the questionnaire from the patient's notes. When the form is completed the consultant and his junior should review it together, the consultant should then return it *as soon as possible* to allow the assessment to take place within six weeks (See 8.9 of the Protocol).

It is hoped that the 'joint' completion of the form will act as an educational process by reviewing the particular case in a manner

4

141   *APPENDIX 3: SUPPLEMENTARY NOTES TO PROTOCOL*

---

not previously attempted. Indeed we hope that the discipline of completing the questionnaire will become the framework of a local mortality review in each surgical unit.

Trainees may write to us under separate cover if they so wish, any communication will be treated with total confidentiality in the same way as other data collected by CEPOD.

9. Assessments

(a) Self. Those completing the form are asked on each questionnaire to assess themselves pre, per and post-operatively (marks out of 10).

(b) External. Once we receive a questionnaire duly completed we will remove any identifying features and send it to an external assessor. He will return the form to us with his own assessment of pre, per and post-operative performance (marks out of 10).

If you wish, the external assessments will be available to you if you correctly identify yourself (See 9.7 of the Protocol). You will not know the identity of the assessor, and the assessor will not know your identity. The study examines major deficiencies in the practice of surgery and anaesthesia, and *not* an individual's practice.

10. Other Hospitals

For the present, deaths related only to NHS hospitals and HM Armed Forces Hospitals are being studied. Deaths in private hospitals are not being studied.

11. The Coroner and Autopsy Findings

Reports made to the Coroner by pathologists after a coroner's autopsy are the property of the Coroner (the Crown). However, the Coroner's Society (letter 10th April 1985) are assisting this Enquiry and these reports could be made available to CEPOD if requested. All the Coroners in the regions have been informed of the enquiry.

5

Association of Anaesthetists   Association of Surgeons

of Great Britain and Ireland   of Great Britain and Ireland

LOCAL REPORTING FORM

Confidential Enquiry into Perioperative Deaths

Please use ball point pen

FORM NO: _____

(PLEASE USE CONSECUTIVE NUMBERS 000 – 100)

ARE THE CONSULTANTS BELOW PARTICIPATING IN THE STUDY? _____ Y/N

SEND THIS FORM AND TWO OF ITS ATTACHED COPIES AS SOON AS POSSIBLE TO NIGEL BUCK, CEPOD, IN THE PREPAID ENVELOPE PROVIDED.

PLEASE RETAIN BOTTOM COPY ONLY FOR YOUR OWN RECORDS

IDENTIFYING DETAILS

NAME OF PATIENT: _____

NAME OF CONSULTANT SURGEON IN CHARGE: _____

NAME AND STATUS OF OPERATING SURGEON: _____

(PLEASE RING)   HS   SHO   REG   S REG   CONS   A SPEC   OTHER

NAME OF CONSULTANT ANAESTHETIST IN CHARGE: _____

NAME AND STATUS OF ANAESTHETIST: _____

(PLEASE RING)   SHO   REG   S REG   CONS   GP   CLIN. ASST   A SPEC

DATE OF DEATH: _____

DATE OF BIRTH: _____

DATE OF OPERATION: _____

HOSPITAL NAME AND ADDRESS: _____

---

12. *Publication of Results*

Results of the Pilot Study in three districts will not be published. It is our intention to hold regional meetings at which pooled data from the main study will be available to consultants. We will *not* publish data which will identify individuals, hospitals, or districts—the Region will be the smallest unit of identification. Results will also be presented to Associations and other professional meetings and committees.

After the regional results meetings and on completion of the Enquiry and analysis of results a report will be published. The names of participating consultants will be given in alphabetical order and their help acknowledged in the report. Similarly the assessors will be thanked.

13. *Funding*

The Nuffield Provincial Hospitals Trust together with the King Edward's Hospital Fund for London are providing the funds for this enquiry.

14.

If you encounter any problems please do not hesitate to contact any of the clinical co-ordinators:

Dr J. N. Lunn   0222 763601 (Direct Line)
Mr H. B. Devlin   0642 603571 (Direct Line)
Professor J. S. P. Lumley   01-600 9000 (Ext. 2560)

NOTES WITH THE QUESTIONNAIRE

OBJECTIVES

The Confidential Enquiry into Perioperative Deaths aims to enumerate the number of deaths which occur within 30 days of a surgical procedure and to identify remediable factors in the practice of surgery and anaesthesia. A fruitful outcome to the Enquiry will be a major achievement by the medical profession in the field of medical audit. These deaths are to be assessed independently in relation to the following items:

   (i) the clinical cause of death (i.e. not just the pathological diagnosis),

   (ii) the contributory factors of the anaesthetic management,

   (iii) the contributory factors of the surgical management including the surgical decisions,

   (iv) the part played by other causes,

   (v) to identify avoidable factors which, if absent, might have contributed to survival,

   (vi) to identify clinical deficiencies,

   (vii) to identify organisational deficiencies.

COMPLETION OF FORM

The consultant is responsible for ensuring that this form is completed correctly. When **completed the consultant should sign the front sheet to mark it as a true record.**

1. It is our recommendation that the consultants ask their junior staff to complete the questionnaire from the patient's notes. When the form is completed the consultant and his junior should review it together, the consultant should then return it AS SOON AS POSSIBLE to allow the assessment to take place within the 6 weeks cycle.

   This "joint" completion is intended as an educative exercise and we hope that the case will be reviewed in this way.

2. Many of the questions are of the yes/no type or there is a list from which a choice may be made. Please give your answer by circling the appropriate word(s) or ticking the correct box.

   e.g. ⟨CONS⟩ or   Yes (✓) No ( )

3. There are 72 questions to answer. Neither the questions nor the lists are intended to suggest standards of good practice: they are designed to assist us in the collection and interpretation of data.

4. Please expand your answers in any way you consider might be helpful.

5. If you are unable to answer any question because there was no record kept please indicate this by placing **NRK** against the question.

6. CONSULTANTS

If you wish to write to CEPOD under separate cover please do so.

TRAINEES

If you wish to communicate some other item(s) of information please do so under separate cover.

7. OPERATING NOTE/AUTOPSY REPORT

Please enclose a facsimile or photocopy of both the operating record and of the autopsy report — any identifying features will be removed prior to assessment.

The Coroner's Society is supporting this Enquiry; Coroner's autopsy reports are valuable to assessors and where appropriate please try to obtain a copy of the autopsy report for us.

3

---

of Great Britain and Ireland

of Great Britain and Ireland

S

Confidential Enquiry into Perioperative Deaths

Six weeks after this form has been returned to the study centre you may telephone 01-580-8697 and the CEPOD office will read the appropriate assessor's scores to you, together with your *own* scores if you wish, provided that you correctly identify yourself, your patient by name and hospital number, the study code number and the telephone number which you have given below. This facility will only be available for six further weeks. No correspondence about individual case reports can be undertaken by anyone concerned in this study. These caveats and conditions are based on legal advice and are entirely to ensure confidentiality.

THIS SHEET WILL BE REMOVED BEFORE ANY ASSESSMENT IS MADE.

THIS WHOLE DOCUMENT WILL BE SHREDDED AT THE COMPLETION OF THE ENQUIRY.

IN ORDER TO PRESERVE TOTAL CONFIDENTIALITY YOU MUST NOT PHOTOCOPY ANY OF THIS DOCUMENT.

All the information you have given us, except your self assessment score, is in the patient's notes. You can consult the notes again after you have received the assessors score back from us.

Please refer to Question 72, then write your telephone number here: _____

CONSULTANTS: Please initial form here once completed _____

       PLEASE WRITE IN BLACK BALL POINT PEN

1

143   *APPENDIX 3: QUESTIONNAIRE. Surgical*

To be completed by the operating team with supervision and **agreement by the Consultant Surgeon.**

Juniors may write to us in confidence about aspects of this case under separate cover if they should wish.

1. Specialty surgical interest of Consultant Surgeon:

   a) GENERAL ( )
   b) GENERAL with special interest in Paediatric ( )
   c) GENERAL with special interest in Urology ( )
   d) GENERAL with special interest in Vascular ( )
   e) GENERAL with other special interest in _____
   f) A & E ( )
   g) CARDIOTHORACIC ( )
   h) DENTAL/ORAL ( )
   i) GYNAECOLOGY ( )
   j) NEUROSURGERY ( )
   k) OPHTHALMOLOGY ( )
   l) ORTHOPAEDIC ( )
   m) OTORHINOLARYNGOLOGY ( )
   n) PAEDIATRIC ( )
   o) PLASTIC ( )
   p) TRANSPLANTATION ( )
   q) UROLOGY ( )
   r) OTHER _____ ( )

OPERATIVE DETAILS

2. *Operation undertaken _____

*If Local anaesthetic given by surgeon — please complete question 39.

MULTIPLE OPERATIONS

If this operation is the most recent in a sequence or was followed by a minor procedure, please enumerate the other operations.

Operation	Date	Specialty of Operating Surgeon
a)		
b)		
c)		
d)		

5

---

8. **MULTIPLE OPERATIONS**

   If there has been more than one operation within 30 days of the main operation indicated in the form, please complete question 2.

9. If any additional information is required one of the clinical co-ordinators will contact you directly.

10. If you have any difficulties please contact the Administrator. —   ***after 1st January, 1986**

Mr Nigel Buck, MSc
14 Palace Court
London W2 4HT
Tel: 01-727-4547

9 Bedford Square
London WC1B 3RA
Tel: 01-580-8697

or one of the Clinical Co-ordinators:
Mr H. B. Devlin, FRCS, 0642 603571 (Direct Line)
Professor J. S. P. Lumley, FRCS, 01-600 9000 (× 2560)
Dr J. N. Lunn, FFARCS, 0222 763601 (Direct Line)

11. PLEASE RETURN THIS FORM **AS SOON AS POSSIBLE** IN THE PREPAID ENVELOPE PROVIDED.

PREOPERATIVE ASSESSMENT

19. Please record all surgical staff who took history before operation?

    (This can be multiple entry) CONS, ASS SPEC, S.R., REG, SHO, HS, MEDICAL STUDENT, OTHER (____)

    Specify any of these who were locums ____

20. Please ring all surgeons who examined the patient before operation

    (This can be multiple entry) CONS, ASS SPEC, S.R., REG, SHO, HS, MEDICAL STUDENT, OTHER (____)

    Specify any of these who were locums ____

21. Working diagnosis by most senior member of surgical team: ____

22. Proposed operation: ____

23. What drug (excluding premedication) or other therapy (including relevant surgical operations) was the patient receiving, (or had received) prior to admission to your hospital? DO NOT include resuscitation therapy

    a) Steroids ____ YES ( ) NO ( )

    b) Antihypertensives ____ YES ( ) NO ( )

    c) H_2 Blockers ____ YES ( ) NO ( )

    d) Diuretics ____ YES ( ) NO ( )

    e) Cardiac or anti-dysrhythmic drugs ____ YES ( ) NO ( )

    f) Contraceptive Pill ____ YES ( ) NO ( )

    g) Cytotoxic drugs ____ YES ( ) NO ( )

    h) Anticoagulants ____ YES ( ) NO ( )

    i) Antibiotics ____ YES ( ) NO ( )

    j) Antidiabetic ____ YES ( ) NO ( )

    k) Other (Specify) ____ YES ( ) NO ( )

    ____

    ____

7

---

3. **Admission:** 1. Elective ( )   2. Urgent ( )   3. Emergency ( )

   Definitions

   1. Elective — at time consented between patient and surgical service.
   2. Urgent — within 48 hours of consultation.
   3. Emergency — immediately following consultation.

4. Admission: Date: ____ Time: ____ (24 hour clock)

5. Was this a day case Patient? YES ( ) NO ( )

6. Date of transfer to surgical team if different from above ____

7. Was the patient transferred from another Hospital? YES ( ) NO ( )

   If yes, a) from Non-NHS ( )
           b) from same District ( )
           c) from same Region ( )

8. Who made the final decision to operate? Cons, Ass Spec, SR, Reg, SHO, HS, Med Student, Other (____)

9. Decision to operate: Date ____ Time ____ (24 hour clock) **Day M T W Th F S S**

9a. **Operation:** Date: ____ Time ____ (24 hour clock) **Day M T W Th F S S**

10. Was the Consultant Surgeon consulted before operation? YES ( ) NO ( )

11. How long before the operative procedure was the decision to operate taken? ____

12. Number of days from admission to operation: ____

13. **Death:** Date: ____ Time: ____ (24 hour clock)

14. Number of days from operation to death: ____

PATIENT DETAILS

15. Date of Birth: ____ / ____ / ____
                    DAY   MONTH   YEAR

16. Sex: a) Male ( )
          b) Female ( )

17. Weight: ____ st ____ lb or ____ kg or Thin ( ) Average ( ) Obese/Overweight ( ) or unrecorded ( )

    Height: ____ ft ____ in or ____ cm or Short ( ) Average ( ) Tall ( ) or unrecorded ( )

    Please indicate the patients physique when for any reason it was not possible to weigh and measure the height of the patient.

18. To which ethnic group did the patient belong?
    a. Europid ( ) b. African ( ) c. Asian ( ) d. Oriental ( )

6

145   *APPENDIX 3: QUESTIONNAIRES. Surgeons*

PLEASE DO NOT PHOTOCOPY

PREOPERATIVE PREPARATION

27. What precautions or therapy were undertaken immediately preoperatively to ensure adequate physiological function? Tick one for each.

	YES	NO	NOT APPLICABLE
a) Pulse rate recording	( )	( )	( )
b) Blood pressure recording	( )	( )	( )
c) Central venous pressure measurement	( )	( )	( )
d) Cardiac support drugs or anti-dysrythmic agents	( )	( )	( )
e) Vasopressors	( )	( )	( )
f) Gastric aspiration	( )	( )	( )
g) Urinary catheter	( )	( )	( )
h) Maintain adequate urine output	( )	( )	( )
i) Intravenous fluid	( )	( )	( )
j) Blood transfusion	( )	( )	( )
k) Optimal preoperative rehydration	( )	( )	( )
l) Diuretics	( )	( )	( )
m) Anticoagulants	( )	( )	( )
n) Antibiotics	( )	( )	( )
o) Chest physiotherapy	( )	( )	( )
p) Oxygen therapy	( )	( )	( )
q) Mucolytics	( )	( )	( )
r) Airway protection e.g. Head injuries	( )	( )	( )
s) Tracheal intubation	( )	( )	( )
t) Mechanical ventilation	( )	( )	( )
u) Stabilization of spinal fractures	( )	( )	( )
v) Stabilization of limb fractures	( )	( )	( )
w) Parenteral feeding	( )	( )	( )
x) Other (Specify)	( )	( )	( )

OPERATION

PLEASE SEND FACSIMILE OR PHOTOCOPY OF THE OPERATION NOTE WITH THIS FORM. Any identification will be removed before assessment. (Please see note 7 on front sheet)

28. Grade of operating surgeon

CONS, ASS SPEC, S.R., REG, SHO, HS,

MEDICAL STUDENT, OTHER (_____)

Specify if locum

9

PLEASE DO NOT PHOTOCOPY

24. Record the results of these preoperative investigations carried out before operation. (Even if not relevant).

	Results	Was the Result available and Noted Preop?
a) Fever greater than 37°C	_____	YES ( ) NO ( )
b) Haemoglobin	_____	YES ( ) NO ( )
c) Blood urea	_____	YES ( ) NO ( )
d) Plasma/sodium	_____	YES ( ) NO ( )
e) Plasma/bilirubin	_____	YES ( ) NO ( )
f) Serum amylase	_____	YES ( ) NO ( )
g) Plasma albumin	_____	YES ( ) NO ( )
h) Blood glucose	_____	YES ( ) NO ( )
i) Cross matching	_____	YES ( ) NO ( )
j) Sickle cell test	_____	YES ( ) NO ( )
k) Coagulation defects test	_____	YES ( ) NO ( )
l) Electrocardiograph	_____	YES ( ) NO ( )
m) Chest X-ray	_____	YES ( ) NO ( )
n) Respiratory function tests	_____	YES ( ) NO ( )
o) Blood gases	_____	YES ( ) NO ( )
p) Urine analysis (Ward or Laboratory)	_____	YES ( ) NO ( )
q) Radiological e.g. C.T. Scan	_____	YES ( ) NO ( )
r) Ultrasound e.g. for gallstones	_____	YES ( ) NO ( )
s) Biopsy	_____	YES ( ) NO ( )
t) Other (specify)	_____	YES ( ) NO ( )

25. Coexisting, active medical diagnoses:
Specify disorder:

a. Respiratory _____
b. Cardiac _____
c. Neurological _____
d. Endocrine _____
e. Alimentary _____
f. Renal _____
g. Musculoskeletal _____
h. Haematological _____
i. Other _____

26. ASA grade (see classification on back sheet) 1 – 5 _____

Note principal abnormalities for Grades 2 – 5 _____

29. Who started the Operation? (Grade) _____

30. Assisted by: _____
(including supervisory surgeon)

CONS, ASS SPEC, SR, REG, SHO, HS,

MEDICAL STUDENT OTHER (_____)

Specify any of these were locums _____

31. Did the operating surgeon, immediately before operation:

(i) identify the patient and notes? YES ( ) NO ( )

(ii) Review the notes and working diagnosis? YES ( ) NO ( )

32. How do you classify this operation?

1. Emergency ( ) 2. Urgent ( ) 3. Scheduled ( ) 4. Elective ( )

Definitions

1. **Emergency** — **immediate** operation, resuscitation simultaneous with surgical treatment (e.g. ruptured aneurysm; head, chest and abdominal injuries). Operation usually within one hour.

2. **Urgent** — **delayed** operation as soon as possible **after** resuscitation (e.g. intestinal obstruction, embolism, perforation, major fractures). Operation usually within 24 hours.

3. **Scheduled** — an early operation but not immediately life saving (e.g. cancer, cardio-vascular surgery). Operation usually between 1 and 3 weeks.

4. **Elective** — operation at a time to suit both patient and surgeon (e.g. cholecystectomy).

33. How many times had the most senior surgeon at the operation undertaken this or similar procedure?

0   <5   <10   <15   <25   >25

34. Time of start of operation:* _____ (24 hour clock)

35. Duration of operation*: _____ H
*(not including anaesthetic time)

36. Was this too long? YES ( ) NO ( ) If yes specify why _____

37. Was there any intra-operative disaster? YES ( ) NO ( )

If yes please specify _____

_____

10

147   *APPENDIX 3: QUESTIONNAIRES. Surgeons*

---

38. How many hours had the operating surgeon been on continuous active duty before

the operation? _____ H

Local Anaesthesia

39. 1. Was local or regional anaesthesia administered by a surgeon in the reported operation?

YES ( ) NO ( ) If NO go to Q40

2. What anaesthesic agent was used? _____

3. Did the solution contain Adrenaline? YES ( ) NO ( )

If yes what concentration? _____

4. Was any other drug administered with the anaesthetic agent? YES ( ) NO ( )

Specify _____

5. What volume and concentration of anaesthetic solution was administered?

_____

6. During what time? _____

7. What was the maximum safe dose of anaesthetic agent permissible for this patient? _____

8. What monitoring was used during the anaesthetic?

a) Pulse rate   YES ( ) NO ( )
b) Blood pressure   YES ( ) NO ( )
c) E.C.G.   YES ( ) NO ( )

9. Were there any adverse effects from the local/regional anaesthetic? YES ( ) NO ( )

If yes, specify _____

10. Was anaesthetic advice sought prior to the local/regional anaesthetic? YES ( ) NO ( )

11. Were facilities for resuscitation including airway management available immediately during this local/regional anaesthetic?

YES ( ) NO ( )

POSTOPERATIVE PROGRESS

INTENSIVE CARE

40. Does your hospital have
a) an I.T.U.?   YES ( ) NO ( )
b) a High dependency area?   YES ( ) NO ( )

41. a) Was the patient admitted to the I.T.U.?   YES ( ) NO ( )
b) Was the patient admitted to a High dependency area? YES ( ) NO ( )

11

	YES	NO	
h) Persistent coma (GCS <7)*	( )	( )	
i) Other organ failure ●	( )	( )	
j) Problems with postoperative analgesia	( )	( )	
k) Other complications	( )	( )	Specify

*Glasgow Coma Scale — Please see Back Sheet

47. Were any antibiotics given postoperatively? YES ( ) NO ( )   Specify which
and why

48. Was parenteral feeding used for this patient? YES ( ) NO ( )

49. Was any other non oral method of feeding used? YES ( ) NO ( )
Specify

DEATH

50. What did you think was the immediate clinical cause of death?

(This need not be a duplication of the death certificate)

51. Other relevant contributory causes of death

52. Which of these did you treat and how?

53. Was there an autopsy?   YES ( ) NO ( )   **Please send photostat of Autopsy Report**
(Please see note 8 on front page)

54. If yes did a member of the team attend?   YES ( ) NO ( )

55. What were the findings?

56. **CAUSE OF DEATH** (this is a facsimile of the death certificate: please complete it accordingly).
i. **Disease or condition directly leading to death**

a)(

due to (or as a consequence of)

13

---

42. Were these facilities adequate?   YES ( ) NO ( )
If no, specify why

43. Date of admission to ITU/HDA: _____ Time of admission _____ (24 hour clock)

44. Date of transfer _____ Transfer destination _____

45. Transfer time: _____ (24 hour clock)
Due to: a) Elective discharge   YES ( ) NO ( )
b) Pressure on beds   YES ( ) NO ( )
c) Death   YES ( ) NO ( )
d) Other, specify

POSTOPERATIVE COMPLICATIONS

46. Was the postoperative period complicated by:

	YES	NO	If yes please give evidence of this
a) Bleeding sufficient to require postoperative transfusion or re-operation	( )	( )	
b) The need for mechanical ventilation			
i) elective	( )	( )	
ii) for respiratory failure	( )	( )	
c) Sepsis			
i) wound or operation site (localized)	( )	( )	
ii) respiratory, urinary or other systematic sepsis including septicaemia	( )	( )	
d) Myocardial disorder	( )	( )	
e) Hepatic failure	( )	( )	
f) Renal failure sufficient to require dialysis	( )	( )	
g) Endocrine system failure	( )	( )	

Antecedent causes
Morbid conditions, if any, giving rise to the above cause stating the underlying condition last

( )
b)( )
c)( )

ii) **Other significant conditions** contributing to the death, but not related to the disease or condition causing it.

( )
( )

GENERAL QUESTIONS

57. Do you have regular local mortality review meetings? YES ( ) NO ( )

If yes, has this death been considered at such a local meeting? YES ( ) NO ( )

58. Was there any delay in getting the patient to the theatre?

YES ( ) NO ( ) If yes due to:

a) Availability of Surgeon? YES ( ) NO ( )
b) Availability of Anaesthetist? YES ( ) NO ( )
c) Availability of Portering? YES ( ) NO ( )
d) Availability of Nurses? YES ( ) NO ( )
e) Availability of Theatre? YES ( ) NO ( )
f) Other — specify

59. Was there any shortage of trained personnel in theatre?

YES ( ) NO ( ) If yes, please specify

60. In your opinion was there any deficiency in preoperative management?

YES ( ) NO ( ) If yes please comment

61. Were there any lack or deficiency of surgical equipment?

YES ( ) NO ( ) If yes please comment

14

149   *APPENDIX 3: QUESTIONNAIRES. Surgical*

62. Was there any technical difficulties or surgical misadventure?

YES ( ) NO ( ) if yes — specify

63. Were there any other measures which could have been taken to improve outcome?

YES ( ) NO ( ) If yes please specify

64. Did any organisational aspects, lack of resources or any other non-clinical factors contribute to the fatal outcome? YES ( ) NO ( ) If yes please specify

65. Who completed this form?

A Operating Surgeon YES ( ) NO ( )
B Trainee other than operating surgeon YES ( ) NO ( )
C Grade: (This can be multiple entry) CONS, ASS SPEC, S.R., REG, SHO, HS, MEDICAL STUDENT, OTHER (_____)

66. Were the patient's notes adequate for you to complete this form?

YES ( ) NO ( ) If no — specify

67. Do you think the previous operation(s) were related to the perioperative death you are now reporting? YES ( ) NO ( )

68. Do you think the surgical assessors should pay particular attention to the anaesthetic questionnaire on this patient?

YES ( ) NO ( ) Why?

69. Score your surgical team between 0 and 10 (e.g. 10, no fault; 7, adequate; 3, avoidable errors; 0, total failure)

a) Preoperatively
b) Peroperatively
c) Postoperatively

70. State what you would do differently next time and detail measures which **may** have prevented or delayed death.

15

S

71. Please add any further information or comments as to why this patient died.

_____
_____
_____
_____

72. Would you like to know the assessor(s) scores?   YES ( ) NO ( )

S

If yes, please make a record of this code number
and write your telephone number on the front sheet.

_____

YOU MUST *NOT* KEEP A COPY
OF THIS FORM

_____

Thank you for completing this questionnaire.

Please reply to:
Mr Nigel Buck MSc,
14 Palace Court,
London W2 4HT

01-727 4547

and after 1st January 1986
9 Bedford Square
London WC1B 3RA

01-580-8697

THIS FORM IS THE PROPERTY OF CEPOD

16

150   *APPENDICES*

GLASGOW COMA SCALE (GCS) (Question 46h)

Eye Opening	Pts	Verbal Response	Pts	Motor Response to Pain (Best Limb)	Pts
Spontaneous	4	Orientated verbal response	5	Obeys commands	5
Eye opening to speech	3	Confused verbal response	4	Localisation	4
Eye opening to pain	2	Inappropriate words	3	Flexion normal/abnormal	3
None	1	Incomprehensible sounds	2	Extension	2
		No verbal response	1	No motor response	1

DEFINITIONS (Question 26)

ASA (American Society of Anesthesiologists) classification of physical status.

Class 1 The patient has no organic, physiological, biochemical, or psychiatric disturbance. The pathological process for which operation is to be performed is localized and does not entail a systemic disturbance. Examples: a fit patient with inguinal hernia; fibroid uterus in an otherwise healthy woman.

Class 2 Mild to moderate systemic disturbance caused either by the condition to be treated surgically or by other pathophysiological processes. Examples: non- or only slightly limiting organic heart disease, mild diabetes, essential hypertension, or anaemia. Some might choose to list the extremes of age here, either the neonate or the octogenerian, even though no discernible systemic disease is present. Extreme obesity and chronic bronchitis may be included in this category.

Class 3 Severe systemic disturbance or disease from whatever cause, even though it may not be possible to define the degree of disability with finality. Examples: severely limiting organic heart disease; severe diabetes with vascular complications; moderate to severe degrees of pulmonary insufficiency; angina pectoris or healed myocardial infarction.

Class 4 Severe systemic disorders that are already life threatening, not always correctable by operation. Examples: patients with organic heart disease showing marked signs of cardiac insufficiency, persistent angina, or active myocarditis; advanced degrees of pulmonary, hepatic, renal or endocrine insufficiency.

Class 5 The moribund patient who has little chance of survival but is submitted to operation in desperation. Examples: the burst abdominal aneurysm with profound shock; major cerebral trauma with rapidly increasing intracranial pressure; massive pulmonary embolism. Most of these patients require operation as a resuscitative measure with little if any anaesthesia.

17

ANAESTHESIA

A

NOTES WITH THE QUESTIONNAIRE

OBJECTIVES

The Confidential Enquiry into Perioperative Deaths aims to enumerate the number of deaths which occur within 30 days of a surgical operation and to identify remediable factors in the practice of anaesthesia and surgery. A fruitful outcome to the Enquiry will be a major achievement by the medical profession in the field of medical audit. These deaths are to be assessed independently in relation to the following items:

(i) the clinical cause of death (i.e. not just the pathological diagnosis),

(ii) the contributory factors of the anaesthetic management,

(iii) the contributory factors of the surgical management including the surgical decisions,

(iv) the part played by other causes,

(v) to identify avoidable factors which, if absent, might have contributed to survival,

(vi) to identify organisational deficiencies.

COMPLETION OF FORM

It is important to appreciate that the consultant is responsible for the correct completion of this form. **The consultant should sign the front sheet to indicate that the form is correct.**

1. It is our recommendation that consultants ask their trainees to complete the questionnaire from the patient's notes. When the form is completed the consultant and his junior should review it together, the consultant should then return it AS SOON AS POSSIBLE to allow the assessment to take place within 6 weeks.

   This joint completion is intended as an educative exercise. We hope that case review in this way will be helpful.

2. Many of the questions are of the yes/no type or there is a list from which a choice may be made. Please give your answer by circling the appropriate word(s) or ticking the correct box.

   e.g. (CONS) or   Yes (✔) No ( )

3. There are 75 questions to answer. Neither the questions nor the lists are intended to suggest standards of good practice: they are designed to assist us in the collection of data.

4. Please feel free to expand your answers in any way you consider might be helpful.

5. If you are unable to answer any question because there was no record kept please indicate this by placing **NRK** against the question.

6. **CONSULTANTS**

   If you wish to write to CEPOD under separate cover please do so.

   TRAINEES

   If you wish to communicate some other item(s) of information please do so under separate cover.

7. **ANAESTHETIC RECORD/AUTOPSY REPORT**

   Please enclose an anonymous facsimile or photocopy of both the anaesthetic record and the autopsy report. Any identifying features will be removed.

   The Coroner's Society is supporting this Enquiry; coroner's autopsy reports are valuable to assessors and wherever appropriate please try to obtain a copy of the autopsy report for us.

3

Association of Surgeons

of Great Britain and Ireland

A

Confidential Enquiry into Perioperative Deaths

of Great Britain and Ireland

Six weeks after this form has been returned to the study centre you may telephone 01-580-8697 and the CEPOD office will read the appropriate assessor's scores to you; together with your *own* scores if you wish, provided that you correctly identify yourself, your patient by name and hospital number, the study code number and the telephone number which you will have given below. This facility will only be available for six further weeks. No correspondence about individual case reports can be undertaken by anyone concerned in this study. These caveats and conditions are based on legal advice and are entirely to ensure confidentiality.

THIS SHEET WILL BE **REMOVED** BEFORE ANY ASSESSMENT IS **MADE**.

THIS WHOLE DOCUMENT WILL BE SHREDDED AT THE COMPLETION OF THE ENQUIRY.

IN ORDER TO PRESERVE TOTAL CONFIDENTIALITY YOU MUST NOT PHOTOCOPY ANY OF THIS DOCUMENT.

Please refer to Question 75, then write your telephone number here: _____

CONSULTANTS Please initial form here once completed _____

PLEASE WRITE IN BLACK BALL POINT PEN

APPENDIX 3: QUESTIONNAIRES. Anaesthetic

1

A

To be completed by the anaesthetist. If this was a trainee the form should be agreed by the consultant anaesthetist responsible, or the one on call, or the chairman of the division of anaesthetics.

BASIC INFORMATION

1. Grade(s) of anaesthetist(s)   SHO   Reg   S. Reg   Cons GP

   Clin. Asst.   Ass. Spec

1a. Specify if Locum

2. **TRAINEES** Has this form been agreed by the consultant responsible?
   YES ( )   NO ( )

3. Did you inform or seek advice from your consultant?   YES ( )   NO ( )

4. What operation was performed? _____

   _____

MULTIPLE OPERATIONS

If this operation is the most recent in a sequence or was followed by a minor procedure please enumerate the other operations

Operation	Date performed
a)	
b)	
c)	
d)	

THE PATIENT

5. Date of Birth: ____ / ____ / ____
   DAY   MONTH   YEAR

6. a) Male ( )
   b) Female ( )

7. Weight: _____ st _____ lb or _____ kg or unrecorded

   Height: _____ ft _____ in or _____ cm or unrecorded

5

---

8. **MULTIPLE OPERATIONS**
   If the patient has been operated on again within 30 days of the main operation indicated in the form, please complete question 4.

9. If any additional information is required one of the clinical co-ordinators will contact you directly.

10. If you have any difficulties please contact the Administrator — **after 1st January, 1986**

    Mr Nigel Buck, MSc
    14 Palace Court
    London W2 4HT
    Tel: 01-727-4547

    9 Bedford Square
    London WC1B 3RA
    Tel: 01-580-8697

    or one of the clinical co-ordinators:
    Mr H. B. Devlin, 0642 603571 (Direct Line)
    Professor J. S. P. Lumley, 01-600 9000 ($\times$2560)
    Dr J. N. Lunn, 0222 763601 (Direct Line)

11. PLEASE RETURN THIS FORM **AS SOON AS POSSIBLE** IN THE PREPAID ENVELOPE PROVIDED.

Indicate the patient's physique to us when this information is not available:

Physique (Weight)   Thin ( )   Average ( )   Obese/Overweight ( )
Physique (Height)   Short ( )   Average ( )   Tall ( )

8.   **ADMISSION:** 1. Elective ( )   2. Urgent ( )   3. Emergency ( )

(For definitions see Back Sheet)

9.   Admission: Date:_____   Time:_____ (24 hour clock)
10. Operation: Date:_____   Time:_____ (24 hour clock) Day M T W Th F S S
11. Death: Date:_____   Time:_____ (24 hour clock)
12. Location of patient at death:
a) Theatre
b) Recovery
c) ITU
d) HDA
e) Ward
f) Home

13. To which ethnic group did patient belong?
a. Europid ( )   b. African ( )   c. Asian ( )   d. Oriental ( )

14. Were you consulted (as distinct from notification, see question 26) preoperatively by surgeons?   YES ( ) NO ( )

15. Did you visit the patient preoperatively?   YES ( ) NO ( )

16. Were any of the following investigations done before the operation?
Answer Yes or No for each and record value/interpretation.

Please record results

a) Chest X-ray _____ YES ( ) NO ( )
b) Haemoglobin _____ YES ( ) NO ( )
c) Blood urea _____ YES ( ) NO ( )
d) Plasma electrolytes _____ YES ( ) NO ( )
e) Electrocardiograph _____ YES ( ) NO ( )
f) Liver function tests _____ YES ( ) NO ( )
g) Urinalysis (Ward (or laboratory)) _____ YES ( ) NO ( )
h) Respiratory function tests _____ YES ( ) NO ( )
i) Blood gas analysis _____ YES ( ) NO ( )
j) Blood glucose _____ YES ( ) NO ( )
k) Sickle cell test _____ YES ( ) NO ( )
l) Other (specify) _____ YES ( ) NO ( )

Ring which of these were noted by you before you started the anaesthetic. (e.g. a,©i,)

a   b   c   d   e   f   g   h   i   j   k   l

6

153   *APPENDIX 3: QUESTIONNAIRES. Anaesthetic*

17. Coexisting active medical diagnoses: Specify disorder:
a) Respiratory _____
b) Cardiac _____
c) Neurological _____
d) Endocrine _____
e) Alimentary _____
f) Renal _____
g) Musculoskeletal _____
h) Haematological _____
i) Other _____

18. What drug (excluding premedication) or other therapy was the patient receiving at the time of the operation (or if relevant to anaesthesia, had received) prior to surgery? Please ring and specify both drug and dose.
a) Antibiotic _____
b) Anticholinesterase _____
c) Anticoagulant _____
d) Anticonvulsant _____
e) Antidepressant _____
f) Antidiabetic _____
g) Antidysrhythmic _____
h) Antihypertensive _____
i) Cardiac glycoside _____
j) Contraceptive _____
k) Cytotoxic _____
l) Diuretic _____
m) Phenothiazine _____
n) Steroid _____
o) Other (specify) _____

19. ASA status 1-5 (see final page) _____
Note principal abnormalities for Grades 2-5 _____

7

PREPARATION

20. Indicate measures you took to improve the respiratory system **before** induction of anaesthesia.

Bronchodilators   YES ( )   NO ( )   Specify nature and dose ___

Chest physiotherapy   YES ( )   NO ( )

Airway management   YES ( )   NO ( )   Specify ___

20a. Were you satisfied with the general preparation of the patient? YES ( )   NO ( )

If no, explain:

21. What was the preoperative blood pressure? ___ / ___ mm Hg

22. Did you prescribe **premedicant** drugs?   YES ( )   NO ( )

If yes, please indicate drug(s) and dosage?

DOSE

Atropine ___
Diazepam ___
Droperidol ___
Fentanyl ___
Hyoscine ___
Lorazepam ___
Morphine ___
Oral barbiturate (specify) ___
Papaveretum ___
Pethidine ___
Phenoperidine ___
Phenothiazine (specify) ___
Other (specify) ___

23. Indicate **pre-operative** precautions you took to minimise the risk of pulmonary aspiration (note question 35)

a) Antacids   YES ( )   NO ( )   Specify nature and dose ___

b) H$_2$ antagonists   YES ( )   NO ( )   Specify nature and dose ___

c) Metoclopramide   YES ( )   NO ( )   Dose ___

d) Stomach tube   YES ( )   NO ( )

---

24. Indicate additional measures you started in order to improve the cardiovascular function **before** and **at the induction** of anaesthesia.

a) Crystalloid I.V. fluids (Ringer lactate, dextrose etc)   YES ( )   NO ( )
    Specify type & volume ___

b) Colloid I.V. fluids (dextran/gelatin etc)   YES ( )   NO ( )
    specify type & volume ___

c) Whole blood transfusion   YES ( )   NO ( )

d) Red cell component transfusion   YES ( )   NO ( )
    specify volume ___

e) Other component transfusion   YES ( )   NO ( )
    specify type & volume ___

f) Inotropes   YES ( )   NO ( )
    specify nature & volume ___

g) Vasopressors   YES ( )   NO ( )
    specify nature & volume ___

h) Other ___   Specify ___

25. Who made the decision to operate?   HO   Reg   SR   Cons   Ass Spec   Other

26. Date and time of **your** notification of need for operation ___

OPERATION

27. Grade of operating surgeon: SHO   Reg   SR   Cons   Ass Spec   HS   Other
(specify if locum)

28. How would **you** classify this operation? — (For definitions see back sheet)

1. Emergency ( )   2. Urgent ( )   3. Scheduled ( )   4. Elective ( )

29. Was there any delay in getting the patient to the theatre?   YES ( )   NO ( )

Due to:

a) Availability of Surgeon?   YES ( )   NO ( )
b) Availability of Anaesthetist?   YES ( )   NO ( )
c) Availability of Portering?   YES ( )   NO ( )
d) Availability of Nurses?   YES ( )   NO ( )
e) Availability of Theatre?   YES ( )   NO ( )

f) Other (specify) ___

If yes to any of the above — please explain ___

THE ANAESTHETIC

30. Is there an anaesthetic record in the notes? YES ( ) NO ( ) **If yes, please send a photocopy.**
(Please note section 7 on the front page)

31. Time of start of anaesthetic _____ (24 hour clock)

32. Time of finish of anaesthetic _____ (24 hour clock)

33. What type of anaesthetic was used?

    a) General _____ YES ( ) NO ( )
    b) Local _____ YES ( ) NO ( )
    c) Regional _____ YES ( ) NO ( )
    d) Combined _____ YES ( ) NO ( )

34. What precautions did you take **at induction** to reduce the risk of pulmonary aspiration?

    Cricoid pressure   YES ( ) NO ( )
    Postural changes head up   YES ( ) NO ( )
                  head down   YES ( ) NO ( )
                  lateral   YES ( ) NO ( )

    Other (specify) _____

GENERAL ANAESTHESIA

35. What agents were used? – please ring agent(s) used e.g. (Halothane)

General anaesthetic agents

Inhalation

                                    Dose

    a) Diethyl ether _____
    b) Halothane _____
    c) Isoflurane _____
    d) Nitrous oxide _____
    e) Trichloroethylene _____
    f) Enflurane _____
    g) Other (specify) _____

Please ring drug(s) or agent(s) used

Parenteral (state dose)   Dose

    a) Alfentanil _____
    b) Diazepam _____
    c) Disoprofol _____
    d) Droperidol _____
    e) Etomidate _____

10

(Please ring drug(s) or system(s) used)

                                      Dose

    f) Fentanyl _____
    g) Ketamine _____ (state route)
    h) Methohexitone _____
    i) Morphine _____
    j) Pethidine _____
    k) Phenoperidine _____
    l) Phenothiazine (Specify) _____
    m) Thiopentone _____
    n) Other (specify) _____

Muscle relaxants (state dose)   Dose

    a) Not used _____
    b) Alcuronium _____
    c) Atracurium _____
    d) Pancuronium _____
    e) Suxamethonium _____
    f) Tubocurarine _____
    g) Vecuronium _____
    h) Other non-depolarising _____

Reversal agents (state dose)   Dose

    a) Not used _____
    b) Atropine _____
    c) Glycopyrronium _____
    d) Neostigmine _____
    e) Other reversal agent _____

Other drug therapy (specify drug and dose)
                                      Dose

    a) Analeptic _____
    b) Antidysrhythmic _____
    c) Antiemetic _____
    d) Anticoagulant _____
    e) Diuretic (excl. osmotic) _____
    f) Electrolyte _____
    g) Hypotensive _____
    h) Inotropic _____
    i) Narcotic antagonist _____

11

PLEASE DO NOT PHOTOCOPY

(Please ring drug(s) or system(s) used)
REGIONAL/LOCAL ANAESTHESIA
Technique
a) Epidural: caudal/lumbar/thoracic/cervical
b) Intravenous regional
c) Nerve or plexus (specify)
d) Spinal

Agent (State Dose)
a) Bupivacaine
b) Cinchocaine
c) Lignocaine
d) Prilocaine
e) Vasoconstrictor (specify)
f) Other drug

36. Did you administer an oxygen rich mixture:-
a) Before and at induction? YES ( ) NO ( )
b) Before tracheal intubation? YES ( ) NO ( )
c) Alone, during the operation? YES ( ) NO ( )

MAINTENANCE

37. What intravenous fluids (excluding blood) were used during the anaesthetic? ____ YES ( ) NO ( ) specify type
Specify volume.
a) Colloid (dextran etc) ____ YES ( ) NO ( )
b) Ringer lactate (Hartmans) ____ YES ( ) NO ( )
c) Dextrose 5% ____ YES ( ) NO ( )
d) Dextrose/saline ____ YES ( ) NO ( )
e) Saline ____ YES ( ) NO ( )
f) Mannitol (specify %) ____ YES ( ) NO ( )
g) Other ____ YES ( ) NO ( ) specify type and volume

38. What was the blood loss? ____ (ml)
Estimated/measured?

39. Was crossmatched blood available? YES ( ) NO ( )

40. What volume of blood was given? ____ (ml)

41. What type (e.g. plasma reduced)?

42. *Which of the following did you display/use/measure to monitor the patient during the operation?
a) Pulse i) Manual ie. palpation YES ( ) NO ( )
     ii) Meter YES ( ) NO ( )
b) Indirect blood pressure (non invasive) YES ( ) NO ( )

*Please note paragraph 3 on the front page.

13

PLEASE DO NOT PHOTOCOPY

(Please ring drug(s) or system(s) used)   **Dose**
j) Oxytocic
k) Steroid
l) Vagolytic
m) Vasopressor
n) Other (specify)

Inhalation breathing system
a) None
b) Absorption
c) Bain
d) Lack
f) Magill
g) No-rebreathing
h) Valveless (eg T.piece)
i) Other (specify)

Ventilation during maintenance
a) Controlled
   Manual
   Machine (specify type)
b) Spontaneous

Tracheal intubation   **Tube size**
a) None
b) Armoured orotracheal
c) Bronchus blocker and orotracheal
d) Double lumen tube (e.g. Carlens)
e) Bronchial
f) Nasotracheal – blind
g) Nasotracheal – direct vision
h) Orotracheal – direct vision
i) Tracheostomy (in existence pre-operatively)

Cuff or pack?
Cuff
Pack

12

c) ECG _____ YES ( ) NO ( )
d) Urine output _____ YES ( ) NO ( )
e) CVP _____ YES ( ) NO ( )
f) Stethoscope _____ YES ( ) NO ( )
g) Ventilation volume _____ YES ( ) NO ( )
h) Airway pressure _____ YES ( ) NO ( )
i) Expired carbon dioxide analysis _____ YES ( ) NO ( )
j) Direct arterial blood pressure (invasive) _____ YES ( ) NO ( )
k) Inspired oxygen analysis _____ YES ( ) NO ( )
l) Peripheral nerve stimulator _____ YES ( ) NO ( )
m) Core thermometry _____ YES ( ) NO ( )
n) Ventilator alarm _____ YES ( ) NO ( )
o) Pulmonary arterial pressure _____ YES ( ) NO ( )
p) Other, please specify _____ YES ( ) NO ( )

43. Was there any lack, or defect, of anaesthetic equipment? YES ( ) NO ( )
If yes, please define.

44. Did you have adequate trained help? YES ( ) NO ( )
If no, please explain

45. If you are a trainee did a consultant come to help you in the management of the anaesthetic? YES ( ) NO ( )
If yes, please explain

46. Did you think your fatigue was in anyway related to the outcome? YES ( ) NO ( )
If yes please explain

47. Was there any misadventure during anaesthetic? YES ( ) NO ( )
If yes, please describe

If yes, was the consultant anaesthetist informed? YES ( ) NO ( ) Not applicable ( )

CARDIAC ARREST

48. Did cardiac arrest occur during the administration of the anaesthetic? YES ( ) NO ( )
If yes, time from induction _____ minutes.

14

49. Did cardiac arrest occur **before** return to the general ward? YES ( ) NO ( )
If no, go to Question 52.

50. Was resuscitation attempted? YES ( ) NO ( ) Not applicable ( )
If yes, give all techniques of resuscitation and drugs used: _____

51. Was resuscitation successful in terms of:
a) Recovery of heart beat _____ YES ( ) NO ( ) Not applicable ( )
b) Recovery of reflexes _____ YES ( ) NO ( ) Not applicable ( )
c) Recovery of consciousness _____ YES ( ) NO ( ) Not applicable ( )

RECOVERY

52. Were adequate recovery facilities **available for this patient?** YES ( ) NO ( )
If no, specify deficiencies:

53. Had the patient recovered consciousness before discharge from theatre/recovery complex to the general ward? YES ( ) NO ( )

54. Had the patient recovered protective reflexes before discharge to the general ward? YES ( ) NO ( )

55. Were you satisfied with the patient's condition on discharge to the general ward? YES ( ) NO ( )
If no, please describe the patient's condition _____

56. Did you see the patient yourself on the ward? YES ( ) NO ( )

POSTOPERATIVE PROGRESS

INTENSIVE CARE

57. Does your hospital have
a) an I.T.U.? YES ( ) NO ( )
b) High dependency area? YES ( ) NO ( )

58. a) Was the patient admitted to the I.T.U.? YES ( ) NO ( )
b) Was the patient admitted to a high dependency area? YES ( ) NO ( )

59. Date of admission:

60. Transfer date: a) Elective discharge
Due to: a) Elective discharge YES ( ) NO ( )
b) Pressure on beds YES ( ) NO ( )
c) Death YES ( ) NO ( )

15

157   *APPENDIX 3: QUESTIONNAIRES. Anaesthetic*

PLEASE DO NOT PHOTOCOPY

61. Time of transfer to general ward: _____ (24 hour clock)

62. What was the indication for admission to the I.T.U./H.D.A.?

    a) Routine   YES ( ) NO ( )

    b) Respiratory failure   YES ( ) NO ( )

    c) Cardiovascular instability   YES ( ) NO ( )

    d) Renal failure   YES ( ) NO ( )

    e) Other (specify) _____ YES ( ) NO ( )

63. Were these facilities adequate?   YES ( ) NO ( )

    If no, specify _____

64. Was the postoperative period complicated by: If yes please give evidence of this

    a) Bleeding sufficient to require postoperative transfusion or re-operation   YES ( ) NO ( )

    b) The need for mechanical ventilation   YES ( ) NO ( )

      i) elective   YES ( ) NO ( )

      ii) for respiratory failure   YES ( ) NO ( )

    c) Sepsis

      i) wound or operation site (localised)   YES ( ) NO ( )

      ii) respiratory, urinary or other systemic sepsis including septicaemia   YES ( ) NO ( )

    d) Myocardial disorder   YES ( ) NO ( )

    e) Hepatic failure   YES ( ) NO ( )

    f) Renal failure sufficient to require dialysis   YES ( ) NO ( )

    g) Endocrine system failure   YES ( ) NO ( )

    h) Persistent coma (GCS <7)*   YES ( ) NO ( )

    i) Other organ failure   YES ( ) NO ( )

    j) Problems with postoperative analgesia   YES ( ) NO ( )

    k) Other complications   YES ( ) NO ( )   Specify _____

*Glasgow Coma Scale — See Back Sheet

PLEASE DO NOT PHOTOCOPY

65. Did any organisational aspects, lack of resources or any other non-clinical factors contribute to the fatal outcome?   YES ( ) NO ( )

    If yes please specify _____

66. Were the patient's notes adequate for you to complete this form?   YES ( ) NO ( )

    If no, specify _____

67. Do you think the anaesthetist assessors should pay particular attention to the surgical form?   YES ( ) NO ( )

    If yes, please explain, _____

68. Do you think that this operation should have been undertaken at this time?   YES ( ) NO ( )

    If no, please explain: _____

69. Was there an autopsy?   YES ( ) NO ( )
(Please note paragraph 7 on the front sheet)

70. If so, what was the cause of death? _____

71. Did you attend?   YES ( ) NO ( )

72. Please add any comments, further information or your account of the sequence of events which led to this patient's death: _____

73. Do you have regular mortality review meetings?   YES ( ) NO ( )

73a. If yes, has this death been considered at such a local meeting? YES ( ) NO ( )

GLASGOW COMA SCALE (GCS) (Question 64)

Eye Opening	Pts	Verbal Response	Pts	Motor Response to Pain (Best Limb)	Pts
Spontaneous	4	Orientated verbal response	5	Obeys commands	5
Eye opening to speech	3	Confused verbal response	4	localisation	4
Eye opening to pain	2	Inappropriate words	3	Flexion normal/abnormal	3
None	1	Incomprehensible sounds	2	Extension	2
		No verbal response	1	No motor response	1

DEFINITIONS

Admission (Question 8)

1. Elective — at time consented between patient and surgical service.
2. Urgent — within 48 hours of consultation.
3. Emergency — immediately following consultation.

Operation (Question 28)

1. **Emergency** — **immediate** operation, resuscitation simultaneous with surgical treatment (e.g. ruptured aneurysm; head, chest and abdominal injuries). Operation usually within one hour.

2. **Urgent** — **delayed** operation as soon as possible **after** resuscitation (e.g. intestinal obstruction, embolism, perforation, major fractures). Operation usually within 24 hours.

3. **Scheduled** — an early operation but not immediately life saving (e.g. cancer, cardiovascular surgery). Operation usually between 1 and 3 weeks.

4. **Elective** — operation at a time to suit both patient and surgeon (e.g. cholecystectomy, hernia, joint replacement).

ASA (American Society of Anesthesiologists) classification of physical status.
(Question 19)

Class 1 The patient has no organic, physiological, biochemical, or psychiatric disturbance. The pathological process for which operation is to be performed is localized and does not entail a systemic disturbance. Examples: a fit patient with inguinal hernia; fibroid uterus in an otherwise healthy woman.

Class 2 Mild to moderate systemic disturbance caused either by the condition to be treated surgically or by other pathophysiological processes. Examples: non- or only slightly limiting organic heart disease, mild diabetes, essential hypertension, or anaemia. Some might choose to list the extremes of age here, either the neonate or the octogenerian, even though no discernible systemic disease is present. Extreme obesity and chronic bronchitis may be included in this category.

Class 3 Severe systemic disturbance or disease from whatever cause, even though it may not be possible to define the degree of disability with finality. Examples: severely limiting organic heart disease; sever diabetes with vascular complications; moderate to severe degrees of pulmonary insufficiency; angina pectoris or healed myocardial infarction.

Class 4 Severe systemic disorders that are already life threatening, not always correctable by operation. Examples: patients with organic heart disease showing marked signs of cardiac insufficiency, persistent angina, or active myocarditis; advanced degrees of pulmonary, hepatic, renal or endocrine insufficiency.

Class 5 The moribund patient who has little chance of survival but is submitted to operation in desperation. Examples: the burst abdominal aneurysm with profound shock; major cerebral trauma with rapidly increasing intracranial pressure; massive pulmonary embolus. Most of these patients require operation as a resuscitative measure with little if any anaesthesia.

19

A

SELF ASSESSMENT BY ANAESTHETIST

74. Score yourself between 0 and 10 (e.g. 10, no fault; 7, adequate, 3 avoidable errors, 0, total failure)

   a) Preoperatively (assessment and management) _____

   b) Peroperatively (anaesthetic) _____

   c) Postoperatively (immediate recovery) _____

If your score is 7 or less for any phase, is there anything you would do differently next time?

_____

_____

A

75. Would you like to know how the assessors scored your management?
                YES ( ) NO ( )

If yes please make a record of this code number _____

and write your telephone number on the front sheet.

DO *NOT* KEEP A COPY OF THIS FORM

THANK YOU FOR COMPLETING THIS QUESTIONNAIRE

Please return to:
Mr Nigel Buck MSc
14 Palace Court
London W2 4HT

Tel: 01-727 4547

After 1st January 1986
9 Bedford Square
London WC1B 3RA

Tel: 01-580 8697

18

159   *APPENDIX 3: QUESTIONNAIRES. Anaesthetic*

5. Were there other departures from ideal practice which are worthy of record? YES / NO / Not assessable

If yes, please specify

6a **ANAESTHETISTS ONLY**
In the same circumstances would you have agreed to anaesthetise this patient? YES / NO

Do you think that the monitoring used was adequate for this patient? YES / NO

6b **SURGEONS ONLY**
In the same circumstances would **you** have decided to operate on this patient? YES / NO / UNKNOWN

7. **ALL**
With this patient's pre-operative circumstances, do you think this patient should have had **any** surgical operation in any centre? YES / NO

COMMENTS (on questions 6a, 6b and 7)

8. **ASSESSORS SCORE**
Score the surgical or anaesthetic management between 0 and 10 (eg. 10, no fault; 7, adequate; 3, avoidable errors; 0, total failure)
a) Pre-operative
b) Peroperative
c) Postoperative

9. **ALL** (NB These are **not** exclusive groups)
DO YOU CONSIDER THAT IN THIS CASE THE DEATH WAS TOTALLY OR PARTLY ATTRIBUTABLE TO:
(i) SURGERY (the fact that an operation took place should not determine an affirmative answer) YES / NO

If yes due to:- (surgical assessor only)
1. Inappropriate operation
2. Inappropriate pre-operative management
3. Inappropriate grade operating surgeon
4. Failure of organisation (system)

Association of Anaesthetists

Association of Surgeons

of Great Britain and Ireland

CONFIDENTIAL ENQUIRY INTO PERIOPERATIVE DEATHS

ASSESSOR'S FORM

Code No:

Please confine your assessment to matters of your own discipline eg: surgery or anaesthesia where indicated.

NAME

Assessor (ring one) — Anaesthetist — Surgeon — Other (specify)

1. Do you require the Clinical Coordinators to request further information in order to make an assessment? YES / NO

If yes — please refer to assessors notes and specify what it is you wish to know and send this form and the questionnaire back to the office:

2. Was the information in the form adequate for you to make an assessment? YES / NO

Do you feel competent to assess this case? YES / NO

3. What in your opinion, was the clinical cause of death in this patient?

4. Were there avoidable elements in the entire management of the patient which, if corrected, would have altered the outcome, or might at least have reduced the chance of death at that time? i.e. Was the death avoidable? YES / NO / Not assessable

SPECIFY

DO NOT PHOTOCOPY

5. Technical failure by surgical team due to:-
   * Inadequate knowledge
   * Failure to apply knowledge
   * Lack of care
   * Lack of experience
   * Inadequate supervision
   * Fatigue
   * Physical impairment
   * Mental impairment
   * Other — specify _____

and/or (ii) ANAESTHESIA   YES / NO
If yes due to:- (anaesthetic assessor only)
   1. Failure of organisation (system)
   2. Failure of equipment
   3. Drug effect
   4. Human (anaesthetist) failure
      Lack of knowledge
      * Failure to apply knowledge
      * Lack of care
      * Lack of experience
      * Fatigue
      * Impairment
      * Other — specify _____

and/or (iii) DISEASE   YES / NO
   Progress of presenting surgical disease _____

   _____

   Progress of intercurrent disease _____

   _____

and/or (iv) UNKNOWN

and/or (v) NOT ASSESSABLE

10. Please write here any other comments you may wish to make.

   _____

   _____

PLEASE RETURN THIS FORM TOGETHER WITH THE QUESTIONNAIRE TO MR N. BUCK, CEPOD, 9 BEDFORD SQUARE, LONDON WC1B 3RA.

161   **APPENDIX 3:**
       ASSESSOR'S
       FORM

CONFIDENTIAL ENQUIRY INTO PERIOPERATIVE DEATHS

NOTES FOR ASSESSORS

OBJECTIVES

The Confidential Enquiry into Perioperative Deaths aims to enumerate the number of deaths which occur within 30 days of a surgical operational procedure and to identify remediable factors in the practice of surgery and anaesthesia. These deaths are to be assessed independently in relation to the following items:-

   i The clinical cause of death.
   ii The extent of contributory factors of the anaesthetic.
  iii The extent of contributory factors of the surgery, including the surgical decisions.
  iv The part played by other causes.
   v To identify avoidable and unavoidable factors.
  vi To identify clinical deficiencies.
 vii To identify organisational deficiencies.

PLEASE CONFINE YOUR ASSESSMENT TO THE EVIDENCE PRESENTED IN THE QUESTIONNAIRE.

If you require further information in order to make your assessment or you have any queries about this particular case, please do not hesitate to contact the appropriate Clinical Co-ordinator; Dr J Lunn, Mr H B Devlin, Professor J S P Lumley, or Mr N Buck, the Administrator, at CEPOD, 9 Bedford Square, London WC1B 3RA (Tel 01-580 8697), and we will endeavour to obtain the details you require from the clinician who completed the form.

If your need to discuss any points about the enclosed questionnaire or the assessment form urgently we can be contacted at work or at home on the following numbers:-

WORK
01-580 8697	Mr N Buck
0642-603571	Mr H Brendan Devlin
01-600 9000	Professor J S P Lumley
ex 2560	
0222-763601	Dr J N Lunn

HOME

It is essential that the highest principles of medical and professional confidentiality are maintained in this study and we would respectfully ask that you do not discuss details which would enable identification of any cases with your colleagues.

It is hoped that you will be able to complete your assessment as soon as possible and at least within ten working days and would ask that you return your form and the questionnaire in the pre-paid envelope.

If it is not possible for you to make an assessment for whatever reason, please do not hesitate to return the forms to us in order that we may approach another assessor on this matter.

THE ASSESSMENT FORM

Please identify which specialty you are assessing.

Questions

1. & 2. If you require more information, please ask. (See above)

3. **Clinical Cause of Death**
The pathological diagnosis is less important than the functional event which culminated in death. We recognise that this is a very difficult question to answer. The answer will often be the same as that of the clinician but occasionally, and importantly, you will spot the *real* event. This is what we want to know.

4. **Avoidable Elements**
Please refer to any event which might have caused the longer survival of the patient.

5. These need not be such that they were even partly causative of the death but may be indicative of a less than ideal standard of practice.

6. & 7. These are questions of clinical judgement about which it is important for the study that *your* opinion is obtained.

8. This is self-evident. It is very subjective and we do not intend to use the match or the mismatch of your score with that of the clinician in any 'pseudoprecise' manner. You understand that their own personal assessment is very subjective and really the question to which you are required to answer is "do you agree with the clinician's answer or is he/she over/underestimating his/her competence?

9. This is the most important question. Please give careful thought before you answer. (The description of deaths other than the subsection for surgery has been agreed by an international group of anaesthetists interested in this subject.) (ref. *Anaesthesia* 1985; 40:79)

IN ORDER TO PRESERVE TOTAL CONFIDENTIALITY YOU *MUST NOT* PHOTOCOPY ANY PART OF THE ENCLOSED QUESTIONNAIRE OR ASSESSMENT FORM.

                      THANK YOU